The MAILBOX®

The Idea Magazine For Teachers®

KINDERGARTEN

2003–2004

YEARBOOK

The Education Center, Inc.
Greensboro, North Carolina

The Mailbox® 2003–2004 Kindergarten Yearbook

Managing Editor, *The Mailbox* Magazine: Leanne Stratton

Editorial Team: Becky S. Andrews, Kimberley Bruck, Karen P. Shelton, Diane Badden, Susan Walker, Karen A. Brudnak, Sarah Hamblet, Hope Rodgers, Dorothy C. McKinney

Production Team: Lisa K. Pitts, Lois Axeman (COVER ARTIST), Pam Crane, Clevell Harris, Rebecca Saunders, Jennifer Tipton Bennett, Chris Curry, Theresa Lewis Goode, Ivy L. Koonce, Troy Lawrence, Clint Moore, Greg D. Rieves, Barry Slate, Donna K. Teal, Tazmen Carlisle, Amy Kirtley-Hill, Kristy Parton, Debbie Shoffner, Cathy Edwards Simrell, Lynette Dickerson, Mark Rainey, Gina Farago

ISBN 1-56234-611-3
ISSN 1088-5528

The Education Center, Inc.
P.O. Box 9753
Greensboro, NC 27429-0753

Look for *The Mailbox*® 2004–2005 Kindergarten–Grade 1 Yearbook in the summer of 2005. The Education Center, Inc., is the publisher of *The Mailbox*®, *Teacher's Helper*®, *The Mailbox*® BOOKBAG®, and *Learning*® magazines, as well as other fine products. Look for these wherever quality teacher materials are sold, or call 1-800-714-7991.

Contents

Arts & Crafts for Little Hands

Arts & Crafts
for Little Hands

Sparkling Stars

Don't shy away from glitter—it's easy and neat with this project! For each child, cut out a star shape from construction paper. Program each star with the phrase "[Child's name] Is a Superstar!" Next, mix some glitter with clear hair gel. Invite each child to use a paintbrush to spread the glittery gel over her star. Once the gel is dry, set it with a little hairspray. Display the finished stars around your classroom door to let everyone know your class is simply heavenly!

Leslie O'Donnell—Gr. K
Sedalia Park School
Marietta, GA

Corn Syrup Chameleon

After sharing Eric Carle's *The Mixed-Up Chameleon,* encourage your kindergartners to make colorful chameleons of their own! In advance, duplicate the chameleon pattern on page 22 onto tagboard to make a class supply. Have each child cut out his pattern. Then mix containers of light corn syrup with various colors of food coloring. Have each young artist dip a finger into the corn syrup paint and fingerpaint his chameleon. Have him add other colors as he desires. Allow the paint to dry thoroughly before displaying these lovely lizards! (Factors such as humidity will affect drying time.)

Leanne Gibbons—Gr. K
Sacred Heart School
Quincy, MA

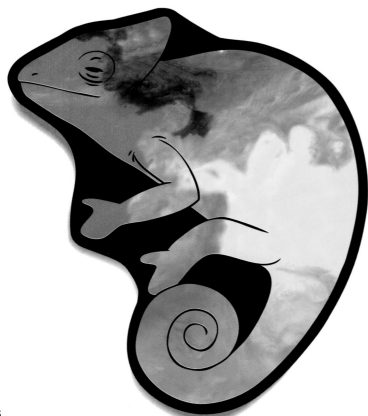

Ant Art

Youngsters will scurry on over to your art center to create these ant farms! To make one, have a child paint the bottom three-fourths of a sheet of brown tagboard or cardstock with diluted glue. Have him sprinkle sand over the glue and then shake off the excess. While the glue is still wet, show him how to use a finger to draw tunnels and passageways in the sand. Then have him glue on a few raisins to represent busy ants inside the farm. Finish the project by writing "[Child's name]'s Ant Farm" at the top. Allow the glue to dry thoroughly before displaying this awesome ant artwork!

S-s-super Snake

This colorful snake is totally tubular! In advance, enlist the help of parents in collecting three toilet paper tubes for each child. To make a snake, punch holes in the ends of the tubes and then thread short pieces of pipe cleaner through the holes, twisting them to secure. Have each youngster cut out from construction paper a snake's head and tail similar to the ones shown. Instruct him to draw eyes and glue a red tongue to the head. Then have him glue the head and tail to opposite ends of the body. To finish, instruct him to glue scraps of construction paper to his snake for decoration. Hiss!

Suzanne Giaimo—Gr. K
Bryant Elementary School
Milwaukee, WI

Arts & Crafts
for Little Hands

Feet and a Treat

Youngsters will step right up to complete this Halloween project! To prepare, print the verse shown onto a sheet of orange construction paper for each child. Paint the bottoms of a child's bare feet with white tempera paint and have him carefully stand on his paper to make prints of his feet. Allow the paint to dry; then have the child use a black marker to add a ghostly face to each footprint. Help him read the verse and ask him to complete the last line by writing or dictating something he'd like to receive when he goes trick-or-treating. Then to complete his paper, have him draw pictures of the treats. "Boo-tiful"!

Kathy Barlow, Southern Elementary, Somerset, KY

Trick or treat!
See my feet!
Here is what I'd like to eat: <u>lollipops</u>.

From Plates to Jack-o'-Lanterns

Transform some paper plates and paper into pretty jack-o'-lanterns for Halloween! Gather the materials listed below; then help each child complete the directions to make her jack-o'-lantern.

Materials for one:

two 9" paper plates	black marker
brown construction paper scrap	scissors
green construction paper scrap	glue
yellow and orange crayons	

Directions:
1. Color the fronts of the paper plates yellow and the backs orange.
2. On one orange side, draw a jack-o'-lantern face. Cut out the features; then trace around them with a black marker.
3. Cut a stem from brown paper and a leaf from green paper.
4. Glue the edges of the two plates together, orange sides out, with the stem wedged between them at the top.
5. Glue the leaf to the stem.

Jeanine Bulber, St. Mary School, Belleville, IL

Beaded Indian Corn

Autumn has arrived, and it's the perfect time to make these pretty beaded magnets! To make one, bend one end of a pipe cleaner half as shown. Have each child thread 20 tribeads in orange, yellow, red, and blue onto her pipe cleaner piece so it resembles Indian corn. Next, cut a six-inch length of raffia for each magnet. Tie the raffia to the free end of the pipe cleaner; then bend the pipe cleaner to secure it. Use tacky glue to attach a length of magnetic tape to this crafty corn, making sure to cover the free ends of the pipe cleaner. How attractive!

Laurel Smith—Gr. K
The Sonshine Place
Fishers, IN

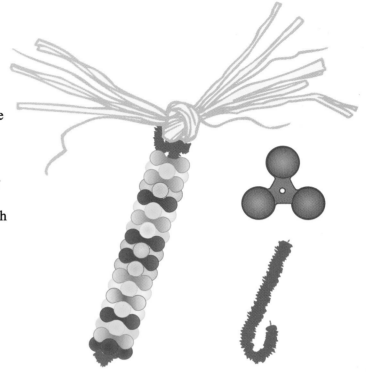

Leaf Suncatcher

Add some whimsy to your windows with this fall project! For each child, lay a piece of clear Con-Tact covering sticky side up on a tabletop. Have each youngster add small pieces of torn tissue paper in fall colors to the covering. Then squirt the paper once or twice with a spray bottle of water to make the tissue colors blend. Once the projects are dry, laminate them and have each child trace a leaf shape onto her laminated paper and cut along the outline. Punch a hole at the top; then use string to hang the suncatcher in a window.

Teresa Harmon
Hillsborough, NC

Masked Bandits

Who are those masked critters? Raccoons, of course! To make one, cut off the top two inches of a brown paper lunch bag. Have each child glue a black construction paper mask shape onto the folded bottom of his bag; then instruct him to cut out circles from both white and black paper and glue them to the mask to make eyes. Next, have each child use a white crayon to trace four hand shapes onto black construction paper. Then have him cut out the shapes and glue them to the bag to represent the raccoon's feet. Instruct him to cut two ears and a nose from brown construction paper. Finally, have him use a black marker to draw stripes and a mouth on the raccoon's body as shown.

Kathleen Rose—Gr. K
Park Falls Elementary
Park Falls, WI

A "Can-Do" Turkey

These beautiful birds will make super centerpieces on Thanksgiving tables everywhere! To make one, cover a 14½-ounce can with white construction paper. Next, have a child make a footprint with brown tempera paint on white poster board. When the paint is dry, cut around the outline and glue it to the covered can, toes down, as shown, to represent the turkey's head and neck. Then have the child trace one of his hands three times onto fall colors of construction paper. Have him cut out the hand shapes and glue them to the back of the can to make tail feathers. Finally, have him glue on a yellow construction paper beak, a red paper wattle, and two paper reinforcements for eyes as shown. How gobble, gobble gorgeous!

Kelly Wilkinson—Gr. K
Holy Family School
New Albany, IN

Santa's "Hand-y" Welcome

These festive welcome signs will grace doors for years to come! To make one, use red, peach, and white fabric paint to paint a child's hand as shown. Have the child make a handprint on the center of a dark felt square. Then have him add blue fingerprint eyes and a red fingerprint nose to the Santa's face, as well as dots of white snow around the Santa. Help the child use a fabric-paint squeeze bottle to write "Welcome" above the Santa and his name and the year below. Glue a craft stick along the top edge on the back. Then glue the ends of a length of ribbon to the two top corners for hanging.

Dorothy Lehto—Gr. K
Wise Owl Preschool
Nashua, NH

From Spoon to Snowman

Use a little paint, craft foam, and fabric to transform a wooden ice cream spoon into a snazzy snowman! First, have a child paint a wooden spoon with plain or textured white craft paint. When the paint is dry, use hot glue to attach a black craft foam hat and a pin back. Have the child use paint or permanent markers to make the snowman's eyes, mouth, and a carrot-shaped nose. For a finishing touch, help the child tie a short length of scrap fabric around the indentation on the spoon to provide her snowman with a warm winter scarf!

Elizabeth Trautman
Greensboro, NC

Earth-Friendly Ornament

Make these cute elf ornaments from recycled CDs and plastic newspaper sacks! To make one, fold down the open edge of a newspaper sack two times to make a cuff. Spread white glue on the printed side of a CD; then slip it into the open end of the sack as shown. After the glue dries, tie the other end of the sack with a short length of yarn; then have a child use scissors to fringe-cut the end of the resulting elf's hat. Instruct him to add paper-reinforcement eyes and glue on a pom-pom nose. Then have him draw a smile with a permanent marker. Tie another length of yarn around the yarn on the hat; then tie the loose ends together to make a loop for hanging.

Dianne Young—Gr. K
Seymour Elementary
Ralston, NE

Colorful Crayon Trees

Crayons on the Christmas tree? Sure! To begin, have each child trace a Christmas tree shape onto the center of a sheet of green construction paper and then cut it out. Have her set the outline aside. Next, instruct each child to use a pencil sharpener to shave old crayons, catching the shavings on a piece of waxed paper laid on the table. When the child is finished, have her fold the waxed paper. Place the waxed paper between layers of brown paper grocery bags on an ironing board. Then use a warm iron to press the paper and melt the crayon shavings for each child. When the paper cools, have the student trim it to fit behind the tree opening on her green paper and then glue it in place. Display the trees on a sunny window to create a festive holiday scene.

Maribeth Foster
Longview, WA

Art "Sew" Easy

Students will stitch these ornaments in a snap! Purchase some large-mesh plastic canvas and several plastic sewing needles with large eyes at your local craft store. Also gather bright or glittery yarns in holiday colors. Cut the plastic canvas into holiday shapes, such as candy canes, stars, snowmen, and trees. Work with a few children at a time, and have each of them choose a shape, as well as some yarn. Help each youngster thread her needle and demonstrate how to begin sewing, weaving the yarn in and out of the holes in the canvas. Then stand back and watch little ones go, go, go as they sew, sew, sew! Add a hook and this ornament's ready for hanging!

Bonnie McKenzie—PreK and Kindergarten
Cheshire Country Day School
Cheshire, CT

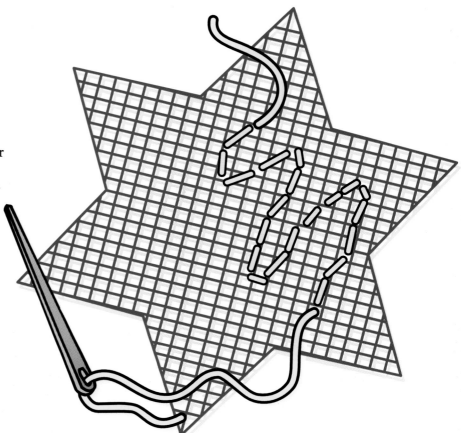

Winter in a Jar

Little ones will love making their very own snow globes to celebrate the winter season! Collect a clean plastic jar with a lid for every child. To make a snow globe, squeeze waterproof glue into each jar lid. Have each child attach small trees, snowmen, or other appropriate figures found at your craft store to the inside of a jar lid. Then allow the glue to dry. Next, have him fill his jar nearly full with water and add a bit of confetti or glitter. Then use more waterproof glue to coat the inside rim of the lid before screwing it in place. When the glue is dry, invite each child to shake his jar and watch the beautiful scene inside!

Darla Cricchio—Gr. K
Sims Elementary
Bridge City, TX

13

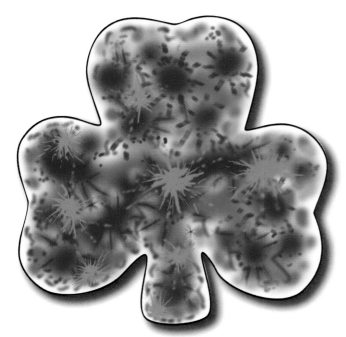

Ping-Pong Ball Painted Shamrocks

Marble painting is always fun, but why not try something a bit different? Put a large piece of construction paper in a box with a lid. Use a plastic spoon to drizzle different shades of green paint onto the paper. Invite a child to drop a Ping-Pong ball into the box, put on the lid, and give the box a few good shakes to make the ball bounce! After the paint has dried, have each student trace a large shamrock on her paper and then cut it out. Use the shapes to decorate your room for Saint Patrick's Day.

Jill Davis—Gr. K
Kendall-Whittier Elementary
Tulsa, OK

Tips for Making a *T. rex*

Here's a creative way to make dinosaur skeletons using cotton swabs. To prepare, duplicate the *Tyrannosaurus rex* outline pattern on page 23 onto tagboard a few times; then cut out the patterns to make tagboard tracers. Duplicate the skull shape onto white copy paper to make a class supply. Then cut a supply of cotton swabs into halves and fourths, and have some full-length cotton swabs available too.

To make a skeleton, a child uses a white crayon to trace a *T. rex* outline onto black construction paper. Then he glues various lengths of cotton swabs over the pattern, outlining the bones. Help him use a hole puncher to punch out the nostrils and eye of the skull pattern where indicated; then have him glue the skull in place on the pattern. "Dino-mite!"

Marcia Murphy—Gr. K
Children's Learning Center at North Kansas City Hospital
North Kansas City, MO

Piggy Banks

Use milk jugs to make these curly-tailed cuties for holding students' pennies! In advance, collect a clean, gallon-size milk or water jug with a lid for each child. For each bank, have a child cut out two triangle ears and a circle snout from pink construction paper and then glue them in place, as shown, with the snout on the jug lid. Have her add two sticky-dot eyes. Next, have her glue four clean plastic condiment cups to the bottom of the jug to form feet. Instruct her to curl a pink pipe cleaner around her finger and then tape one end of the tail to the back of the pig. Finally, have an adult cut a slit in the top of the bank for dropping in coins. Encourage each child to take her bank home to hold her savings. When she wants to dip into her savings, she simply pops off the jug lid to retrieve the money!

Barb Miles—Gr. K
Charles A. Upson Elementary
Lockport, NY

Rainbow Spirals

Celebrate the coming of spring with these spirals! To make one, have a child paint both sides of a thin white paper plate with many different colors of watercolor paint. Encourage her to completely cover one side with colorful designs, allow it to dry, and then completely cover the other side. To make the spiral, begin cutting at the outer edge of the plate, and cut a continuous strip (about an inch wide), until you reach the center. Punch a hole in the center end of the spiral, and then thread through it a length of yarn. Tie the yarn into a loop to create a hanger.

Susan DeRiso
Barrington, RI

Anne M. Cromwell-Gapp—Gr. K
Connecticut Valley Child Care Center
Claremont, NH

15

Arts & Crafts
for Little Hands

Sounds Like Rain

Tippita, tappita…Is that rain outside? No, it's this clever rain stick! To make one, cut from tagboard two circles sized to fit over the ends of a paper towel tube. Tape one circle to one end of the tube. Then decorate the tube with crayons, markers, stickers, or paint pens. Roll or crumple a large piece of aluminum foil; then twist it into a spiral shape and fit it inside the tube. (Be sure to use enough foil to reach both ends of the tube.) Pour in about a quarter cup of small dried beans, lentils, or rice. Then tape the second tagboard circle to the open end of the tube. Flip the stick from end to end to hear the sound of falling rain!

Michelle Barnea—Educational Consultant
Dover, NJ

Oatmeal Bunnies

Invite youngsters to hop on over to your art table to make these Easter baskets from oatmeal canisters! Prepare the canisters by peeling off the labels and cutting a large oval on one side of each canister. Have a child paint an entire canister with tan, white, or gray tempera paint. When the paint is dry, have her glue a cotton ball tail on one end and paper ears and eyes, a pink pom-pom nose, and some pipe cleaner whiskers on the other end as shown. Stuff some Easter grass into the opening; then add Easter treats and colored eggs to this cute bunny!

Cindi Zsittnik, Hanover, MD

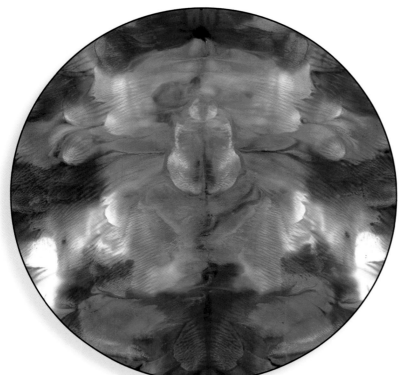

Earth Day Painting

Celebrate Earth Day with these easy-to-make paintings of our world! Have a child spoon a little green, white, and blue tempera paint onto a white construction paper circle. Then have her fold the circle in half and press from the fold outward. Have her unfold the paper and observe the beautiful mix of blue, green, and white that resembles our planet!

Laura Dickerson—Grs. K and 1
Seawell Elementary
Chapel Hill, NC

Impressive Eggs

These eggs will leave a colorful impression! Give each child an egg shape cut from white construction paper. Have her cut or tear enough small pieces of bright colors of tissue paper to cover the egg. Then have her paint white vinegar over the egg shape. Have her lay the tissue paper pieces on top of the egg, painting more vinegar over each one. When the egg is covered with colorful tissue, leave it to dry. When dry, the tissue paper pieces will fall right off, leaving behind a pretty design.

Leanne Gibbons—Gr. K
Sacred Heart Elementary School
North Quincy, MA

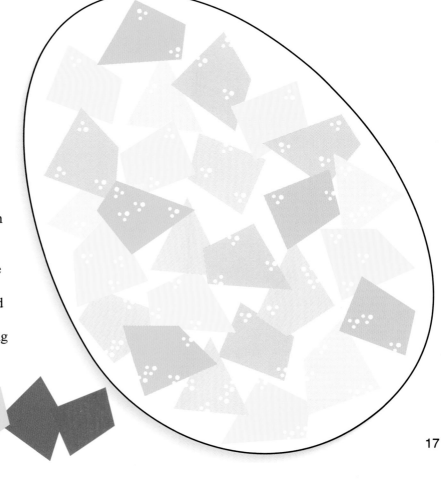

Arts & Crafts
for Little Hands

The Early Bird

These spring robins are adorable! To make one, cut a red semicircle and a smaller brown semicircle from construction paper. Have each child glue the two shapes onto background paper, as shown, to form the bird's body and head. Instruct him to draw two feet and add two paper reinforcement eyes. Next, direct him to use a black marker to color in the center of each eye. Then have him glue on a craft feather for the tail. Instruct him to cut out a yellow construction paper triangle for a beak and glue it just along its top edge. Then fold the beak up and glue a real Gummy Worm candy underneath it. See? This early bird really *did* get a worm!

Diane Bonica—Gr. K, Deer Creek Elementary, Tigard, OR

Fancy Bonnets

These pretty hats make wonderful wall hangings for Easter or Mother's Day. To make one, use craft glue to glue the rim of a heavy-duty paper bowl to the bottom of a heavy-duty paper plate. Decorate the hat with paper die-cuts of flowers, greenery, and butterflies. Add a yarn loop for hanging the hat on a wall. Then glue a bow or two long ribbons at the bottom of the hat to complete the project.

Seema R. Gersten—Gr. K
Harkham Hillel Hebrew Academy
Beverly Hills, CA

Linda Oesterle—Gr. K
Eggert Road Elementary
Orchard Park, NY

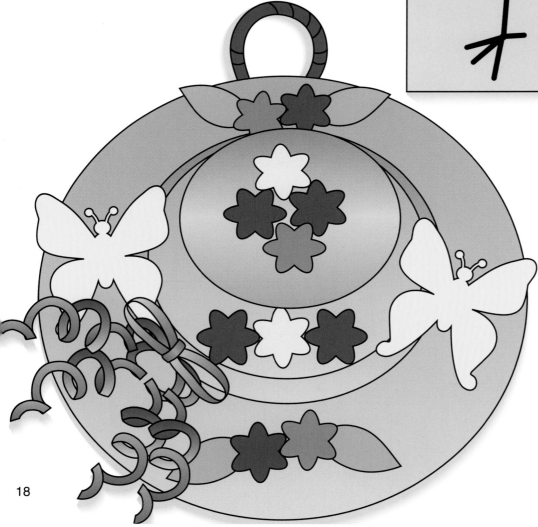

A Pencil Cup for Dad

Dads everywhere will proudly display these pencil cans on desks and kitchen counters!

Materials for one cup:
empty 14.5 oz. clean vegetable can (edges taped)
copy of page 24
1" square of craft foam
thin marker
crayons
glitter glue
scissors
glue

Directions:
1. Use the marker to write three words to describe your dad (or another special person) on the left side of the label.
2. On the right side of the label, write your name.
3. Color the label and the ribbon. Add glitter glue for decoration.
4. Cut out the label and the ribbon.
5. Glue the square of craft foam to the circle on the label. Glue the ribbon to the craft foam.
6. Wrap the completed label around the soup can and glue where indicated.

Lucia Kemp Henry
Fallon, NV

Dandelion Fireworks

'Tis the season for dandelions to sprout up everywhere! Put them to good use for this painting project. Take your class on a nature walk and collect a large supply of dandelions. Back in your classroom, set out shallow trays of tempera paints in a variety of colors. Have a child dip a flower into paint and then *lightly* print on a sheet of white art paper. Have him continue with other flowers and other colors to make a dazzling display that resembles fireworks!

Amanda Renchin—Gr. K
Kid Zone
Lakeville, MN

Father's Day Message Board

These memo boards will make memorable Father's Day gifts! To make one, start with two 9" x 12" sheets of craft foam in two different colors. Trim one to make it slightly smaller than the other. To the smaller sheet, glue a craft foam frame and a 4" x 5" rectangle of craft foam in a third color to serve as a corkboard. Cut a slit and add a small pad of paper. Also glue on a small loop of craft foam to form a pencil holder as shown. Glue the smaller sheet of craft foam to the larger one. Then have each child decorate the board with peel-and-stick craft foam shapes. Instruct her to glue her school photo to a small piece of paper cut to fit the craft foam frame and then write the message "Happy Father's Day!" next to it. Slip this into the frame on the memo board. Place a pencil in the loop and, if desired, a couple of thumbtacks in the corkboard section. Hot-glue a paper-clip hanger to the back of each project. Then wrap up the gift and send it home to a deserving dad!

Tina Bellotti—Gr. K
G. A. Jackson Elementary
Jericho, NY

Stained Glass Fish

Decorate your classroom windows with a school of these beautiful fish! Duplicate a simple fish pattern onto white paper to make a class supply. Then cut out a class supply of waxed paper sheets. Staple a waxed paper sheet over each fish pattern. Have a child use a Sharpie pen to trace the pattern onto the waxed paper. Then have her use diluted white glue to attach small scrap pieces of colorful tissue paper all over the fish. When the glue is dry, have her cut out the fish. Display the projects in your classroom windows.

Skila Brown—Gr. K
Christian Center School
South Bend, IN

Sensational Sunflowers

Welcome summer with these three-dimensional blooms! Give each child a small white paper plate. Have her paint the center of the plate brown. Then have her cut a large supply of yellow tissue paper squares. Show her how to crumple each square into a ball and then glue it to the unpainted rim of the plate. When the outer rim is covered with yellow "petals," have her glue a few real sunflower seeds to the brown center. Display these summery beauties with green paper stems and leaves on a bulletin board.

Leanne Gibbons—Grs. K and 1
Boston Public Schools—Mattapan
Mattapan, MA

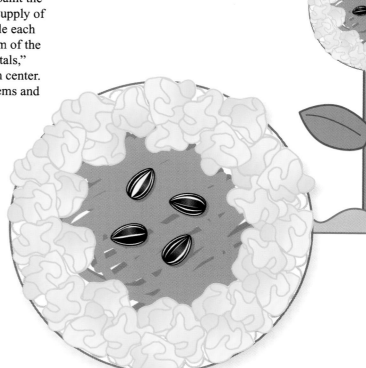

Charming Chimps

These construction paper chimps will look great hanging around in your classroom! To begin, have each child trace her hands and feet on tan paper and cut them all out. For each chimp, cut an oval body from a sheet of 9" x 12" brown paper, a head from 6" x 9" brown paper, and four 4" x 12" rectangles for arms and legs. Also cut an oval mouth area from a piece of 4" x 8" tan paper and two ears from 3" x 3" tan paper. Accordion-fold the arms and legs; then assemble the parts as shown. Have each youngster use a black marker to add eyes, a mouth, and details for the ears. Display the chimps right-side up or upside-down from walls and ceilings to give your room the feeling of a rain forest!

Johanna Litts—Gr. K
North Central Elementary
Hermansville, MI

21

Chameleon Pattern

Use with "Corn Syrup Chameleon" on page 6.

Can Label

Use with "A Pencil Cup for Dad" on page 19.

Glue here.

Love,

Glue ribbon here.

I think you are...

and

ribbon

Number **1**

Building Math Skills

Building

Nonstandard measurement

Markers for Measuring

Looking for an easy unit of nonstandard measurement? Grab a handful of markers! Simply connect markers end to end by fitting the cap of one marker onto the end of another. Have kindergartners use the markers to measure their classmates, the chalkboard, a table, or a window. Help students compare the number of markers it took to measure each person or item, using terms such as *fewer, fewest, more, most, longer, shorter,* and *equal.*

Vada Boback—Gr. K
Alliance Christian School
Morgantown, WV

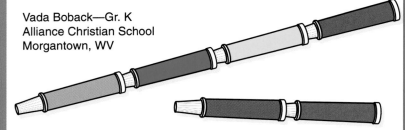

Counting
Numeral recognition

Rodeo Roundup

Yee-haw! Encourage your young cowpokes to count and corral some horses with this easy math game! To prepare, duplicate page 36 to make a class supply. Have each child color and cut out the horses at the bottom of her sheet. Then have students play the game in pairs. One child at a time rolls a die and identifies the number rolled. Then she covers the corresponding number on her reproducible with one of her horses, ending her turn. If she rolls a number she has already covered, her turn ends. The first child to cover all her numbers—and have all her horses in the corral—is the winner!

Rhonda L. Chiles—Gr. K
South Park Elementary School
Shawnee Mission, KS

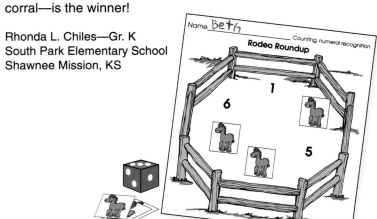

Randy Rectangle

Shapes

Space Shapes

Make learning about shapes truly out-of-this-world with the help of some visitors from outer space! First, create a simple spaceship from a cardboard box. Each time you introduce a new shape, have students help you create a construction paper character made entirely of that shape. Then enlist youngsters' help in naming the character. Have this space shape emerge from the spaceship periodically to teach your little ones about the characteristics of his shape. Also use the character to call on students or to give high fives for correct answers.

Joe Montgomery—Gr. K
St. Mary of the Assumption School
Herman, PA

Math Skills

Number identification
Number order

A Fine Number Line

Encourage youngsters to take a walk on this nifty number line! Label the back sides of ten carpet squares with numbers from 1 to 10. Lay the numbered squares on the floor, in order, to create a number line. Then have students walk along the line, counting from 1 to 10. Next, instruct students to close their eyes as you remove one of the squares. Have youngsters determine which number is missing. To vary the activity, have one child at a time walk the line as you ask a question such as the following:

• What number comes before number ___?
• What number comes after number ___?
• What number comes between number ___ and number ___?

Linda Rasmussen—Gr. K
Donner Springs Elementary
Reno, NV

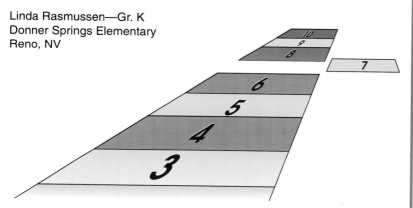

Counting
Sorting
Family involvement

A Multitude of Manipulatives

Here's an idea that will ensure you'll always have plenty of math manipulatives on hand. Each month, ask students and their families to collect a particular type of manipulative and bring their donations to school for use in your math center. You might have them collect milk jug lids, film canisters, or bottle tops. There will be a lot of items for students to count and sort, and even the busiest families can do their part to help their children learn!

Nancy Jergensen—Gr. K
Halstead Academy
Baltimore, MD

Shapes

Circle Art

Studying circles? Bring in some sweet circular treats for eating—and painting! Provide large marshmallows and shallow trays of various colors of paint. Have each youngster dip one end of a marshmallow into paint and then print circles on a sheet of paper. After they have printed several circles, encourage children to draw pictures incorporating their circles. For example, a child might draw a car with marshmallow-print wheels or a flower with a marshmallow-print center. After the projects are complete, allow each youngster to eat a fresh marshmallow treat. Mmm...marshmallow math!

Cami Baldivid—Preschool and Gr. K
Speech & Hearing Center/Achieve
Chattanooga, TN

27

Number identification Counting

Jack's Teeth

Smile! Here's a fun, seasonal way for your students to practice counting sets to five. Cut five pumpkin shapes from orange felt. Use a black marker to give each one a simple jack-o'-lantern face with a big smile but no teeth. Then label each pumpkin with a different number from 1 to 5. Cut 15 tooth shapes from black felt. Place the pumpkins and teeth on a flannelboard with the teeth to one side. Have a child identify the number on a pumpkin and add the corresponding number of teeth to its smile.

Jennifer Barton—Gr. K
Elizabeth Green School
Newington, CT

Number sequence

Calendar Order

Each month, bring out a seasonal set of calendar pieces to give kindergartners practice with numerical sequence. Have a student lay the calendar pieces out on a table or on the floor in order from 1 to 10, 1 to 15, or 1 to 30, depending on the child's skill level.

Leanne Gibbons—Grs. K and 1
Boston Public Schools—Mattapan
Mattapan, MA

Name_____   Graphing
Bunch o' Bones
🖍 Color.

6					
5					
4					
3					
2					
1					
	skull	bone	foot	hand	ribs

Sorting Graphing

Sweet Skeletons

For a yummy Halloween math activity, purchase a package of Brach's Dem Bones Tart & Tangy Candies. Give each child a scoop of candy to sort by shape (skulls, ribs, bones, feet, and hands). Then give each child a copy of the graph on page 37. Have each youngster color in the spaces on the graph to reflect his candy collection. After graphing, have each child assemble a skeleton from his candies. Then invite everyone to bite into the bones!

Sue Lein
Wauwatosa, WI

Math Skills

Patterning

Jell-O Patterns

Make snacktime into math time with this simple patterning activity! Prepare two or three different colors of Jell-O gelatin according to package directions. Give each child a clear plastic cup and a plastic spoon. Have her spoon gelatin into her cup, creating a pattern. For example, she might make an AB pattern of red and yellow gelatin. When everyone's pattern is complete, invite your young mathematicians to eat their creations!

Melissa Auchenbach
Harleysville, PA

Counting by fives

"Hand-y" Math

Here's a tasty way to help your kindergartners count by fives! Prepare a batch of sugar cookie dough; then have each child use a hand-shaped cookie cutter to make a hand cookie. Instruct each child to count to five as she presses five M&M's candies onto the cookie fingertips to create fingernails. Bake the cookies. Place each one on a different paper plate, and then line them up on a tabletop. Have the class count by fives as you point to each hand cookie. Give your class a hand for their counting; then invite them to eat up!

Barbara Meyers
Fort Worth, TX

Sorting

Feathers or Fur?

Ask youngsters to bring in their Beanie Babies stuffed animals or other small stuffed animals for this sorting activity. (Make sure each child's stuffed animals are labeled with his name.) Have students sort the animals by various criteria, such as color, number of feet, feathers or fur, and wild or tame. They're soft and cuddly…and educational!

Rebecca VanderWilt—Gr. K
Hospers Christian School
Hospers, IA

Building

Estimating Counting

Snowball Estimation

The snowballs in this activity will never melt, but they *will* help youngsters with estimation and counting! Label each of three sandwich-size zippered plastic bags: one "A," one "B," and one "C." Put a varying number of small foam balls into each bag. Program a recording sheet as shown; then duplicate the sheet to make a supply for use in your math center. Encourage a child at this center to write down his estimate for each of the bags. Then have him open each bag, count the snowballs, and record the actual total for each bag. For added fun, provide mittens for youngsters to wear while they work!

Mary Grant—Gr. K
Westminster Preschool
Charleston, SC

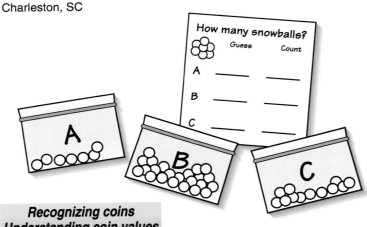

Recognizing coins
Understanding coin values

Calendar Coins

Make calendar time even more valuable by adding money skills to your daily routine. Duplicate patterns of pennies, nickels, dimes, and quarters so that you have a supply of each. Each day, count out coins to match the number of the day of the month and post the coins near your calendar. Use only pennies at first, adding nickels, dimes, and quarters as the year progresses. By May, your kindergartners will be counting coins like pros!

Kay Thomas—Gr. K
Thomas Homeschool
Greenfield, IN

Writing numerals
Creating sets

This Snowman's Buttons

The ten snowmen in this booklet will be well dressed by the time your little ones are finished with them! To prepare the booklet, make a cover with the title "This Snowman" and a place for the child to write her name. Add a drawing of a plain snowman with no buttons. Then create the booklet pages by programming a page similar to the illustration. Duplicate a cover and ten pages for each child. Have the child add a face to the snowman on the cover and write her name in the space provided. Then have her write the numerals 1 to 10 on the succeeding pages and draw a corresponding number of buttons and a face for each snowman. Or for an added challenge, have students write the appropriate number word on each page instead of each numeral. What a "math-terpiece"!

Judi Lesnansky—Title I
New Hope Academy
Youngstown, OH

Math Skills

Measurement

Snowman Sticks

These snowman measuring sticks are fun to make *and* use! Ask a local home improvement store to donate a class supply of paint stirring sticks. Spray-paint all the sticks white. Have each child glue a black craft foam hat to the handle end of his stick. Then have him use permanent markers to draw eyes, a nose, and a mouth for his snowman. Tie a scrap piece of fabric around the indentation to serve as a scarf. Help each child mark off five inches from the bottom of the stick. Then just wait for the snow to fall and the measuring to begin! After youngsters return to the classroom, encourage them to use their snowman sticks to measure mittens, pencils, and more!

Angela Fulk—Preschool and Kindergarten
Homeschool
Garner, NC

Counting
Addition

Math Names

This activity adds up to fun! On a long strip of bulletin board paper, write a child's first and last name as shown. Each child counts the letters in her first name, writing the numeral below each letter, and then does the same with her last name. Have her write the total of the letters in each name above it. Then show her how to add plus and equal signs to create a math sentence. Finally, have her count and label the letters in her combined name to find the sum of her math name.

Janette Phelan—Gr. K
Abiqua School
Salem, OR

$$3 + 5 = 8$$
Joi + Smith = Joi Smith
123   12345   123 45678

Graphing

Super Bowl Math

Got football fever before the Super Bowl? Try this activity to sharpen graphing skills. Program a sheet of paper with a two-column graph, each column labeled with one of the teams playing in the Super Bowl. Duplicate the page for each student. For each child, prepare a tagboard football and label each side of it with the first letter of a Super Bowl team. Then give one to each student and have him toss the football. Instruct him to look to see which team's letter lands on top; then have him color in one square in that team's column. He continues tossing and graphing until one team's column is completely colored in. Touchdown!

June Holoch—Gr. K
Wakonda Public School
Wakonda, SD

SUPER BOWL FEVER!

Panthers   Titans

P   T

31

Tally marks

Musical Tally Marks

Help your students understand tally marks with this musical approach! Give each child an individual whiteboard or chalkboard to use. Play one note at a time on a xylophone, and instruct students to make a tally mark each time they hear a note. When you get to five, run the hammer down the xylophone keys instead of sounding a single note. Have students make a diagonal line across their four existing tally marks when they hear that sound. After several minutes, have youngsters count by fives to determine the total sounds played.

Sadie Day—Gr. K
Carbondale Attendance Center
Carbondale, KS

**Coin recognition
Collecting data**

Heads or Tails?

Introduce your kindergartners to the penny with a fun game of Heads or Tails. To prepare, duplicate the penny patterns on page 38 to make a large supply. Laminate the penny patterns, cut them out, and store them in a small bag in your math center. Make a copy of the recording sheet on page 38 for each child. After showing students a real penny and discussing what is on the heads side and what is on the tails side, invite them to visit your math center for this game of chance! Have each child write his name on a recording sheet. Then have him draw out one penny pattern at a time, coloring in a box in the heads or tails column as appropriate. He continues to draw out pennies and record until one column is full. That side "wins" the game!

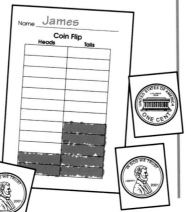

Tammy Lutz—Gr. K
George E. Greene School
Bad Axe, MI

**Counting to 100
Comparing numbers**

100 Hearts

Mark the 100th day of school with this colorful jar of candy! Cut a giant jar shape from bulletin board paper and post it on a classroom wall. Then have students work together to color 100 paper hearts. As each heart is finished, have a child tape it to the jar. When the jar is full, extend the math lesson by counting and comparing the number of hearts in each color.

Teresa Mirra—Gr. K
P.S. 215 Queens
Far Rockaway, NY

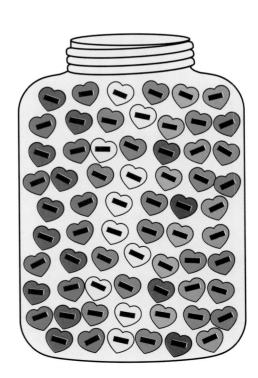

Math Skills

Lucky Measurement

How does a leprechaun measure things? In Lucky Charms cereal pieces, of course! And your lucky little ones will love to measure that way too! Just choose some classroom objects to measure. Have students first estimate and then measure an object's length or width in cereal pieces. Extend this seasonal tip for nonstandard measurement to other times of the year by using candy canes at Christmas or jelly beans at Easter.

Tiffany Gosseen—Gr. K
Salisbury Elementary
Salisbury, MO

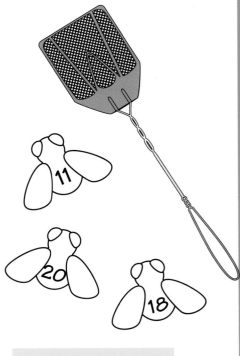

Counting by twos

Peekaboo, Count by Twos!

Here's a tip for helping students visualize the numbers as they count by twos. After your students have had lots of experience with counting by ones on a large hundred chart, use small Post-it notes to cover the odd numbers. These numbers will still be slightly visible, but the even numbers will stand out as you guide students in counting by twos.

Dawn Hernandez—Gr. K
Hebron Elementary
Hebron, IN

Recognizing numerals

Swat the Fly

This activity is sure to be a hit! Duplicate several copies of a fly pattern similar to the one shown. Cut them out and laminate them; then use a washable marker to label each one with a different numeral you want students to recognize. Scatter the flies on the floor. Working with one small group at a time, give a child a new, clean flyswatter. Call out a number and have her find it and swat that fly! Then give the next child a turn. After students have mastered numerals, invite them to swat flies labeled with number words.

Karen Bannis—Gr. K
Metropolitan Christian School
Dallas, TX

33

Building

Critical thinking

How Many Eggs?

Help your kindergartners with the concept of addition or subtraction with a basket full of Easter eggs! To prepare for this small-group activity, hide a number of plastic eggs in Easter grass in a basket. Give a child a clue about the number of eggs in the basket, such as "I put one egg in the basket and then I put in three more. How many eggs are in the basket?" Have the child guess the number and then find and count the eggs to verify that he's correct. Reward correct guesses with a holiday sticker. Vary the number of eggs in the basket and repeat the activity. Continue until every child in the group has had a turn to guess how many eggs you've hidden.

Judi Lesnansky—Title I, K–4
New Hope Academy
Youngstown, OH

Addition

Take a Giant Step

Make great strides toward teaching youngsters about addition when you create a giant number line! Simply roll out a long piece of bulletin board paper or nonadhesive paper shelf liner. Draw lines with a wide black permanent marker at evenly spaced intervals. Then label each line with a numeral. Give an addition problem such as "Two plus six." Have the child stand at the number 2 and then take six steps, ending at number 8. Hey...addition is easy!

Cathy Peterson—Gr. K
Old Suwanee Christian School
Buford, GA

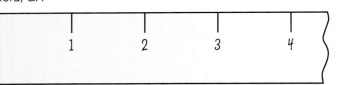

1   2   3   4

Ordinal numbers

Ordinal Countdown

Here's a math game your youngsters will find first-rate! Have everyone line up at your door. Choose an ordinal number (first through tenth) and start at the front of the line, counting by ordinal numbers until you reach the stated number. Have that child leave the line, choose another ordinal number, and be the counter. After she takes her turn, have her move to the end of the line. Continue until you are ready to move your line of students.

Sue White—Gr. K
Creekside Elementary
Harvest, AL

Math Skills

Buggy Bottles

Students will bug you to let them use these counting bottles again and again! To make a set of bottles, clean out several clear plastic bottles and allow them to dry thoroughly. Into each one, pour about a half cup of Karo syrup. Then add a different number of small, lightweight plastic bugs to each bottle. Hot-glue the caps in place. Invite a child at your math center to choose a bottle, count the number of bugs he finds inside, and then write the number on an index card.

Shannon Martin—Gr. K
Children's World
Frankfort, IL

Subtraction

Fishy Subtraction

Kindergartners will be hooked on this yummy subtraction activity! To start, give each child a blue napkin, a paper plate, and ten Goldfish crackers. Have each child put his crackers in the water (on the napkin). Then chant the rhyme below, having each child move the specified number of fish from the napkin to the plate when they are caught. At the end of the verse, write the corresponding number sentence on your chalkboard. Then repeat the rhyme as many times as you like, changing the starting number and the number subtracted as desired. Reward your hardworking fishermen by having them eat the crackers when math time is over!

[Ten] fish are swimming in the sea.
[One] got caught on a hook by me!
How many fish are still swimming free?

Stephanie Zettlemoyer—Gr. K
Turbotville Elementary
Turbotville, PA

Ordinal numbers

Colorful Rows

Review the idea of rows (and columns) and emphasize ordinal numbers with this Geoboard activity. Give each child an individual Geoboard and a set of five rubber bands or fabric weaving loops in various colors. Give a direction, such as "Put a blue band around the first row of pegs." Model this on your own Geoboard. Continue giving directions for adding different colors to the second, third, fourth, and fifth rows. Then ask questions, such as "Which color band is around the third row?" If desired, have students remove all the bands and give a new set of directions for the first through fifth columns on the Geoboard.

Deb Shank—Gr. K
Greencastle Elementary
Greencastle, PA

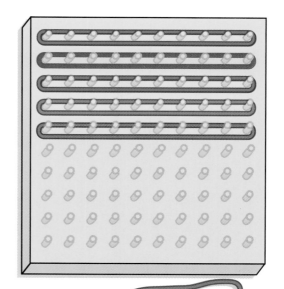

35

Rodeo Roundup

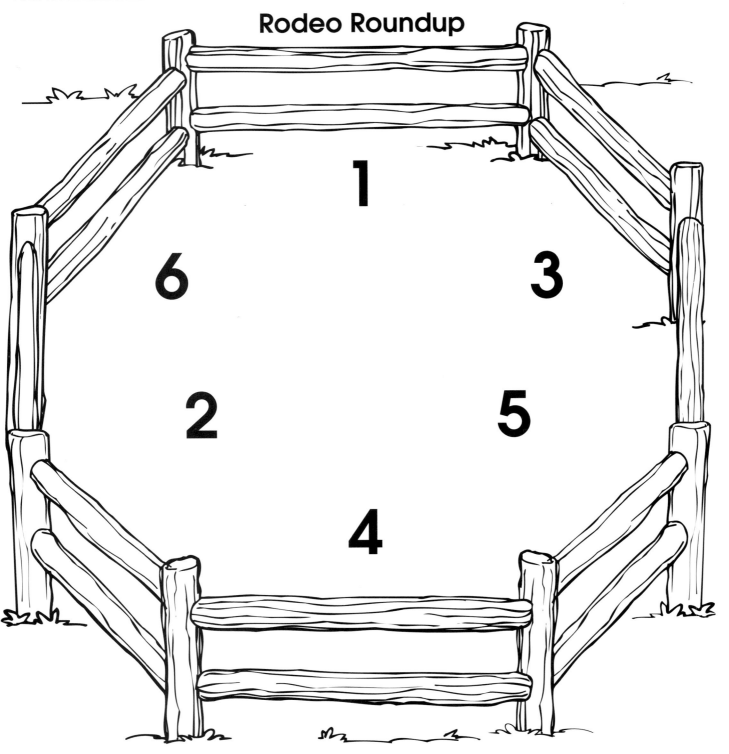

1

6

3

2

5

4

Note to the teacher: Use with "Rodeo Roundup" on page 26.

Bunch o' Bones

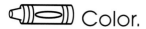 Color.

	skull	bone	foot	hand	ribs
6					
5					
4					
3					
2					
1					

Note to the teacher: Use with "Sweet Skeletons" on page 28.

Recording Sheet

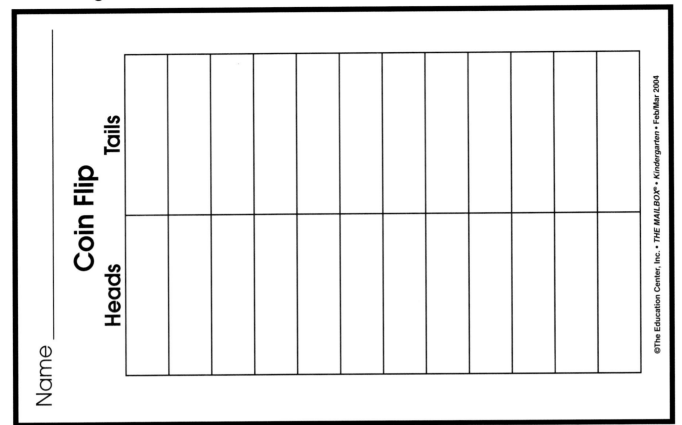

Name

Coin Flip

Heads	Tails

©The Education Center, Inc. • THE MAILBOX® • Kindergarten • Feb/Mar 2004

Note to the teacher: Use with "Heads or Tails?" on page 32.

Penny Patterns
Use with "Heads or Tails?" on page 32.

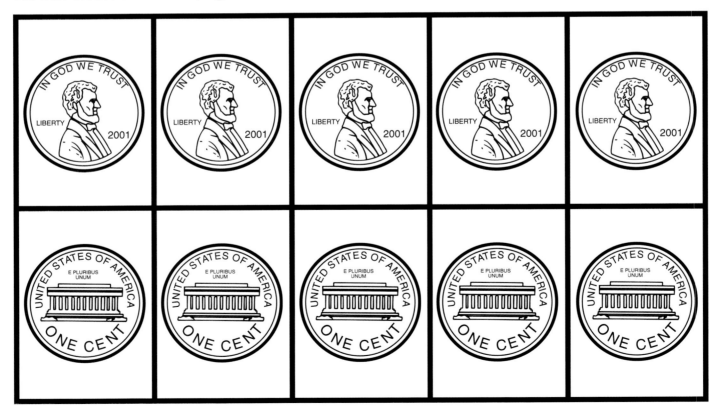

©The Education Center, Inc. • THE MAILBOX® • Kindergarten • Feb/Mar 2004

CIRCLE TIME

Circle

Skill-Based Group

Nimble Names
• • • • Name Recognition, Gross-Motor Skills • • • •

Help your new kindergartners learn one another's names with an activity that'll have them jumping for joy! Put an unlit candle in a candlestick on the floor in your group area. Invite each child, in turn, to jump over the candle as the class recites the nursery rhyme "Jack Be Nimble." Of course, you'll replace the name "Jack" with the name of the jumping student! If desired, post a copy of the rhyme where everyone can see it and use sticky notes with the children's names to change the verse each time you recite it.

Paula Uthoff—Gr. K, Amvet Boulevard School, North Attleboro, MA

Like a Quarter
• • • • Social Studies • • • •

How is a person like a quarter? Find out with this simple activity, which will teach youngsters about the likenesses and differences in people. Give each student in your class a quarter. Have students examine their quarters closely. Make a list on chart paper of the ways that their quarters are alike and the ways that they are different. Then remind students that although the quarters don't look exactly alike, they are all worth the same amount. Guide little ones to see that the quarters are like people— all different, but equally valuable. For safety purposes, make sure to collect the same number of coins that were distributed.

Jan Messali—Gr. K, Canyon View Elementary, San Diego, CA

Bring a Friend
• • • • Social Skills • • • •

Encourage youngsters to get to know their classmates with this fun transition to circle time. Begin with students at their seats. Tap a child and invite her to hold your hand as you continue to walk around your students' tables or desks. Have her ask, "May I bring a friend?" Answer yes, and then have her choose someone to tap. Have that child ask to bring a friend, and continue until everyone is in one long line. Then snake your way to your group area and invite everyone to have a seat!

Jana Sanderson
Rainbow School
Stockton, CA

Time!
Activities and Games

Hoop-de-doo!
• • • • • **Color Recognition** • • • • •

Review colors at the start of the year with a quick game of Hoop-de-doo! In advance, gather Hula-Hoop toys in four different colors. Then program four index cards, each with a color corresponding to one of your hoops. Put the cards in a paper lunch bag. To play, lay the hoops on the floor. Play some music as students walk around the hoops. When you stop the music, direct everyone to stand inside (or put a foot inside) one of the hoops. Then pull one of the cards from the bag. Each child inside the matching hoop must then find something in your classroom in the corresponding color. When each child has found a color match, start the game again.

Millie Morris—Gr. K, Berkmar United Methodist School, Lilburn, GA

Skill-Packed Seven-Up
• • • • • **Listening Skills, Attributes** • • • • •

Try this twist on the classic game of Seven-Up. Choose seven students to stand at the front of the group. Ask the remaining students to put their heads down and put one of their thumbs up. In a whisper, instruct the seven students to tap the thumbs of children who meet a criterion set by you, such as children wearing red, children with blonde hair, or children wearing sneakers. Continue the game by having the tapped children try to guess who tapped them. Then have the class guess the attribute that you chose for that round of play. Heads up!

Cathy Fontana

Whipping Up Colors
• • • • • **Color Mixing** • • • • •

Here's a delicious follow-up to *Mouse Paint* by Ellen Stoll Walsh. Bring in three large tubs of Cool Whip whipped topping, along with some red, blue, and yellow food coloring. Have students help as you mix one color into each tub of topping. Then, in a separate bowl, combine a dollop of red and a dollop of blue topping. Have student volunteers take turns stirring as they observe the effect of mixing the colors. Continue by mixing colors to create green and orange whipped topping too. Then give each child a paper cup and a clean plastic spoon; invite him to enjoy a scoopful of his favorite color!

Chip Davis, Potter Street Elementary School, Bainbridge, GA

Parts of a Pizza
• • • • • **Language** • • • • •

Hungry for a way to improve students' skills in retelling a story? Try this flannelboard follow-up to the story *The Pizza That We Made* by Joan Holub. Before sharing the book, make simple felt pieces to represent the various parts of a pizza. Read the book aloud, placing the pieces on the flannelboard when appropriate. Then have youngsters take turns retelling the story using the felt pieces on your flannelboard. Store the pizza parts in a clean pizza box. Place the box at a center for youngsters to use in retelling the story again and again!

Angela Van Beveren, Alvin, TX

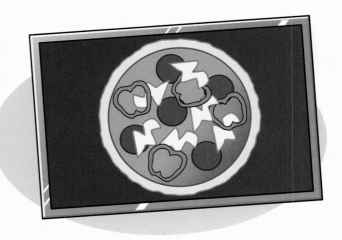

Kindermunch
• • • • • **Social Studies** • • • • •

What special foods do your kindergartners eat at home? Find out with this family project! Send home a letter asking each family to take a turn sending in a store-bought or homemade dish that reflects its culture, its ethnicity, or a family tradition. Stress that they need to send only enough food for each child to have a taste. Also send a simple questionnaire for parent and child to fill out together, asking for the name of the food and when the family eats it. Have the child draw a picture of the food on the form. For each student's turn, invite her to tell about the food and then have her classmates sample it. What a yummy way to learn about one another!

Laura Boeve—Gr. K, Beverly Elementary, Beverly Hills, MI

Kindermunch

Name of your food:
Kugel

When do you eat it?
Rosh Hashanah

Take Your Pick
• • • • • **Self-Esteem, Theme Review** • • • • •

Encourage students to take the lead at circle time with a boxful of ideas! For each theme you teach, make individual index cards with songs, group activities, and charades youngsters can perform. Keep the cards in a file box in your group area. Each day, invite one student to choose a card from the section devoted to your current theme. Have her lead the song or activity or act out the charade for her classmates. What's happening at circle time today? It's up to you!

Sharon Tessier—Gr. K, Children's World Learning Centers
Lake in the Hills, IL

Act like a turkey.

Five Little Turkeys

Do the turkey twist dance.

Time!

Activities and Games

Night Fliers
• • • • • Science • • • • •

Invite youngsters to be like bats with an activity that emphasizes the meaning of *nocturnal*. After discussing bats and explaining to your students that bats like to be awake and fly around at night, have each of them pretend to be a bat. Demonstrate to youngsters how to flap their "wings" and pretend to fly around, emphasizing that each child should fly in his own space to avoid bumping into others. Then have the bats "go to sleep" until night falls—or you turn out the lights! When the room is dark, they may fly around, but when the lights come back on, they must wrap their wings around their bodies and pretend to sleep. Turn the lights off and on several times to give youngsters a chance to go batty!

Melissa Auchenbach, Harleysville, PA

Mystery Object
• • • • • Language • • • • •

Here's a skill-packed idea for show-and-tell! Each week, ask each youngster to find an object at home whose name begins with your featured letter. Have her practice three clues at home that will help her classmates guess her object. On the designated day, instruct each child to present her three clues to the class, and have students guess the object before it's shown. Wow! Speaking and listening skills, critical thinking, and letter sounds all in one idea!

Deb Risse—Gr. K, Rhinelander, WI

It shines in the dark.

Thankful Buddies
• • • • • Social Studies • • • • •

Here's a fun Thanksgiving activity to share with an older buddy class. In advance, prepare a turkey cutout for each of your students and each student's buddy. Label half the cutouts with uppercase letters and the other half with the corresponding lowercase letters, making sure each letter has a match.

When the buddy class arrives, give each of the older students a turkey with an uppercase letter and each of your kindergartners a turkey with a lowercase letter. Have each of your kindergartners find the buddy holding the uppercase match to his letter. Then have the pairs sit together and take turns telling the whole group what they are thankful for.

adapted from an idea by Debra Bousquet—Gr. K, Edward Fenn Elementary, Gorham, NH

Circle
Skill-Based Group

Name Bingo
• • • • • Language • • • • •

This game makes name writing and name recognition tons of fun! Give each child a copy of a large bingo grid like the one shown. Have each student walk around the classroom and ask classmates to write their names in the open spaces on her grid. When everyone has a card complete with a name in every space, play Name Bingo. Call out a name and have each child with that name on her grid cover it with a marker of your choice. When someone covers a row across or down, she says, "Name Bingo!"

Katie Zuehlke—Gr. K
Bendix Elementary
Annandale, MN

Name Bingo		
A.J.	Sarah	Drew
Chanel	Jacoby	Ian
Duncan	Shakira	Li
Max	Robbie	Rebecca

Snowball Counting
• • • • • Math • • • • •

These snowballs are soft, white, and perfect for counting! Seat students in a circle; then place a sand bucket with a large supply of white cotton balls in the center. Add two sand shovels—or in this case, *snow* shovels—and you're set! Call on two students at a time. Give them a number of snowballs to count out from the bucket. Have them use the shovels to remove the snowballs as the group helps them count aloud. Then have them return to the circle with their piles. Continue with two more students until everyone has a pile of snowballs. Have students recount their snowballs and then compare their sets with a neighbor. Next, have each pair share its comparison results with the class. Then it's time for that traditional kid favorite—a snowball toss into a bucket!

adapted from an idea by
Cathy Peterson—Gr. K
Old Suwanee Christian School
Buford, GA

Alphabet Soup
• • • • • Letter Review • • • • •

Cook up some fun at circle time! Give each child a disposable bowl and a handful of magnetic letters. Call out one letter at a time. Any child who has that letter may add it to his bowl of "alphabet soup." Whose soup will be done first? Continue until every child has put all his letters in his bowl. Then change the activity by calling out a word and having each student place the correct beginning letter in his bowl. Soup's on!

Michele Tunstall—Gr. K
Cambria County Christian School
Johnstown, PA

Time!
Activities and Games

Penguins Afloat
• • • • • **Number, Letter, and Shape Review** • • • • •

These perky penguins will help you review basics with your youngsters and then provide more fun during center time! Make a class supply of simple penguin patterns and then laminate them. Label the back of each penguin with a letter, a number, or a shape. Have each child cut out a penguin. Tape a flat toothpick to the back of each student's penguin. Have her insert the free end of the toothpick into a piece of scrap foam packaging.

Before circle time, partially fill your water table or a small pool with water. Gather students and call out a number, a letter, or a shape. The child with that penguin may then place it in the water. Continue until all the penguins are afloat. At center time, invite youngsters to play with the penguins and encourage them to sort the penguins into three groups: letters, numbers, and shapes.

Sandy Burchette—Gr. K
Newport Grammar School
Newport, TN

Morning News by All of Us!
• • • • • **Language** • • • • •

Include everyone in "writing" your morning news with this neat idea! Write all the words from your daily news on individual notecards. Pass out the cards to students; then have everyone help put the news together! (Use a similar format each day so that students will become familiar with the order of key words.) Put the news together by inserting the cards into a pocket chart. Or prepare the cards for use on a flannelboard and post the news there each day.

Deborah Patrick—Gr. K
Park Forest Elementary
State College, PA

Today	is	Monday.
We	go	to	art.
Today	is	Nina's	birthday!

She is wearing red shoes.

Special Helper Clues
• • • • • **Self-Esteem, Listening Skills** • • • • •

Identify your special helper of the day in a very special way! Have all students stand; then begin giving clues about the special helper of the day, such as "She is a girl" and "She has brown hair." If the clue does not apply to a child, he sits down. Keep going until only the special helper is left standing and your students have had plenty of practice with listening and identifying characteristics!

Tania Haynes—Gr. K
Webster Niblock School
Medicine Hat, Alberta, Canada

Círcle
Skill-Based Group

Come Read to Us!
• • • • • **Language** • • • • •

Ask some special guest readers to help your class commemorate Dr. Seuss's birthday on March 2. Copy the poem shown. Add the specific information and blanks you wish to use at the bottom of your letter. Then enjoy a day full of rollicking rhyming.

Brenda Saunders—Gr. K
Beale Elementary, Gallipolis Ferry, WV

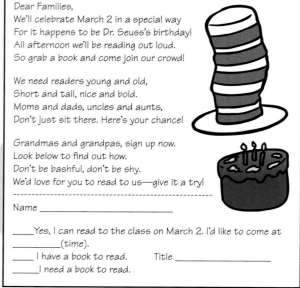

Dear Families,
We'll celebrate March 2 in a special way
For it happens to be Dr. Seuss's birthday!
All afternoon we'll be reading out loud.
So grab a book and come join our crowd!

We need readers young and old,
Short and tall, nice and bold.
Moms and dads, uncles and aunts,
Don't just sit there. Here's your chance!

Grandmas and grandpas, sign up now.
Look below to find out how.
Don't be bashful, don't be shy.
We'd love for you to read to us—give it a try!

Name _____

_____Yes, I can read to the class on March 2. I'd like to come at
_____(time).
_____ I have a book to read.   Title _____
_____I need a book to read.

Kid Patterns
• • • • • **Patterning** • • • • •

Have students really get a feel for patterning when they use themselves! Seat students in a circle. Choose one child to start the pattern. Ask him to take a position to represent an object of his choice. He might sit hugging his knees to be a rock, sit cross-legged to be a pretzel, stand straight to be a stick, or stand in jumping jack position to be an X. Then have the child next to him choose a different position/object. Establish the pattern (for example, say, "Rock, pretzel"); then have the next child in the circle assume the correct position to keep the pattern going. Continue until everyone is part of the pattern!

K Casey—Gr. K
Tiny Tots Preschool and Kindergarten
Auburn, NH

Full of Love
• • • • • **Self-Esteem, Social Skills** • • • • •

Love abounds in February, so why not concentrate on compliments and kindness with your students? Discuss what a compliment is and how it can make a person feel. Give each child in your group a compliment to demonstrate how it's done. Then bring out a heart-shaped latex balloon. Explain that just as compliments fill a person's heart with love, you're going to fill the balloon! Have students volunteer compliments for one another. Each time a compliment is given, blow some air into the balloon. When it's full, explain that you're going to let the balloon go so the kind words can blow through the classroom and be used by everyone throughout the day. Then release the balloon and watch the delight on children's faces! (Be sure to carefully dispose of the balloon afterward.)

Michele Branda
Kindercare Learning Center, Toms River, NJ

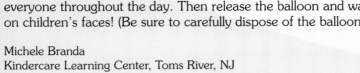

Time!
Activities and Games

Add 'em Up!
• • • • • Addition • • • • •

Introduce youngsters to the plus sign and addition with this giant-size idea! Cut two strips of paper, each about 18 inches long. Lay them on the floor in front of your group to form a plus sign. Discuss what the sign is and what it means. Then call on two students to stand on one side of the plus sign, facing the group. Ask one more student to stand on the opposite side of the plus sign, also facing the group. Demonstrate how to read the resulting number sentence (2 + 1). What's the answer? Direct students to count all the standing students to arrive at the sum of three. Continue with other student volunteers and different addition equations.

Heather Keller—Gr. K
Valley Brook Country Day School
Long Valley, NJ

Play Dough Pictionary
• • • • • Critical Thinking, Creativity • • • • •

This guessing game with a textured twist is great fun anytime! In advance, think of several objects students can create out of play dough, such as grapes, spaghetti, a snowman, a snake, a hot dog, and a sun. Write the name of each object on a separate slip of paper, and draw a picture of the object next to it to help non-readers. Keep the slips in a basket near your group area, along with a container of play dough and an old cookie sheet. At circle time, have a child draw out a slip, identify the object, and create it from the play dough. Have him show his creation to the group; then have his classmates guess what he's made. The first student with a correct guess then gets a turn to draw a slip and create an object.

Sue Lein
Wauwatosa, WI

I like the way you used a period at the end of each sentence.

Happy Thoughts
• • • • • Writing, Communication Skills • • • • •

Encourage positive feedback for your young writers when you ask students to share their happy thoughts. After a child shares his writing, have classmates give him compliments on it. The compliments might refer to the writer's content, the child's spacing skills, or the use of periods at the ends of sentences. Just watch kindergartners grow more confident as they both give and receive these positive words!

Kathleen Reddy—Gr. K
Knights Elementary, Plant City, FL

Circle
Skill-Based Group

A Different Kind of Egg Hunt
• • • • • Science • • • • •

Get youngsters thinking about characteristics of animals with this unique egg hunt! Collect three class supplies of plastic eggs. Into each egg, put a slip of paper with a word or two that could describe an animal, such as *four legs, claws, furry, yellow, wings, beak,* or *webbed feet.* Scatter the eggs around your classroom. At circle time, instruct each child to find three eggs and return to her seat. Have her open her eggs and then help her read the descriptions. Encourage each child to draw an animal with those characteristics on a sheet of construction paper. Some may look real, and some may be really fantastic! Have students name their animals; then display the drawings on a bulletin board for everyone to enjoy.

Bonnie Elizabeth Vontz—Gr. K
Cheshire Country Day School, Milldale, CT

On the Overhead
• • • • • Creating Sentences • • • • •

Put leftover laminating film to good use when teaching your kindergartners to create sentences! Cut the film into rectangles; then label each one with a sight word or vocabulary word you want students to practice and label a few with punctuation marks. Each day, have a student volunteer help you use a few of the words to make a sentence on the overhead projector. At the end of the week, review the sentences made. You'll be amazed at the number of words your students will learn!

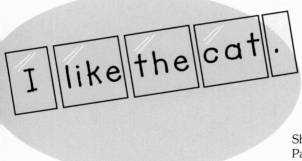

Sharon DeSplinter—Gr. K
Padgett Elementary, Lakeland, FL

Positions, Please!
• • • • • Positional Words • • • • •

Turn a traditional tic-tac-toe grid into a tool for teaching youngsters positional words, such as *left, right, top, middle,* and *bottom.* Draw a tic-tac-toe grid on your board. Then tape a spring-themed cutout in each square. During group time, call out a position, such as "top, right." Have a student volunteer come to the board and remove the cutout in that position. Continue until only one cutout remains. Then challenge students to name the position of the last cutout. Once students have the hang of this activity, invite them to do the position calling as well as the removing of the cutouts. And, if desired, make enough of two different cutouts so that this activity can end in a real game of tic-tac-toe!

Angie Kutzer—Gr. K
Garrett Elementary, Mebane, NC

Time!
Activities and Games

Word Reach
• • • • • **Sight Words** • • • • •

A traditional Twister game is fun, but just wait 'til your youngsters try Word Reach! To make the Word Reach board, use a permanent marker to write lowercase letters all over a clear shower curtain. (Be sure to repeat some letters, especially vowels.) Lay the curtain on a carpeted area. Call out a three- or four-letter word, challenging a child to spell it out by putting her hands, feet, and even her head on the letters needed! What tangled-up fun!

Lisa McDaniel—Gr. K
Foust Elementary, Greensboro, NC

Rhythm Phonics
• • • • • **Language** • • • • •

Add some movement to words when you teach kindergartners this rhythmic way to spell! To begin, write a simple word on your chalkboard, such as "pig." Point out that the *p* and *g* are consonants and the *i* is a vowel. Explain that you're going to clap each time you see a consonant in a word and stomp each time you see a vowel. Draw a hand under each consonant letter and a foot under the vowel as cues. Then have students say the letters with you, clapping or stomping for each letter. Clap and stomp your way through new words each day!

Vada Bobec—Gr. K
Alliance Christian School, Morgantown, WV

Ending Sounds in a Circle
• • • • • **Language** • • • • •

Help your students recognize ending sounds with this speedy circle-time game! Have the class form a circle facing in. Then have one child stand in the center, looking out at one of the children in the circle. This will be her opponent for the first word. Call out a word that ends with a consonant letter. The first of the two opponents to say the word's ending letter wins the round. If the child in the middle wins, she simply turns and faces the next child in the circle. If the child in the outer circle wins, he changes places with the student in the middle and faces the child who was beside him for the next word. Continue play as time and interest allow.

Diana Cubeta—Gr. K
Minue School, Carteret, NJ

49

Circle
Skill-Based Group

Puzzler Perfect
• • • • • **Sequencing Letters** • • • • •

Sequencing the alphabet is easy when you work together! Bring in an alphabet floor puzzle for your group to assemble. Give each child a letter piece. Then have the child holding the letter *A* start the assembly by putting her piece on the floor in front of the group. Have the child with the letter *B* then attach his piece. Keep going until the puzzle is complete. Then invite everyone to sing the "ABC Song" together!

As a variation, give the letter sounds rather than the letter names as each piece is attached.

Joanne Gallagher—Gr. K
St. Bernadette's School
Drexel Hill, PA

Greetings!
• • • • • **Literacy, Communication Skills** • • • • •

Incorporate beginning and ending sounds into your morning hellos! When you gather in the morning, ask all students whose names begin with the same sound to come up and say hi to one another. Or ask children with the same ending sound in their names to greet one another. Continue naming various sounds until every child has had a chance to start the day in a pleasant way!

Deborah Patrick—Gr. K
Park Forest Elementary
State College, PA

Pocket Words
• • • • • **Forming Compound Words** • • • • •

Help your kindergartners practice forming compound words with the help of a shoe bag. Purchase an over-the-door shoe bag with several pockets. Then write on index cards short words that when put together can form compound words, such as *pop* and *corn* or *butter* and *fly*. Put one short word card into each of the shoe bag pockets. Then play a game similar to Concentration. Have a child choose two pockets and read the two words inside. If he can put the two words together to form a compound word, he keeps the cards. If not, he returns the word cards to the pockets and another player takes a turn. The game continues until the pockets are empty and all the compound words have been formed.

Elouise Miller—Gr. K
Lincoln School, Hays, KS

50

Time!
Activities and Games

June

Ordinal Number Review
• • • • • **Month of the Year, Ordinal Numbers** • • • • •

Add even more math practice to your calendar time with this simple idea! After reviewing the name of the month, use it to review ordinal numbers. Ask a child to tell you the first, second, fourth, or whichever letter in the month name. What a first-rate way to review ordinals every day!

Susan McGuirl—Gr. K
Minue School
Carteret, NJ

How Tall Is It? *Really* Tall!
• • • • • **Math, Height** • • • • •

Here's a way to help kindergartners conceptualize heights taller than the ceiling of your classroom, such as those of the giant dinosaurs. Measure a length of string to match the height you want to see. Mark the string in one-foot increments by tying a ribbon around the string at each foot. Then tie one end of the string to a ruler and the other to a bunch of helium-filled Mylar balloons. Outdoors or in a gymnasium with a high ceiling (depending on the height you're measuring), have a child stand on the ruler and let go of the string. Wow—*that's* tall!

Betsy Saunders—Gr. K
The Steward School
Richmond, VA

Time for Baseball
• • • • • **Time** • • • • •

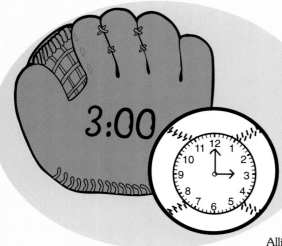

This game for practicing time to the hour is sure to be a hit! Duplicate the baseball and mitt patterns on page 52 to make as many pairs as you wish. Label each mitt with a time to the hour; then make a matching clock on a baseball pattern for each glove.

To play a game, divide your class into teams. Have one team hold the mitts and stand to one side of the room in the outfield. Have the other team line up to bat. The teacher-pitcher hands a baseball to the first batter, who looks at the clock, finds the outfielder holding the matching time, and sits in front of her. If he is correct, he earns a point for his team. If he is incorrect, he gets an out. Then he is guided to the correct outfielder. The two teams change places whenever there are three outs or when everyone has had a turn at bat. Continue the game until each team has had a predetermined number of times at bat.

Allison Pratt—Gr. K
Onalaska Kindergarten Center
Onalaska, WI

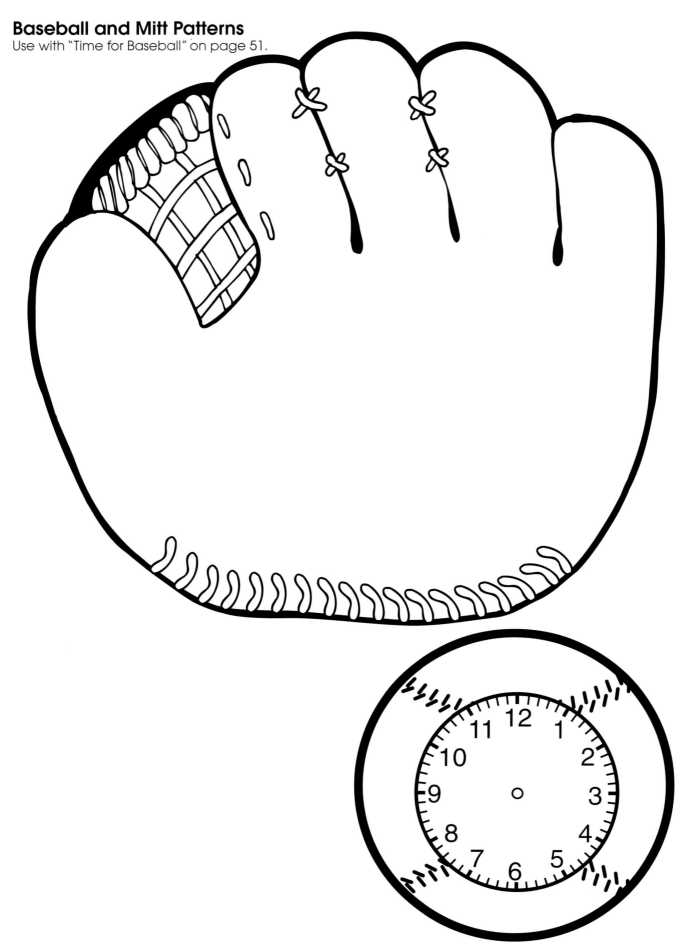

Classroom Displays

CLASSROOM DISPLAYS

Ms. Moss's Class Is "Soup-er"!

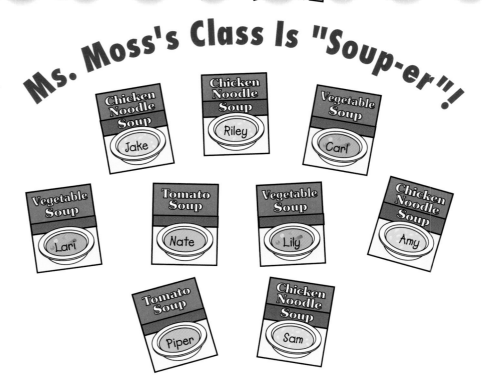

Dish up this cute display to welcome your little ones to kindergarten! In advance, collect a soup label for each child. Fold each label in thirds so that only the front shows. Write a different child's name on each label. Then attach the labels to a wall along with the title shown. Soup's on!

Gail Moss—Gr. K
Westwood School
Camilla, GA

Alert kindergartners to the great things in store for them with this informative picture display! To prepare, locate pictures taken of activities your class participated in during the previous year. To create the display, label a different construction paper balloon cutout with each event and then attach each one to your display near the appropriate set of pictures. At a glance, youngsters will know that kindergarten is going to be a lot of fun!

Marcia Longo—Gr. K, Hancock North Central Elementary, Kiln, MS

After a visit to a pumpkin patch or after having a pumpkin-carving experience, save some pumpkin seeds for this display of pumpkin punctuation! Cut a large pumpkin shape from orange and green bulletin board paper and mount it on a wall. Have each child tell something about the class experience. Record each child's response as a complete sentence on the pumpkin. Then invite her to glue a dried pumpkin seed at the end of her sentence to represent the period. After everyone has contributed, you'll have a fine display about pumpkins…period!

Lin Attaya—Gr. K
Hodge Elementary
Denton, TX

Pumpkins grow on vines. They have seeds inside them. Pumpkins are green before they turn orange. Lots of pumpkins grow in a pumpkin patch.

Show off your youngsters' nursery rhyme knowledge with this bulletin board! Have each student create a square for a nursery rhyme quilt by making a collage picture representing one rhyme. Add the typed verse and the artist's name to each square. Display the squares in quilt fashion on a bulletin board. Then, whenever you have time, say a rhyme!

Taryn Lynn Way—Gr. K, Los Molinos Elementary, Los Molinos, CA

Creativity rules this decorative, triangle-shaped tree! To prepare, cut a supply of green construction paper sheets into 9" x 9" squares. Then cut each square on a diagonal to create two triangles. Have each child decorate a triangle with markers, stickers, or small bows. Attach the finished projects to a wall as shown. For a final touch, add a brown construction paper trunk to the tree. Now that's a one-of-a-kind tree!

Brandy Bowen—Gr. K, Basin Elementary, Idaho City, ID

Kindness is the focal point of this special bulletin board. Discuss with students the meaning of kindness and then have each child write a kind deed that she will do on a sheet of paper. Next, give each child a sheet of tagboard and a piece of holiday gift wrap of the same size. Instruct each youngster to glue her gift wrap to her tagboard and then attach a bow. Staple the pretend present to her writing. Display the projects on a hallway bulletin board along with the title shown. Then encourage passersby to take a peek inside the gifts!

Jennifer Stinnett, Arlington Elementary, Arlington, TN

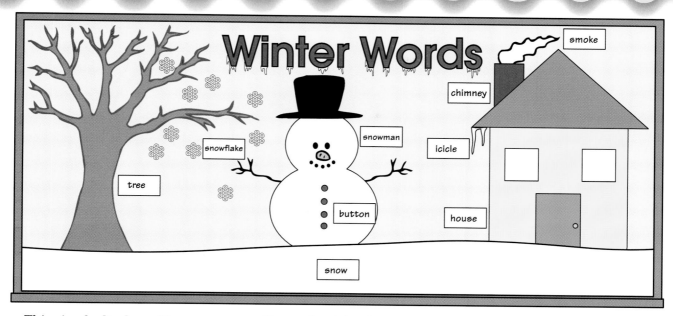

This simple display will encourage reading and writing during the winter season. Have students help you create a winter scene similar to the one shown. Label each part of the scene on an index card. Then add the title shown. Encourage youngsters to read the words and refer to them when they write. Cool!

Carrie Herzog—Gr. K, Lincoln Elementary, West Allis, WI

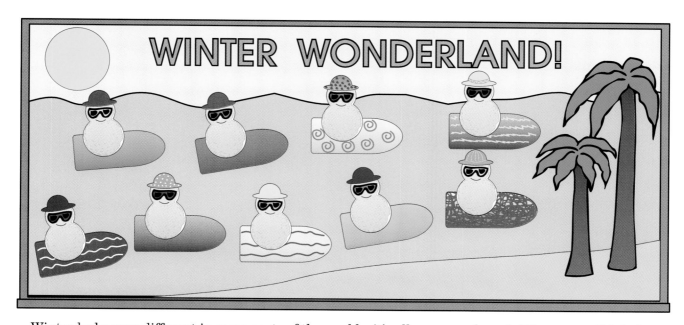

Winter looks very different in some parts of the world—it's all sunny and sandy! To prepare this bulletin board, draw a simple sand person, similar to a snowman, and a surfboard on a sheet of paper. Then make a tagboard photocopy for each child. Give each child a copy and have him color the surfboard and the sand person's hat and sunglasses as desired. Then instruct him to brush glue over his sand person pattern and sprinkle sand on it. Have him shake off the excess sand and then allow the glue to dry. Cover your bulletin board with blue and tan paper as shown. Add bulletin board paper palm trees and a sun. Then staple the sand people to the boards and add the title shown. Surf's up!

Theresa Collins and Marsha Keefer—Grs. K–3 EMH/Primary, Florine Abel Elementary, Sarasota, FL

Grab your magnetic letters! They're an important part of this interactive display. Provide little ones with construction paper hearts (or any shape that fits your theme) and craft items. Invite each youngster to decorate her heart as desired. Post the hearts on a magnetic whiteboard. Put a large supply of magnetic letters in a basket near the board. Have students complete the display by using the letters to form words that label and describe the hearts. Pretty and simple!

Becky Auerbach—Gr. K
Summit View Elementary
Waukesha, WI

Youngsters are eager to learn their addresses to complete this simple bulletin board. To prepare, cover a bulletin board with red paper. Write each child's name and address on a business-size envelope. Take a photo of each student. Cut each picture with pinking shears to create a stamp. Glue each picture to the corner of the appropriate envelope. Randomly staple the envelopes to the board along with a mailbox cut from blue bulletin board paper. As each youngster memorizes her address, use a date stamp to add a postmark to the envelope. Now that's first-rate!

Johanna Litts—Gr. K, North Central Elementary, Hermansville, MI

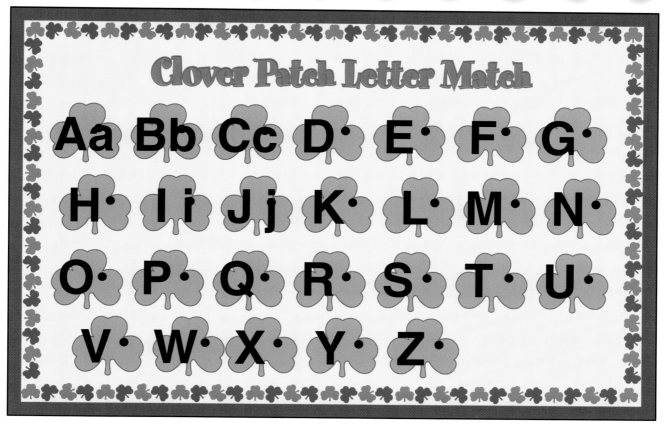

Reinforce letter matching with this bulletin board. In advance, die-cut 26 shamrocks and a set of uppercase letters. Glue one letter to each shamrock and laminate them for durability. Laminate additional paper and then die-cut a set of lowercase letters. Put a piece of a Velcro fastener (hook side) on each shamrock and another piece (loop side) on each lowercase letter. Staple the shamrocks to the board and add the title shown. Place the lowercase letters nearby. Then have each youngster attach the lowercase letters to the appropriate shamrocks.

Melissa Auchenbach—Gr. K, Lower Gwynedd Elementary, Ambler, PA

There will be a buzz in your classroom as students make and write about these clever bugs! To begin, provide each child with construction paper, craft items, scissors, and glue. Instruct him to use the items to make a bug. Then have each child name his bug using his own name as part of its name, like "Kent-beetle" or "Carley-hopper." Then have him write about his bug. Attach the projects and writings to a wall and title the display "Kinder-bugs."

adapted from an idea by Leah Treen
Hillwood Baptist Preschool, Huntsville, AL

Watch your kindergarten kindness garden grow with this blossoming bulletin board! To prepare, cover your board with blue bulletin board paper. Staple green Easter grass along the bottom to represent grass. Cut out a large supply of colorful flower shapes from construction paper. Each time a student does a kind deed, write her name and a brief explanation of her kind act on a different flower shape. Add the title shown to complete the display. Over time your classroom garden will grow and grow with kindness!

Judi Lesnansky—Title 1 Grs. K–4, New Hope Academy, Youngstown, OH

This beautiful rainbow will have students, teachers, and parents taking a closer look to discover what makes its colorful stripes. In advance, have students cut pictures of flowers from discarded gardening magazines. Instruct youngsters to sort the pictures by color. Draw large rainbow stripes on a piece of bulletin board paper. To get students started, use the appropriate marker to label each stripe with a different color of the rainbow. Then instruct each child to glue his pictures to the appropriate stripe of the rainbow. Hang the rainbow in your hallway for all to admire. Beautiful!

Barbara Alley—Multi-age Grs. K–2
Moorestown Children's School
Moorestown, NJ

Lara Renfroe—Gr. K
Heber Springs Elementary School
Heber Springs, AR

Moms will be touched when they view this student-created display on the anatomy of a mother. To prepare, trace the outline of an adult on a long length of bulletin board paper. Have students color the shape to show clothes, shoes, and hair and draw a face to represent a mom. Cut out the mom shape. Then help students decide what each body part of a mom is used for, such as two arms to hug us, a lap for us to sit on when we read, two feet to dance with us, and two eyes to watch us grow. Have each child write one of the characteristics on a sentence strip. Post the mom and strips on a wall with the title shown. She's perfect!

Fran Morcone—Gr. K, Memorial Elementary School
Milford, MA

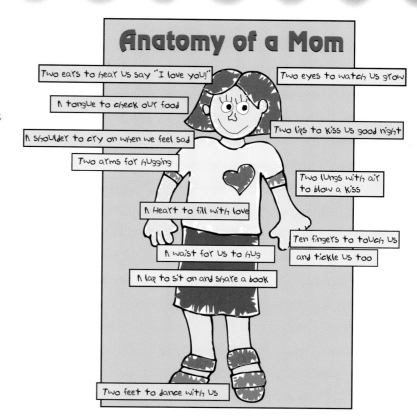

Anatomy of a Mom

Two ears to hear us say "I love you!"

Two eyes to watch us grow

A tongue to check our food

A shoulder to cry on when we feel sad

Two lips to kiss us good night

Two arms for hugging

Two lungs with air to blow a kiss

A Heart to fill with love

Ten fingers to touch us

A waist for us to hug

and tickle us too

A lap to sit on and share a book

Two feet to dance with us

Dropping In on Spring!

This simple springtime bulletin board shows youngsters' artistic talents. In advance, take a photo of each child and have the film developed. Cut out hot-air balloon and basket shapes from tagboard for each student. Invite each child to paint a balloon shape with bright paint. Have him glue his picture to a basket. Then instruct him to glue lengths of yarn to his balloon and basket to connect them as shown. Display the projects on a bulletin board with the provided title.

Melissa L. McCarter—Title 1 Reading and Math, Marlowe Elementary, Hagerstown, MD

Can your students believe you were once their age? They will when you create this display! Title a bulletin board "[Your name] Was in Kindergarten Too!" On the board, post photos and work you've saved from your own kindergarten year. Both students and parents will love this glimpse into your past!

Pablo Millares—Gr. K
Palm Springs North Elementary
Pembroke Pines, FL

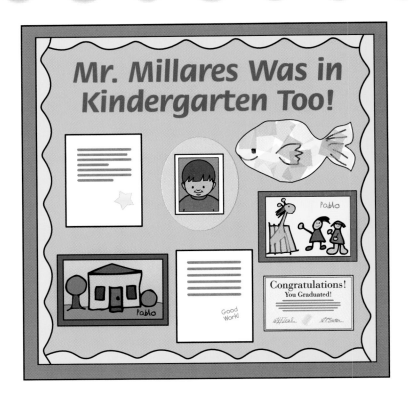

Showcase your kindergarten graduates with this cute display! Have each child decorate a paper plate to look like herself, including yarn for hair. Post all the faces on a bulletin board; then add black paper graduation robes to each figure. Cut black caps and add yarn tassels to resemble graduation caps. Attach the caps above the heads as if they've been thrown into the air. Then add the title shown. Good luck in first grade!

Amy Koch—Gr. K, Kelly Elementary, Benton, MO

Getting Your Ducks in a Row

Tooth Bags

Get ready for lost teeth and proud smiles by preparing these tooth bags at the start of the school year! Simply affix a cute tooth sticker to each one in a supply of resealable plastic bags. Store the bags in a convenient location. Then, when a child comes to you with a tooth, slip it into a bag and use a permanent marker to label the bag with the child's name and the date. Have him put the tooth bag in his backpack for safekeeping.

Ginny Calame
Sonshine School
Salem, OR

Quiet-Time Shelf

Dedicate one shelf in your classroom as the Quiet-Time Shelf. Stock the shelf with quiet, individual activities, such as puzzles, lacing cards, and sequencing activities. These activities will come in handy whenever you need students to be quietly occupied for a few minutes, such as when students finish their work early or you need to leave someone else in charge of your classroom for a minute or two. Rotate the activities periodically to maintain students' interest.

Shelly Fales—Gr. K
Whittemore-Prescott Early Childhood Center
Whittemore, MI

No More Marker Mess

Here's an easy way to keep markers (or pencils) organized and neat! From your local discount store, purchase one or two ice trays designed to make cylindrical ice for sports bottles. Use the trays to store markers instead! The markers fit perfectly in the cylinders and the trays make it easy to move them from one table or center to another.

Karen Hagelstein—Gr. K
Germantown Grade School
Germantown, IL

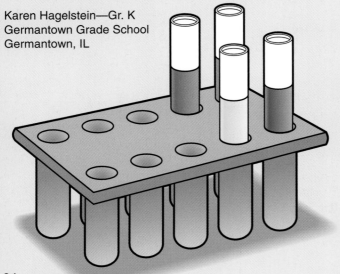

Easy As A, B, C

Want to make collecting and filing papers a snap? Call students in alphabetical order whenever you collect papers or projects you plan to file. Soon students will be in the habit of turning in their work in order, and when it comes time to file, it'll be as easy as A, B, C!

Sheila Weinberg—Gr. K
Warren Point School
Fair Lawn, NJ

Hallway Song

Encourage your little ones to walk quietly in the hallway by having them sing this song with very soft voices.

(sung to the tune of "Battle Hymn of the Republic")

We're going down the hallway just as quiet as can be!
We're going down the hallway just as quiet as can be!
We're going down the hallway just as quiet as can be!
And the quietest one is me!

Tracie Watson
Peter H. Craig Elementary
Augusta, GA

Getting Your Ducks in a Row
Management Tips for the Classroom

Oct. 16

If I went pumpkin picking...

Journal Labels

Use your computer and a sheet of self-adhesive labels to make journal prompts easy! Simply type in the date and the prompt on a label template; add clip art if desired. Then print out a sheet of labels. Affix one label to a page in each child's journal, and you're ready for writing time!

Kelly J. Sickle—Gr. K
Oak Grove Primary
Oak Grove, MO

Restroom Signal

Help keep interruptions to a minimum by teaching your students to signal silently when they need to use the restroom. Show everyone the sign language signal for "toilet." Have each child fold in the middle, ring, and pinky fingers of her left hand. Then have her place her thumb next to her middle finger and bend her index finger down on the outside of her thumb. Anytime a child needs to go to the restroom, have her put up her hand and wave this sign language signal. You'll know what she needs without a word!

Kelly Payne—Gr. K, P. S. 20, Staten Island, NY

From Bathroom to Classroom

Use inexpensive shower curtain liners to minimize mess in your classroom. Use the liners to cover tables for art or cooking projects, or use them under your easel to protect the floor. The liners wipe clean easily and air-dry quickly. If you have desks instead of tables, simply cut the liner into placemats!

Carolyn Kaplan—Gr. K
Rosa G. Maddock School
Burbank, IL

Musical Cleanup

Encourage little ones to clean up quickly and quietly with the help of a music box or musical water globe. Wind the music box or globe; then challenge students to clean up before the music stops. They'll also want to clean quietly so they can hear the music!

Bobbie Redd-Hallman, Don Stowell School, Merced, CA

You Be the Teacher

Give each child a chance to play the part of the teacher with a transitional activity that encourages quiet. As students are finishing their work (or anytime you have a few minutes to fill), have one child sit in the teacher's chair and observe his classmates. Have the junior teacher call on someone who is sitting quietly; then have the two switch places. The new teacher chooses another quiet child, and the activity continues as time allows.

Pam Ferguson—Gr. K, Holy Family School, St. Petersburg, FL

Talking Cubes

Give all your students an equal chance to share during circle-time discussions with this idea. Pass around a basket of Unifix counting cubes and have each child take one. Invite students to share their ideas in any order (rather than going around the circle). Once a student shares what she wants to say, she drops her cube back in the basket, and it becomes someone else's turn. Talkative students will think more carefully about what they want to share, and shy students can have more time to think about their ideas before speaking.

Erin Green—Gr. K
Rosewood Elementary
Rock Hill, SC

A December to Remember

A candy cane, some clothespins, and some inexpensive treats will help keep little ones on track during December. Draw a simple candy cane on poster board, labeling it as shown. Write each child's name on a separate clothespin. At the beginning of the week, clip all the children's clothespins to the bottom section of the candy cane. Each time you see a child exhibiting good behavior, move his clothespin up to the next reward stripe. At the end of the week, reward students whose clothespins are in the three labeled spaces with the specified treats: stickers, lollipops, or inexpensive treats such as pencils or party favor toys.

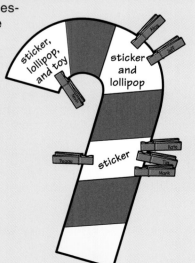

sticker, lollipop, and toy

sticker and lollipop

sticker

Millie Morris—Gr. K
Berkmar Preschool
Lilburn, GA

The M&M's Candy Game

Encourage good behavior with this reward that's also a game of chance! Keep a jar of M&M's candies in your classroom. Each day, have a child choose a "color of the day" for the jar. When you reward a student for good behavior, reach into the M&M's candy jar (without looking) and pull out a candy. If the candy is not the color of the day, the child receives it and the reward is complete. But if the candy *is* the color of the day, you reach in again and the child gets a second candy. Keep going until you pull out a candy that is not the color of the day.

Helen Gayness—Gr. K
Richmond Christian School
Chesterfield, VA

Scissors Storage

You'll be hooked on this idea for storing students' scissors! Attach a class supply of self-adhesive plastic hooks to an old dry-erase board (or other durable surface). Put the board in a location that's handy and easy for children to reach. Above each hook, write a different child's name. Have each youngster hang his scissors on his hook and then take them down when it's time to use them.

Andrea Rothrock—Gr. K
Bowling Green Primary School
Milford, VA

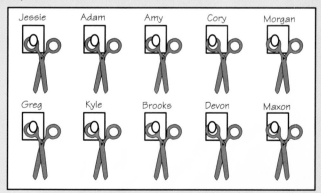

Easy Poster Storage

Keep posters looking new when you store them away in these easy-to-make pockets! Glue together two sheets of poster board along three sides. Laminate the resulting pocket; then slit open the unglued edge. You've got a sturdy poster-size storage pocket!

Patrice Clynes—Gr. K
Plantsville Elementary
Plantsville, CT

The Glue Song

This tune will help remind little ones that just a dot of glue will do!

(sung to the tune of "Mary Had a Little Lamb")

All you need is a little dot, little dot, little dot.
All you need is a little dot
When you use your glue!

Crystal Elliers—Gr. K
Lacoste Elementary
Chalmette, LA

Get More From a Field Trip

Get the most learning possible from a field trip with this easy preview-do-review approach! Before the trip, ask youngsters what they expect to learn and what they want to know. Record this preview on a chart. After the field trip, review the chart and check off what your kindergartners saw and learned. Record this information; then display your field trip chart for students and classroom visitors to read.

Brenda J. Hume
Flowertown Elementary
Summerville, SC

Sunnyvale Farm

Our Questions

• Will we see horses, cows, and pigs?
• How much does a horse eat?
• Will the pigs be muddy?
• Do they have chickens?

What We Learned

Music to a Sub's Ears

Help your substitute's day go smoothly by leaving her easy access to the songs you and your class use throughout the day. Record your class singing songs you use for circle time, transitions, cleanup, or curriculum areas. Then leave the tape where your sub can easily find it—with your lesson plans or near your tape recorder.

Barbara Meyer—Gr. K
Lincoln Elementary
Dayton, KY

Handy Canisters

Do you spend too much time counting out manipulatives for your students to use during math lessons? Try this! Label a film canister for each child. Put ten round counting chips into each canister. Now getting ready for math will be as easy as 1, 2, 3!

Dianne Joseph—Gr. K
Bayou Vista Elementary
Morgan City, LA

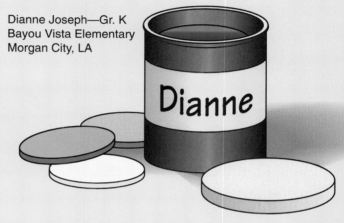

Snack Bucket

Use a decorated ice-cream bucket to make collecting class snacks supersimple! Each day, send the bucket home with a different child. Have the family put a class snack in the bucket and return it to school the next day. Now your snacks will arrive fresh and unbroken!

Dell Tideman
Bryant Elementary
Superior, WI

Getting Your Ducks in a Row
Management Tips for the Classroom

Sub Tub

Make an unexpected absence easier by preparing a Sub Tub ahead of time! Type up your daily schedule, one or two days' worth of lesson plans, a list of your students' names or a seating chart, and the names of helpful students or teachers. Put all the information in a plastic tub, along with stickers or other rewards for students. And don't forget a thank-you note and a candy bar for the sub!

Laura Arnold
Creative Corner Child Care
High Point, NC

Tracy Pearcy—Gr. K
Audubon School
Merritt Island, FL

Musical Cleanup

Teach youngsters this tune to help them stay focused during cleanup time.

(sung to the tune of "Are You Sleeping?")

Are you cleaning, are you cleaning
Our classroom, our classroom?
It is time to clean up.
It is time to clean up.
Let's all help; let's all help!

Laura Butts—Gr. K
Thorndale Elementary
Thorndale, TX

Circle-Time Poem

Use a variety of poetry to help call your students back to your circle area after a project. Choose a poem and begin reciting it when you want students to come to the circle. Encourage everyone to be seated before the poem ends. Keep this activity interesting by changing poems every week or two. Post your current poem on a wall so that it's easy for you to see and students can use it when they read the room.

Kristen Gregory—Gr. K
Binger-Oney Public School
Binger, OK

Pockets Full of Borders

Store your bulletin board borders neatly and within easy reach with an over-the-door shoe organizer. Purchase an organizer with see-through pockets and hang it inside a closet door in your classroom. Store one rolled-up border in each clear pocket. You can see at a glance which borders you have and you'll save space too!

Pam Siudak—PreK and K
Peace Lutheran School
Antigo, WI

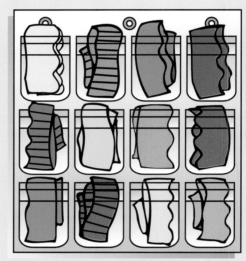

Line Inspection

Try this fun tip to get your students to line up quietly. Keep a small magnifying glass handy in a pocket. Once in a while, pull it out as students are lining up. "Inspect" each child by looking him up and down with the glass. Watch as your students stand straight and still to pass this silly inspection!

Jolene Letourneau—Junior Kindergarten
Elmwood School
Ottawa, Ontario, Canada

Kindergarten Café

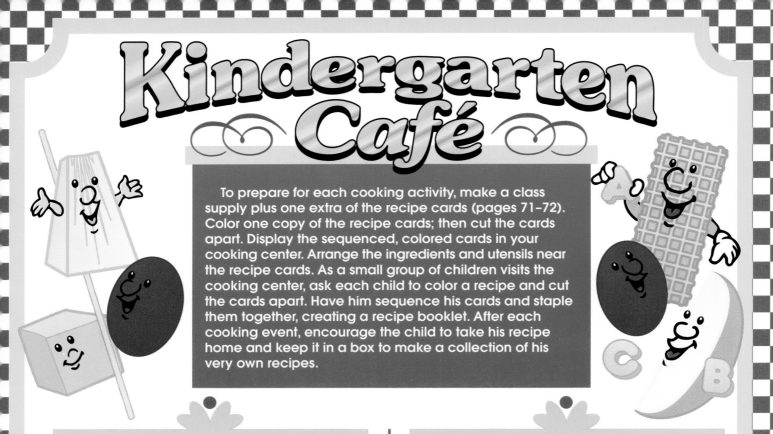

Kindergarten Café

To prepare for each cooking activity, make a class supply plus one extra of the recipe cards (pages 71–72). Color one copy of the recipe cards; then cut the cards apart. Display the sequenced, colored cards in your cooking center. Arrange the ingredients and utensils near the recipe cards. As a small group of children visits the cooking center, ask each child to color a recipe and cut the cards apart. Have him sequence his cards and staple them together, creating a recipe booklet. After each cooking event, encourage the child to take his recipe home and keep it in a box to make a collection of his very own recipes.

Shape Kabob

Ingredients for one:
3 pineapple tidbits (triangular prisms)
3 red seedless grapes (spheres)
3 cheese cubes (cubes)

Utensils and supplies:
paper plate for each child
wooden skewer for each child

Teacher preparation:
- Use clean kitchen shears to cut the pointed end off each skewer.
- Arrange the ingredients, utensils, and supplies for easy student access.

Teresa Kelley—PreK
Broward Estates Elementary
Ft. Lauderdale, FL

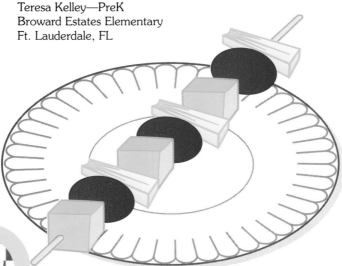

ABC Tree

Ingredients for one:
4 green apple slices (palm leaves)
2 sugar wafers (trunk)
3 red seedless grapes (coconuts)
large spoonful of Alpha-Bits cereal

Utensils and supplies:
paper plate for each child

Teacher preparation:
- Core and cut apples into thin slices.
- Arrange the ingredients, utensils, and supplies for easy student access.

Angie Choate
Mustang Trails Elementary
Mustang, OK

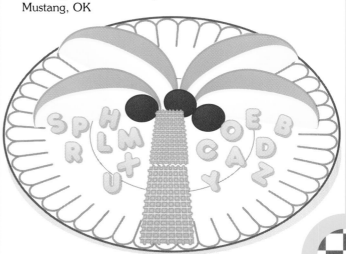

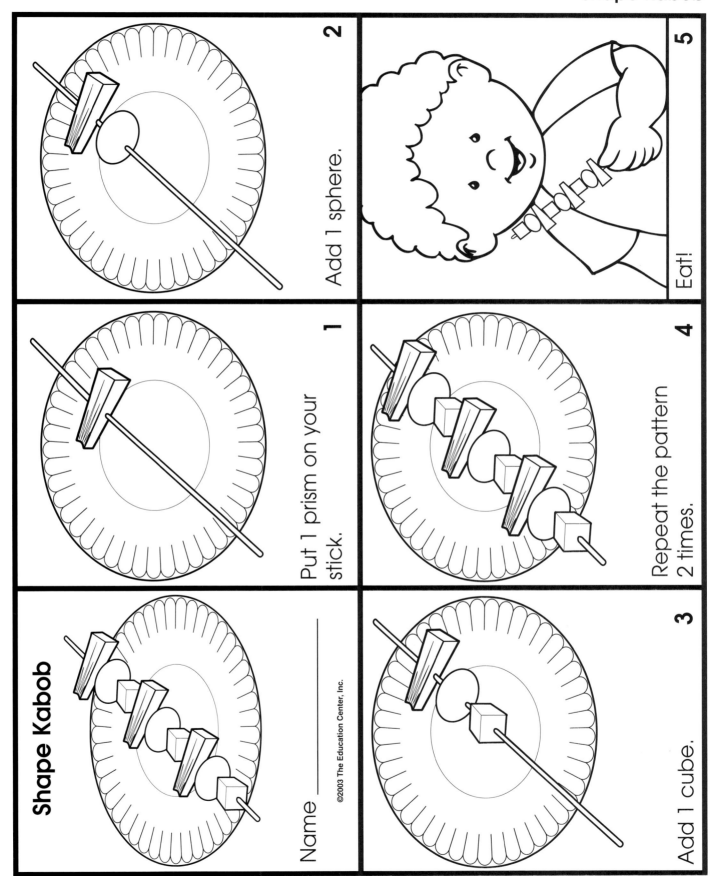

2 Add 1 sphere.

5 Eat!

1 Put 1 prism on your stick.

4 Repeat the pattern 2 times.

Shape Kabob

Name _____

©2003 The Education Center, Inc.

3 Add 1 cube.

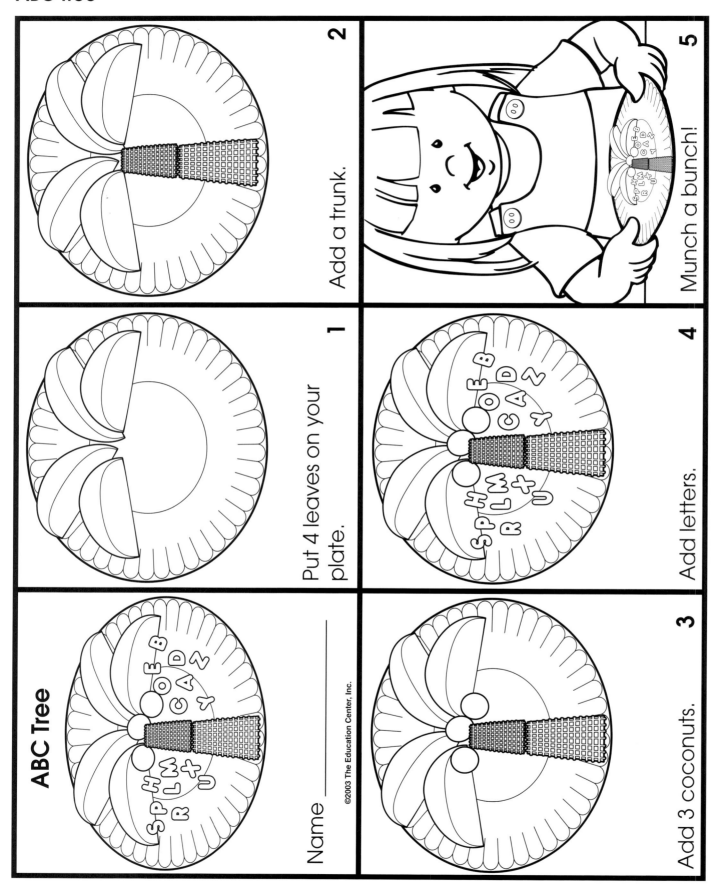

2 Add a trunk.

5 Munch a bunch!

1 Put 4 leaves on your plate.

4 Add letters.

ABC Tree

Name _____

©2003 The Education Center, Inc.

3 Add 3 coconuts.

Kindergarten Café

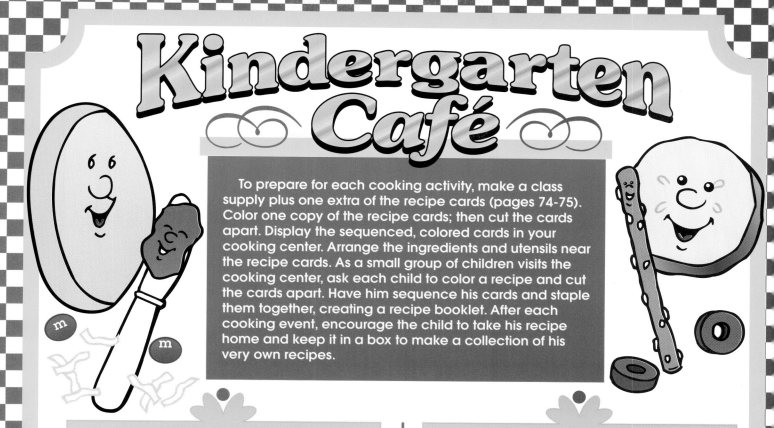

To prepare for each cooking activity, make a class supply plus one extra of the recipe cards (pages 74-75). Color one copy of the recipe cards; then cut the cards apart. Display the sequenced, colored cards in your cooking center. Arrange the ingredients and utensils near the recipe cards. As a small group of children visits the cooking center, ask each child to color a recipe and cut the cards apart. Have him sequence his cards and staple them together, creating a recipe booklet. After each cooking event, encourage the child to take his recipe home and keep it in a box to make a collection of his very own recipes.

Pretend Pizza

Ingredients for one:
sugar cookie (crust)
strawberry jam (tomato sauce)
shredded coconut (cheese)
4 red M&M's candies (pepperoni)

Utensils and supplies:
paper plate for each child
plastic knife for each child

Teacher preparation:
- Put the jam in a bowl and stir until smooth.
- Arrange the ingredients, utensils, and supplies for easy student access.

Rachel Meseke Castro
Castro's Kids
Albuquerque, NM

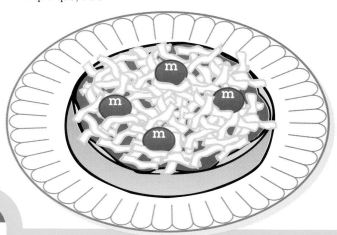

A Spider Bite

Ingredients for one:
cucumber slice (body)
ranch dip
2 black olive slices (eyes)
8 pretzel sticks (legs)

Utensils and supplies:
paper plate for each child
plastic spoon for each child

Teacher preparation:
- Slice cucumbers.
- Drain olive slices.
- Arrange the ingredients, utensils, and supplies for easy student access.

Irene T. Winslow
Cleveland, OH

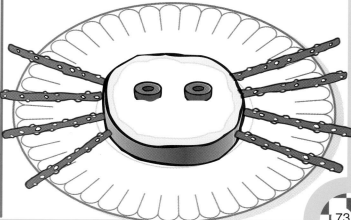

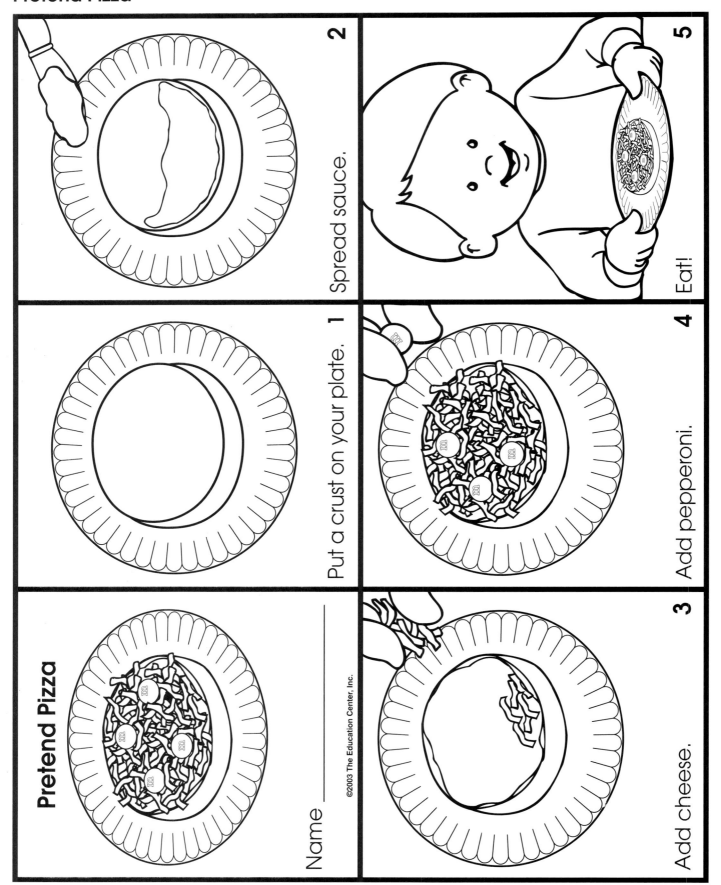

2 Spread sauce.

5 Eat!

1 Put a crust on your plate.

4 Add pepperoni.

Pretend Pizza

Name _____

©2003 The Education Center, Inc.

3 Add cheese.

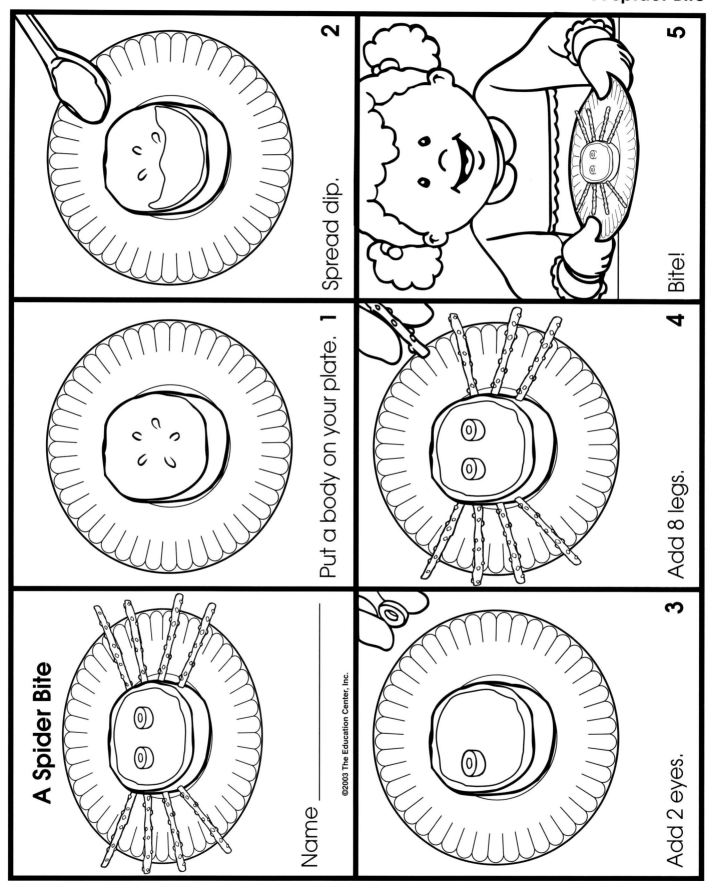

2 Spread dip.

1 Put a body on your plate.

5 Bite!

4 Add 8 legs.

3 Add 2 eyes.

A Spider Bite

Name _____

©2003 The Education Center, Inc.

Kindergarten Café

To prepare for each snack activity, make a class supply plus one extra of the recipe cards (pages 77–78). Color one copy of the recipe cards; then cut the cards apart. Display the sequenced, colored cards in your snack center. Arrange the ingredients and utensils near the recipe cards. As a small group of children visits the snack center, ask each child to color a recipe and cut the cards apart. Have him sequence his cards and staple them together, creating a recipe booklet. After each snack event, encourage the child to take his recipe home and keep it in a box to make a collection of his very own recipes.

A Warm Snowflake

Ingredients for one:
8" flour tortilla
melted butter
powdered sugar (snow)

Utensils and supplies:
paper plate for each child
clean school scissors
shaker for powdered sugar
pastry brush

Teacher preparation:
- Wash several pairs of scissors in a dishwasher to clean them.
- Wrap tortillas in damp paper towels and microwave for 15 to 30 seconds.
- Melt butter in a bowl.
- Put powdered sugar in a shaker container.
- Arrange the ingredients, utensils, and supplies for easy student access.

Allison Pratt—Gr. K
Onalaska Kindergarten Center
Onalaska, WI

Snowman S'more

Ingredients for one:
half a graham cracker (two sections)
2 large marshmallows
vanilla frosting
black cake-decorating gel
orange cake-decorating gel

Utensils and supplies:
paper plate for each child
plastic knife for each child

Teacher preparation:
- Break graham crackers in half.
- Arrange the ingredients, utensils, and supplies for easy student access.

adapted from an idea by Shannon Martin—Gr. K
Children's World
Frankfort, IL

2

Cut out shapes.

5

Sprinkle snow and eat!

1

Fold your tortilla.
Fold it again.

4

Brush it with butter.

A Warm Snowflake

Name _____

©2003 The Education Center, Inc.

3

Unfold your snowflake!

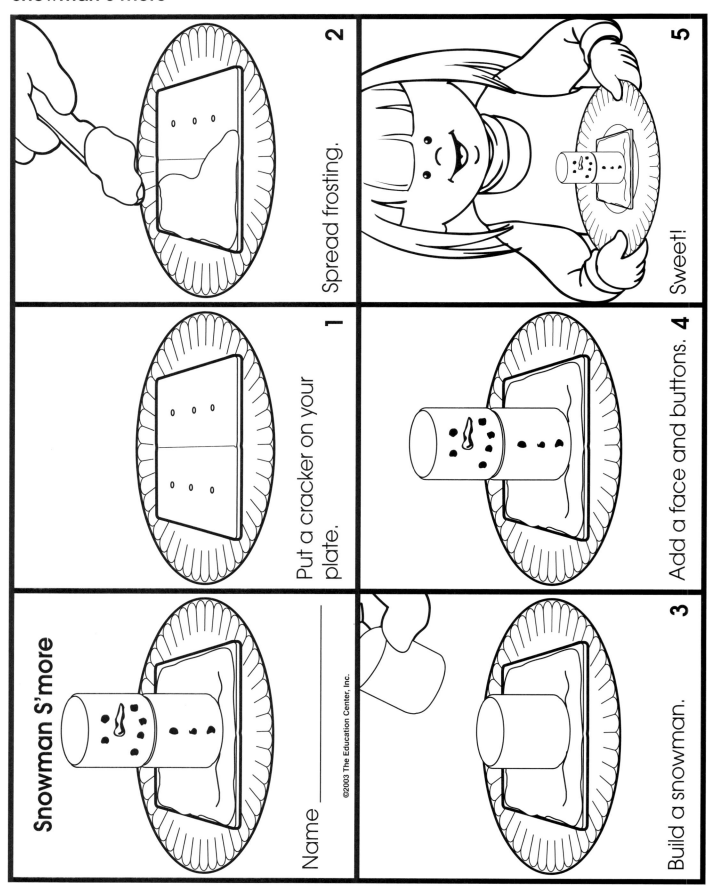

2 Spread frosting.

5 Sweet!

1 Put a cracker on your plate.

4 Add a face and buttons.

Snowman S'more

Name _____

©2003 The Education Center, Inc.

3 Build a snowman.

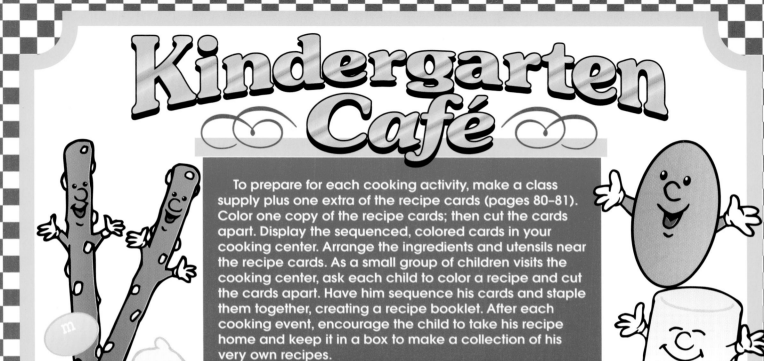

Kindergarten Café

To prepare for each cooking activity, make a class supply plus one extra of the recipe cards (pages 80–81). Color one copy of the recipe cards; then cut the cards apart. Display the sequenced, colored cards in your cooking center. Arrange the ingredients and utensils near the recipe cards. As a small group of children visits the cooking center, ask each child to color a recipe and cut the cards apart. Have him sequence his cards and staple them together, creating a recipe booklet. After each cooking event, encourage the child to take his recipe home and keep it in a box to make a collection of his very own recipes.

Bacon and Eggs

Ingredients for one:
2 pretzel sticks (bacon)
vanilla baking chips, melted (egg whites)
2 yellow M&M's candies (yolks)

Utensils and supplies:
piece of waxed paper for each child
plastic spoon for each child
access to a refrigerator

Teacher preparation:
- Right before making this recipe, melt baking chips in the microwave until smooth.
- Arrange the ingredients, utensils, and supplies for easy student access.

Emily Porter—Gr. K
Garth Elementary School
Georgetown, KY

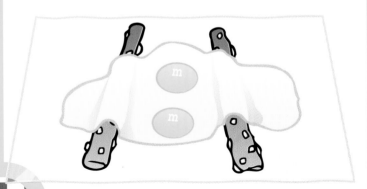

A Hat Snack

Ingredients for one:
vanilla wafer
vanilla frosting
large marshmallow
red decorating gel

Utensils and supplies:
paper plate for each child
plastic knife for each child

Teacher preparation:
- Arrange the ingredients, utensils, and supplies for easy student access.

Pam Arntson—Gr. K
Colfax Elementary School
Colfax, WI

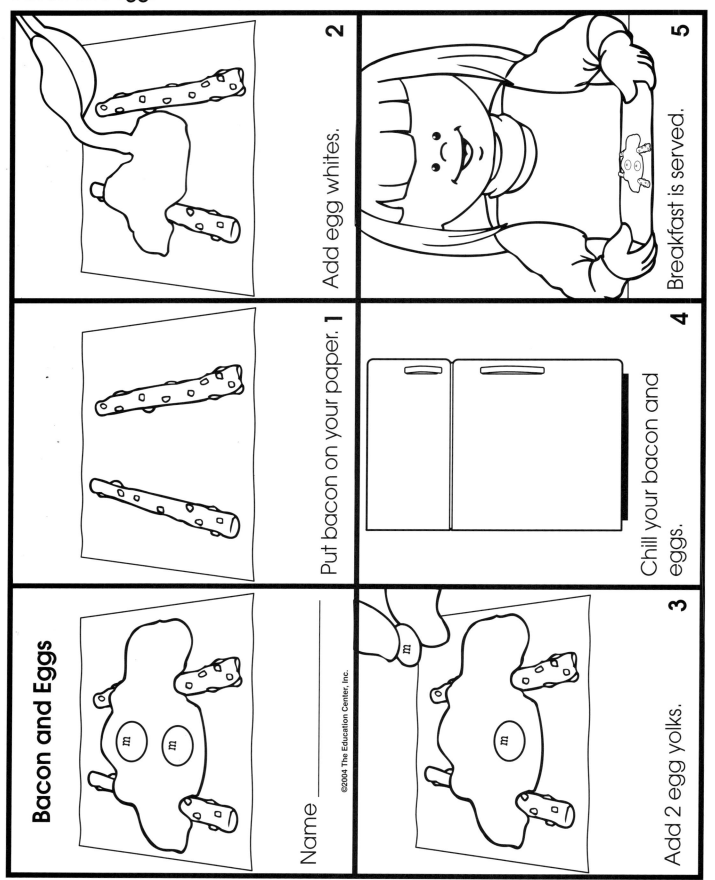

Bacon and Eggs

Name _____

Put bacon on your paper. 1

Add egg whites. 2

Add 2 egg yolks. 3

Chill your bacon and eggs. 4

Breakfast is served. 5

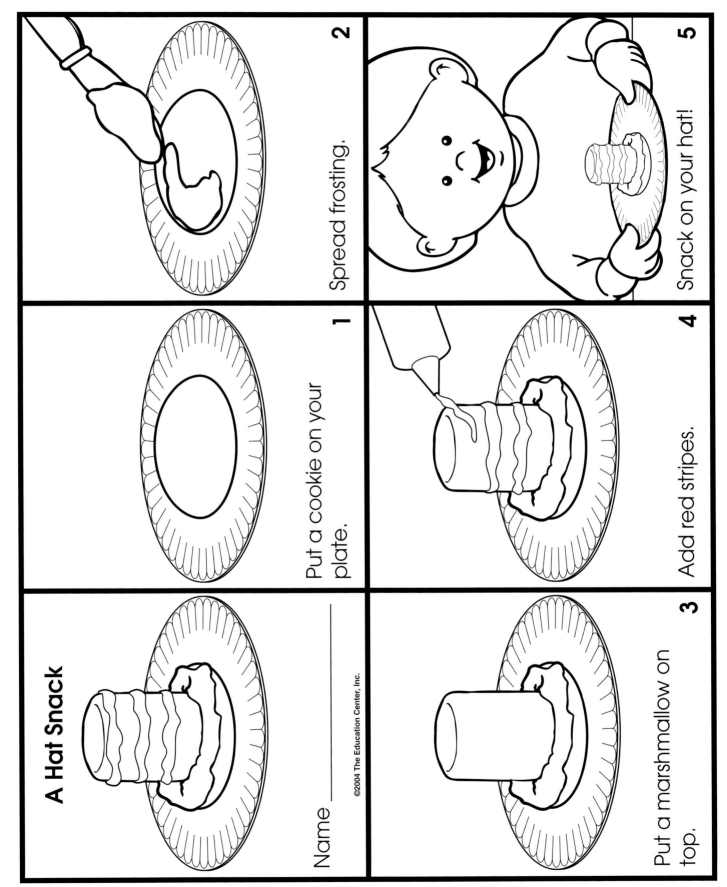

2 Spread frosting.

5 Snack on your hat!

1 Put a cookie on your plate.

4 Add red stripes.

A Hat Snack

Name _____

©2004 The Education Center, Inc.

3 Put a marshmallow on top.

Kindergarten Café

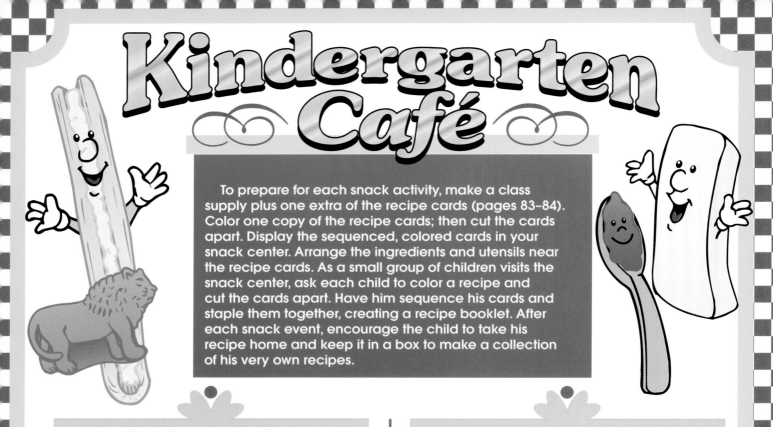

To prepare for each snack activity, make a class supply plus one extra of the recipe cards (pages 83–84). Color one copy of the recipe cards; then cut the cards apart. Display the sequenced, colored cards in your snack center. Arrange the ingredients and utensils near the recipe cards. As a small group of children visits the snack center, ask each child to color a recipe and cut the cards apart. Have him sequence his cards and staple them together, creating a recipe booklet. After each snack event, encourage the child to take his recipe home and keep it in a box to make a collection of his very own recipes.

Animal Parade

Ingredients for one:
4" celery stick
strawberry-flavored cream cheese
3 animal crackers

Utensils and supplies:
paper plate for each child
plastic knife for each child

Teacher preparation:
• Arrange the ingredients, utensils, and supplies for easy student access.

Alyson Sykes—Grs. K–5
Covenant Christian Day School
Greensboro, NC

Red, White, and Blue Roll-Up

Ingredients for one:
slice of white bread (no crusts)
blueberry jam
strawberry jam

Utensils and supplies:
paper plate for each child
2 plastic spoons for each child
access to a small rolling pin

Teacher preparation:
• Arrange the ingredients, utensils, and supplies for easy student access.

adapted from an idea by Allison Pratt—Gr. K
Onalaska Kindergarten Center
Onalaska, WI

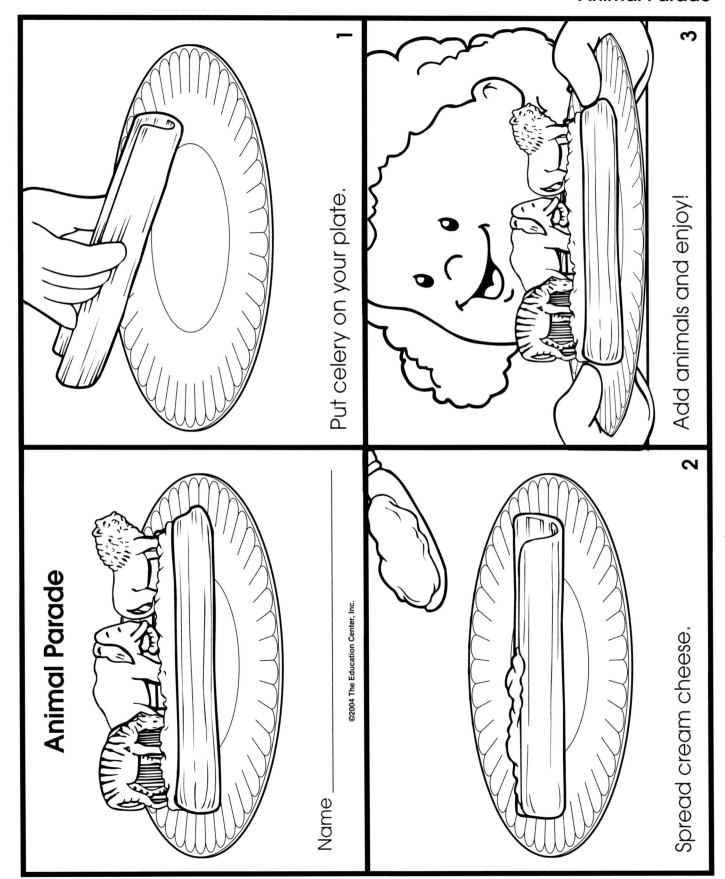

1

Put celery on your plate.

3

Add animals and enjoy!

Animal Parade

Name _____

©2004 The Education Center, Inc.

2

Spread cream cheese.

Recipe Cards
Red, White, and Blue Roll-Up

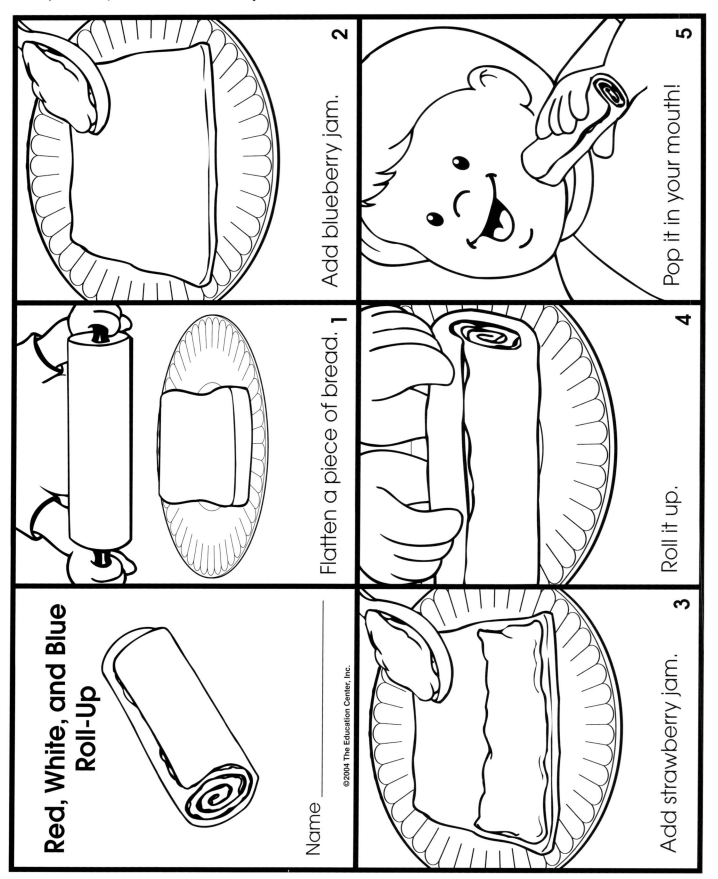

2 Add blueberry jam.

5 Pop it in your mouth!

1 Flatten a piece of bread.

4 Roll it up.

Red, White, and Blue Roll-Up

Name _____

©2004 The Education Center, Inc.

3 Add strawberry jam!

©The Education Center, Inc. • *The Mailbox®* Kindergarten • TEC42013 • June/July 2004

LEARNING CENTERS

Learning Centers

Game Center

A Twist on the Twister Game

Make learning left and right as well as colors more interesting by transforming a Twister game mat! Over each of the colored circles, place a clip-art picture of a school supply. For example, cover the blue circles with blue crayons, the red circles with red pencils, the yellow circles with yellow glue bottles, and the green circles with green scissors. Use clear Con-Tact paper to keep the clip-art pictures in place. Then spin the spinner and start playing. Right hand, red pencil!

Sheila Crawford—Five-Year-Olds
Kids Kampus
Huntington, IN

Language Center

Classmate Memory Game

Your new kindergartners will love being the focus of a game that helps them learn one another's names and faces. To prepare, take a head-and-shoulders photo of each child. Order double prints when you have the film developed. Mount each photo on a separate piece of tagboard, write each child's name below her picture, and then laminate the resulting cards for durability. Have students play the game by matching the cards as in a traditional game of Memory. If your class is large, have students use just the boys, just the girls, or some other subgroup at first. It's a match!

Leanne Gibbons—Grs. K and 1
Boston Public Schools—Mattapan
Mattapan, MA

Social Studies Center

Helpers Galore

Invite youngsters to think about a variety of community helpers with this artistic idea! Make a template of the person pattern on page 98. Cut out a large supply of people from a variety of skin-toned colors of paper. Make several tagboard tracers of the shirt and pants patterns. Place the cutouts, the tracers, scissors, crayons, construction paper, and glue at a center. Encourage each child to trace and cut out a shirt and pants to make a particular community helper; for example, he might cut out blue pants and a blue shirt for a police officer. Have him glue the clothes in place on a person cutout. Then invite him to use crayons and construction paper to add details, such as a hat, badge, and walkie-talkie. With these simple patterns, the possibilities are endless!

Terry Schreiber—Gr. K, Holy Family School, Norwood, NJ

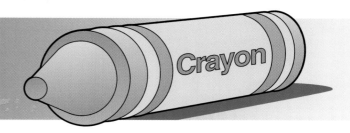

Typewriter Tasks

Give your youngsters an old-fashioned writing experience when you bring in a manual typewriter! Search for one at garage sales or thrift stores. Then invite your students to use the typewriter for a variety of tasks (see the list below). Students may even come up with their own typing activities!

- Type the letters of the alphabet in order.
- Type numbers from 1 to 10.
- Type your full name.
- Type classmates' names (from a list).
- Type color words.

Jamie Nolan—Gr. K, P.S. 58, Maspeth, NY

On a Roll

For some mouthwatering math manipulatives, try this easy idea! Cut six or more circles from tan craft foam. Drizzle white puffy paint over the top of each circle so that it resembles a cinnamon roll. Allow the paint to dry completely. Then store the rolls in a clean, resealable package from real frozen cinnamon rolls! Invite students at your math center to use the imitation rolls for counting, adding, and subtracting. Sweet!

Colleen Dabney

Itty-bitty Beans

What do you get when you combine soap dishes, soybeans, and tweezers? An activity to improve your kindergartners' fine-motor skills! Begin by purchasing a few inexpensive suction cup soap holders, a few pairs of tweezers, and a bag of soybeans. Place the beans, soap dishes, and tweezers on a tray in your fine-motor area. Have each child use tweezers to pick up one bean at a time and place it into one of the suction cups on a soap dish. Have her continue in this manner until each suction cup is filled.

Barbara Blalock
Tutor Time
Phoenix, AZ

Learning Centers

Dramatic-Play Center

Firefighters to the Rescue!

Invite little ones to dress as firefighters with these easy-to-make air packs. For each pack, cut a 7½" x 12" piece of cardboard. Spray-paint the cardboard and an empty three-liter soda bottle yellow. Next, cut two 34-inch lengths of 1½-inch-wide black grosgrain ribbon. Tie each length into a loop; then use duct tape to attach the loops to one side of the cardboard as shown. Add black electrical tape to the tank to create stripes. Use a heavy-duty adhesive to glue the painted bottle, neck down, to the other side of the cardboard. Invite a child to wear the air tank like a backpack and to don a child-size pair of swim goggles for a final touch. Where's the fire?

Jean Muse—Gr. K
Hazelwood Elementary
Waynesville, NC

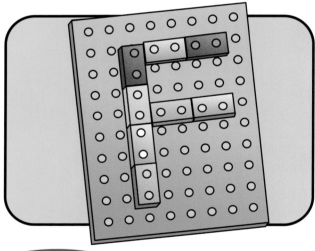

Literacy Center

Letters From LEGO Blocks

Build students' interest in letter formation with the help of LEGO building blocks! Give each child in the center a green LEGO baseplate and a supply of LEGO blocks. Have her make the letters found in her name, your letter of the week, or letters of her choice. What a fun, multisensory approach to learning letters!

Susan Westley—Gr. K
Poinciana Elementary School
Naples, FL

Math Center

Dot-to-Dot and Count a Lot!

Help your kindergartners practice counting and number sequence with laminated dot-to-dot pictures! Simply place a variety of laminated dot-to-dot activity sheets at your math center, along with dry-erase markers and a box of tissues. Have a student use a marker to follow the dots on a page, using a tissue to erase any mistakes and to clean the page after he's admired the finished picture. Ready for another sheet? There are lots of dots at this center!

Wanda Rikli—Gr. K
Beaver City Elementary
Beaver City, NE

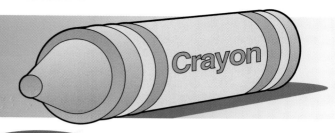

Logo Memory Game

Motivate young readers with this game that involves environmental print. Gather pairs of logos that youngsters will likely recognize, such as those from cereal boxes, toy ads, or supermarket ads. Glue each logo to a separate tagboard card; then laminate the cards for durability. Encourage students to try to match pairs of cards as they would for a game of Memory. Have them read aloud the words on the logo each time they turn over a card. Hey! I can read that!

Donna Hafner—Gr. K
Maryvale Primary School
Cheektowaga, NY

Math Center

Pattern Cans

Take those chip cans from potatoes to patterning! To make a pattern can, cover a Pringles potato crisps can with white paper. Then lay the can on its side and draw a simple pattern along the length of the can. Drop the matching manipulatives inside the can and pop the top back on. You might use counting cubes, teddy bear counters, cereal pieces, or links. At your math center, have each child pour out the manipulatives and then copy and extend the pattern on a tabletop.

Toni Osterbuhr—Gr. K
Price-Harris Elementary
Wichita, KS

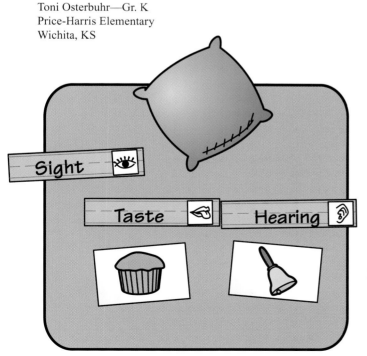

Science Center

"Sense-ational"!

This activity is sure to spark discussions and help your students better understand the five senses. Plus, it's fun! To prepare, make two copies of the pictures on page 99 and cut them apart. Color the pictures if desired. Use Sticky-Tac adhesive to attach each one (except for the senses) to cover an X or an O on a Toss Across gameboard. Then label five sentence strips with the five senses and glue on the corresponding symbols from page 99; then attach them to your chalkboard or a wall.

To play, have a child toss a beanbag onto the Toss Across board. When the square that is hit stops spinning, have the child remove the picture on it. Ask her to place the picture under one of the senses headings and explain why she thinks it belongs there. Invite a discussion by asking a question such as "Does anyone have another idea of where the picture could go?" Continue until all the pictures have been placed on the board.

Sharon Cornwall—Gr. K
Tarawa Terrace 1 Primary
Tarawa Terrace, NC

Learning Centers

Block Stories

Add a language link to your block area when you encourage kindergartners to compose stories about their structures! When a child's building is complete, have him write a story about his block creation. Take a photo of the child next to his block structure; then display the photo and story together in your block center. Watch as students' creativity grows and leads to imaginative stories!

Kathy Massengale—Gr. K
Woodward Academy
Riverdale, GA

The Candy Castle
My casal is mad from candy bloks.

Kent

Literacy Center

Shoveling Sounds

Learning beginning sounds is "snow" much fun with this idea! To prepare, label each of three sand shovels with a different letter you wish your students to focus on. Next, die-cut a supply of snowflakes or laminate a supply of small paper doilies to serve as snowflakes. On each snowflake, glue a clip art picture of an item with one of the three chosen letters as its beginning sound. Have the snowflakes "fall" in your literacy center; then invite three students to shovel the snow! Have each child choose a shovel and look for flakes with the corresponding letter sound at the beginning. Have the child put her shoveled snow into a sand pail or small bucket. For an added challenge, glue a clip art picture of an item ending with one of the letters to each flake in a different set. Then repeat the activity, having youngsters sort the pictures by beginning or ending sounds. When all the snow has been shoveled, have each child sort her flakes into two piles—beginning and ending sounds.

Andrea Singleton—Gr. K
Waynesville Elementary
Waynesville, OH

Reading Center

Logo Discovery Bottle

Here's a fun twist on letter identification! Cut out a large, familiar logo from packaging, such as a cereal box or soda carton. Then cut out the letters to spell the brand name from craft foam. Fit the foam letters into a 20-ounce clear soda bottle. Then fill the bottle with water and cap it securely with glue around the inside of the cap. Have a child twist and turn the bottle to find each of the letters to spell the logo. Can he spell any other words?

Jill Davis—Gr. K
Kendall-Whittier Elementary
Tulsa, OK

SMILE-Os

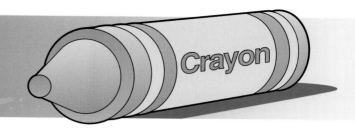

Math Center

Stuff the Stockings

Ho, ho, ho! Candy canes and stockings provide an especially festive way to practice counting! Cut out 15 stocking shapes from construction paper. Label each one with a number from 1 to 15. Have a child identify the numeral on each stocking and then count out a corresponding number of mini candy canes to "fill" each one.

Vary the skill for this activity by labeling the stockings with number words instead of numerals.

Andrea Singleton—Gr. K
Waynesville Elementary
Waynesville, OH

Sensory Center

Gel? Gee!

Add a little water and voilà—swell gel! Visit your local craft store to purchase pellets of houseplant potting medium that turns to gel when water is added. Put several vials in your sensory table; then add water as directed. The substance will increase in volume and resemble crushed ice. Invite your young explorers to feel the gel and to use a variety of containers to see which will hold the most or least gel. Encourage them to pour the gel from one container to another and explore the volume of the various containers. And after the gel sits for a day, you can add food coloring to make it even more interesting!

Tania Haynes—Gr. K
Webster Niblock School
Medicine Hat, Alberta, Canada

Literacy Center

Trim a Tree

Trim a tree with any letters you wish for this activity with holiday flair! To prepare, cut out three large Christmas trees from green construction paper. Add a yellow paper star to the top of each tree; then label each star with a different letter you want to reinforce. Next, glue clip art pictures of items with your chosen letters' beginning sounds onto simple construction paper circles. To use the center, a child chooses a paper ornament, identifies the picture's beginning sound, and adds it to the corresponding tree. He continues until he's trimmed all the trees with all the ornaments. Ah, how festive!

Andrea Singleton

91

Learning Centers

Literacy Center

Oh, My—Cherry Pie!

Take note of Washington's birthday with this cherry pie activity, which gives youngsters practice with word families. Label three disposable aluminum pie tins, each with a different word family. Then die-cut a supply of circles from red craft foam to serve as cherries. Glue a picture to each cherry, showing an object that belongs to one of the three word families on the pie tins. Have a youngster take one cherry at a time from a pail and sort it into the correct pie tin. When she's sorted all the cherries, add extra flavor (and learning) to this activity by having her write a list of all the words in one of the pies.

Andrea Singleton—Gr. K
Waynesville Elementary
Waynesville, OH

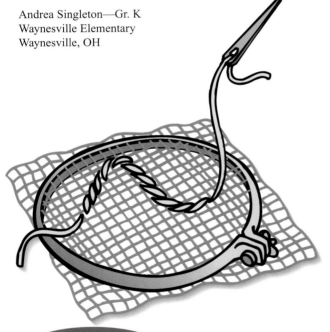

Fine-Motor Center

Mesh Masterpieces

Sewing cards are wonderful tools for fine-motor development, but un-sewing them when youngsters are done can be tedious. Here's an alternative! Cut out pieces from the mesh bags that fruit and vegetables come in at the grocery store. Place a piece of mesh in an embroidery hoop; then have a child use a large plastic needle and yarn to sew a design on the mesh. When he's done, take the mesh piece out of the hoop and invite him to take it home. Then simply snap in a new piece of mesh for another child. Easy!

Ann Gordon—Grs. K–2
HiMount Community School
Milwaukee, WI

Science Center

Animal Twister Game

Here's an active game that reinforces families in the animal kingdom! Take an old Twister game mat. Cover each dot on the mat randomly with a picture of a different bird, fish, reptile, or mammal. On the game's spinner, write those category names randomly on the colored circles of the spinner. To play, one child spins and calls out the direction, such as "Right hand, bird!" A player must put his right hand on any bird on the mat. The spinning and twisting continue until each player loses his balance and falls, leaving one winner just as in the original game. Meanwhile, students are classifying animals as they have fun!

Jill Davis—Gr. K, Kendall-Whittier Elementary
Tulsa, OK

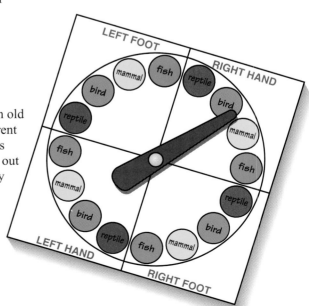

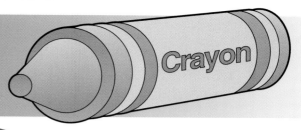

Clippin' Clothes

Little ones will find the miniature clothes and clothespins in this activity irresistible! Cut several different pieces of clothing from colorful half sheets of construction paper. Laminate the clothing pieces for durability. Then label each one with a different number word or a simple addition problem. Put the clothing and a supply of colorful miniature plastic clothespins (found at craft and discount stores) at your math center. A child reads the number word and attaches the corresponding number of clothespins to the garment. Or she solves the addition equation and clips on the number of clothespins equal to the sum. Watch as your students' math skills develop at a fast clip!

Brenda S. Beard—Gr. K, Greenbrier Elementary
Greenbrier, TN

Kids in the Candy Store

Sweet treats seem to be everywhere in February, so why not set up a candy store in your dramatic-play area? Put a cash register and some play money, as well as napkins and paper plates in the center. Have students help you make candy from play dough or clay. To make lollipops, roll the clay into long snakes, coil them, and add craft stick handles. Also press clay or dough into candy molds (sold at your local craft store). Be sure to stock the center with some waxed paper so students can wrap their candy creations. And, of course, add some empty candy boxes (especially heart-shaped ones) for those who want to buy a special someone a selection of sweet treats!

Jennifer Feldmann—Gr. K
Walnut Creek Day School
Columbia, MO

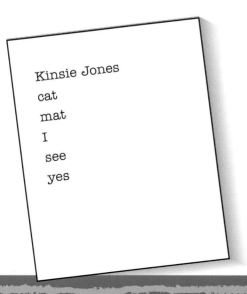

I Can Type!

This idea for your writing center will have youngsters developing fine-motor skills! In advance, prepare an individual index card with each child's name on it. Put these in your writing center, along with an old typewriter and a supply of paper. Invite each child to type her name on a sheet of paper, using her card as a guide. Then have her type any other words she knows. Invite each youngster to share her list with the class. Rat-a-tat-tat!

Andrea Henderson
Jefferson Brethren School
Goshen, IN

Learning Centers

Dig It!

Spelling at the sand table? Sure! Bury a large supply of magnetic letters in the sand of your sand table. Near the table, place a magnetic board and a stack of word cards with sight words or vocabulary words you want students to learn. Have a child choose a card and then dig for the letters needed to spell it on the magnetic board.

Jean Ricotta—Lead Teacher
Signal Hill Elementary, Dix Hills, NY

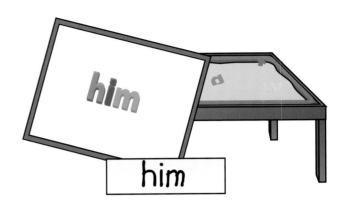

How Many Pieces of Pasta?

Name_____ Measuring, predicting, and counting

I predict...   I count...

1 cup

½ cup

⅓ cup

¼ cup

1 cup

Math Center

Pasta Procedure

Help your kindergartners practice measurement, prediction, and counting with this neat noodle center! To prepare, make a class supply of the recording sheet on page 100. Place the sheets at your math center, along with a corresponding set of measuring cups and a full cup of uncooked pasta, such as bow-tie or rotini. Have a child at this center first measure the pasta into the one-cup measuring cup. Have him record his prediction of how many pieces are in the cup. Then have him count the pasta to determine the actual answer. Have him repeat the procedure with the ½-cup, ⅓-cup, and ¼-cup measuring cups.

Carole Beckman—Gr. K
Sea Gate Elementary, Naples, FL

Dramatic-Play Area

Milk the Cow

Your kindergartners will get a kick out of milking this pretend cow as part of a dramatic-play farm! To make the cow, cover with white bulletin board paper and black spots a large cardboard box with one open side. To make the udder, cut a hole in the bottom of a plastic tumbler. Pull a rubber glove over the tumbler as shown, and then staple it in place. Push the glove and tumbler into a hole cut in the box as shown. Use a needle to punch tiny holes in each finger of the glove. Then set the box between two chairs as shown. Finally, attach a cow puppet for the head. Put some raffia below the cow along with a pail or pan to catch the milk. Pour some milk into the cup. Invite one child at a time to reach below the cow and "milk" it by pulling on the fingers of the glove. "Moo-velous"!

Nancy Read—Lead Teacher and Beth Stewart—Paraprofessional
Rebecca Minor Elementary, Lilburn, GA

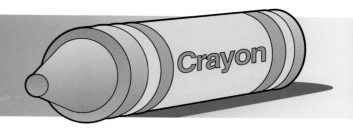

Math Center

Bunny Teeth

Hop to it and create this fun springtime center for helping youngsters practice addition! To prepare, cut out several bunny face shapes. Draw eyes, a nose, and whiskers on each one, but no mouth. Laminate the bunny math mats for durability, if desired. Next, program a set of sentence strips with various addition problems. Put the bunny mats, the addition problems, and a supply of white Chiclets gum pieces in your math center. Direct a child to select a math problem and then place the gum pieces—the bunny teeth—on a bunny mat to solve the problem.

Bonnie Elizabeth Vontz—Gr. K
Cheshire Country Day School
Milldale, CT

Literacy Center

Alphabet Eggs

Have youngsters take a crack at improving their letter-sound skills with this fun Easter egg activity! Gather 26 plastic eggs. Into each one, put a small item or picture representing a different letter of the alphabet, such as an apple-shaped eraser for *A* or a ball for *B*. Place the eggs in a center, along with a class supply of photocopied sheets showing the entire alphabet. A child at this center opens an egg, looks at the item inside, determines its beginning letter, and then marks that letter off his alphabet sheet. He continues until he's found an item for every letter.

Leanne Gibbons—Grs. K and 1
Mattapan-Boston Public Schools
Mattapan, MA

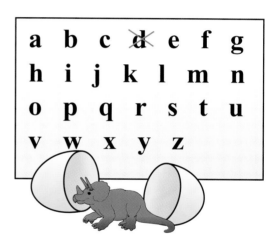

Writing Center

Grab Bag Journal Writing

Do your students sometimes struggle to think of ideas for journal writing? Help them out with this great grab bag! Fill a bag with various small toys and other interesting items. When a student needs an idea, have him pull three items from the bag. Then ask him to write a story incorporating all three items. A red truck, a space alien, and Santa's sleigh? Now *there's* a great story waiting to be written!

Holly Gibson-Coe—Gr. K
Great Bridge Presbyterian School
Chesapeake, VA

Learning Centers

Planting a Garden

If you're exploring a garden theme in your sensory center, add this "sand-sational" tub! Fill a small plastic pool with wet sand. Add silk or plastic flowers, small shovels, and plastic sand rakes. Then set your young gardeners to work planting and replanting rows of beautiful blooms!

Diane Bonica—Gr. K
Deer Creek Elementary
Tigard, OR

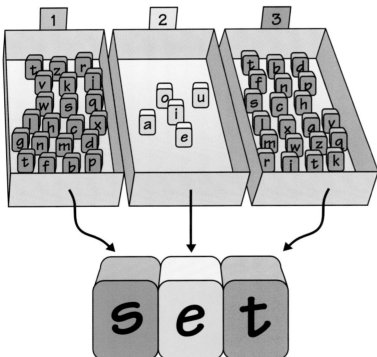

Block Words

Help youngsters learn to spell simple CVC words with this color-coded block system. Choose three colors of wooden counting cubes, or use plain wooden blocks and three colors of dot stickers. Write consonants on two of the block (or sticker) colors. Write only vowels on the third color. Arrange the blocks in three boxes as shown. Direct a child at this center to choose one block from each box to form a CVC word. Provide paper and pencils so that youngsters can record the words they form.

Kiva English
Cato-Meridian Central
Cato, NY

A to Z Tic-Tac-Toe

Use a simple game of tic-tac-toe to help your students with letter formation! Instead of having players use *X* and *O* on the game grid, ask them to write two letters you wish for them to practice, such as *R* and *L* or *K* and *W*.

Juli Engel—PreK & Kindergarten
Homeschool Playgroup
Midland, TX

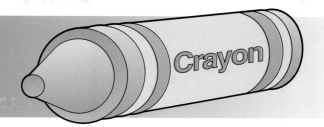

Spelling Center

Sight Word Stamping

Help youngsters learn sight words letter by letter! Write several sight words on the inside of a file folder. Add an illustration for each one. Then put the folder and a set of alphabet stamps at your spelling center, along with blank paper and ink pads. Have a child at this center stamp the letters to spell each sight word on his own paper.

Kim Lockley—Gr. K
Hawk Ridge Elementary
Charlotte, NC

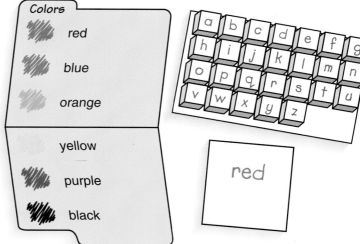

Math Center

I Spy

Some fabric and your photocopier will help you prepare for this marvelous math activity! Purchase a yard of interesting fabric that ties in to your current theme. On the photocopier, duplicate various images from the fabric to make a reproducible similar to the one shown. Spread the fabric over a table; then ask studens to search the design and count the number of each image on their recording sheets. Have students fill in the numbers or the number words for the totals they find.

Laurie Bushnell and Laura Kwiatkowski—Gr. K
Boardmanville Elementary
Olean, NY

Reading Center

Gift Match

Use some pretty packages to present this matching activity! Wrap several boxes in wrapping paper or Con-Tact paper. Label each package with a word in lowercase letters. Then label a corresponding number of bows with the same words, this time using a different font. Have a student match the word on each bow to the word on each package. If desired, make the activity self-checking by taping an index card on the bottom of each package that shows the word written both ways.

Judi Lesnansky—Title I, K–4
New Hope Academy
Youngstown, OH

Person and Clothing Patterns
Use with "Helpers Galore" on page 86.

How Many Pieces of Pasta?

I predict...   I count...

Lighting the Way
to Literacy

Nifty Names

Help new kindergartners learn the letters in their names with this pretty project! To prepare, die-cut the letters in each child's name. Invite each youngster to use art materials, such as bingo daubers or stamps, to decorate his letters. Then glue the letters of each name to a sheet of white construction paper. Have the child add more decorative accents around his name if desired. Then instruct him to use a black marker to outline the letters before you laminate the page. Display the names on your classroom walls; then use them for spur-of-the-moment literacy lessons, asking questions such as "Whose name begins with *E?*" or "Whose name has two *t*'s?"

Cheryl Mesch—Grs. K–2 Special Education
Northwood Elementary
West Seneca, NY

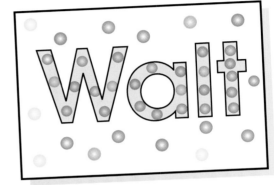

ABC Tree

A few fun props will encourage youngsters to reenact the favorite tale *Chicka Chicka Boom Boom* by Bill Martin Jr. and John Archambault. Hot-glue five large coffee cans end to end to form a palm tree trunk. Spray-paint the trunk brown. Use more hot glue to attach green craft-foam palm leaves and some brown-painted foam balls for coconuts. Put the tree in your literacy center along with a supply of magnetic letters. Then watch those letters move to the top of the coconut tree!

Patrice Clynes—Gr. K
Plantsville Elementary School
Plantsville, CT

Circle Story Mat

If you give a kindergartner a story mat, he'll improve his story retelling! Using a circle story, such as *If You Take a Mouse to School* by Laura Joffe Numeroff, make a story mat to prompt your students to recall the story's events. Use permanent markers to draw and label simple pictures around the edge of a round vinyl tablecloth to represent the sequence of the story. Write the story's title in the center; then place the mat in your literacy center along with a copy of the book. Let the retelling begin!

Jan Gleason—Gr. K
Chatham Elementary School
Chatham, MA

to Literacy

Rhyme Time Slide Show

Take a trek into technology when you create this rhyming lesson! Using a computer program with a slide show option, create slides that show pairs of objects, some of which rhyme and some of which do not. Run the slide show on the computer for a small group and have students give a thumbs-up if the word pairs rhyme and a thumbs-down if they do not. Or print out the slides for use with a large group.

As an alternative, use slide film to photograph pairs of objects. Run the slide show the traditional way with a projector, and have students respond with a thumbs-up or a thumbs-down for each slide.

Donna Hill—Gr. K
Murfreesboro, TN

Color-Combination Names

Mix a little science into this literacy lesson focused on writing names. Use a yellow highlighter to write a child's name on a white piece of paper. Then have the child choose a blue or a pink highlighter to use to trace over the letters. Look! The letters changed color! Neat!

Karen Crow—Gr. K
Emerson School
Lorain, OH

The Very Busy Kindergartner

Keep track of kindergarten experiences and children's growth with this yearlong book project based on Eric Carle's *The Very Hungry Caterpillar.* For each child, program a set of pages similar to the one shown, making a page for each month of the year. Each month, ask the child to write her name on the top blank and then dictate or write about something she did in school that month. For the summer months, have her write about what she'll do during school vacation. For the final month, have her draw herself as a big first grader! Bind the completed pages together; then make a cover featuring photos of the child at the beginning and the end of the school year.

Lisa Wilkinson and Janet Shlegle—Gr. K
Benjamin Banneker Elementary
Loveville, MD

Lighting the Way

Early Experiences in Reading & Writing

Out-of-Order Alphabet

Use a "magic letter finder"—an eraser—to make letter identification fun for your kindergartners! To prepare, write the letters of the alphabet out of sequence within students' reach on a dry-erase board. Give a child the eraser and have her find a particular letter. Instruct the class to chant the verse below as the child searches for and erases the letter. Keep going until everyone's had a turn and all the letters are gone.

You can find a letter; you can find it today
With the magic letter finder! Hip, hip, hooray!

Tiffany Reynolds—Gr. K
Edgemont Primary
Covington, VA

Geoboard Book

Stretch students' interest in letter formation by using Geoboards and rubber bands! Have each child stretch rubber bands over the pegs of a Geoboard to form a letter. Then have him record the letter on a piece of paper programmed with the same dot pattern as the pegs on the Geoboard. After he's recorded several letters, have him staple the papers together to make a Geoboard book.

Katie Zuehlke—Gr. K
Bendix Elementary
Annandale, MN

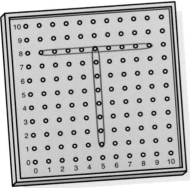

Candies From *A* to *Z*

Here's a post-Halloween project to help youngsters review the alphabet *and* the fun they had trick-or-treating! Ask students to bring in wrappers from the Halloween candy they received. Label 26 sheets of paper, each with a different letter. Then have students sort their candy wrappers by the first letter of the candy name. Next, instruct them to glue the wrappers onto the labeled papers. For pages without wrappers, have students make up pretend candies. Then bind the pages together in alphabetical order for a mouthwatering class book!

Heather Oliver
Kinkeade Early Childhood School
Irving, TX

to Literacy

Name Search

Have students practice reading one another's names with this search-and-find activity. Give each child a pencil and a photocopied class list on a clipboard. Instruct her to look around the room and check off each name as she finds it. Encourage youngsters who have trouble to check out cubbies, tables, mailboxes, or other spots labeled with students' names.

Katie Zuehlke—Gr. K
Bendix Elementary
Annandale, MN

Animal Alphabet Apron

Enhance your teaching of the alphabet with this animal-themed apron. For each letter, sew the hook side of a small piece of Velcro fastener to an apron. For each letter, collect a tiny stuffed animal or laminated picture of an animal whose name begins with that letter. Sew or glue the loop side of a Velcro piece to each animal or picture. As you introduce each letter, show students the animal. Talk about the letter sound at the beginning of its name; then add the animal to your apron. When all the animals are in place, use the apron to review letters and sounds.

Kendi Morris—Gr. K
Beale School
Gallipolis Ferry, WV

Pretzel Letters

Help youngsters form letters with this yummy activity! Give each child five large twist pretzels and five pretzel sticks, a sheet of paper, and a pencil. Have each student break or take bites from a pretzel in order to shape it into a letter of the alphabet. Then have her record on her paper the letter she makes. Have her repeat her letter nibbling with her remaining pretzels. Who knew learning could take place during snacktime?

Johna Heflin—Gr. K
Florence Elementary School
Florence, MS

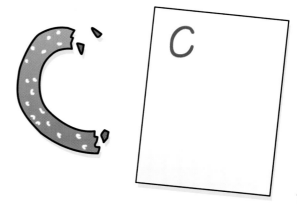

Snowfriends

After reading aloud Lois Ehlert's *Snowballs,* talk about all the interesting objects used to decorate the snowpeople in the book. Then encourage students and their families to create some cool snowfriends with this family project! For each child, send home a large sheet of white paper with a simple snowman (three blank circles) drawn on it. Send along instructions for the family to create any kind of snowperson (or snow animal) they wish, using common objects such as shoelaces, yarn, cereal pieces, pasta, fabric, plastic utensils, shells, or any craft materials. When the snowfriends are returned to your classroom, have each child write a sentence telling about her family's creation. Then display the snowfriends and sentences on a wall or bulletin board for everyone to admire. Welcome, snowfriends!

Michele Michalski—Gr. K
Calvary Academy
Lakewood, NJ

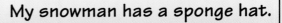

My snowman has a sponge hat.

Ellis

elephant
gray
big
squirting
water
heavy

Picture This

Want to get students writing creatively in their journals? Try some picture prompts! Cut out interesting pictures from magazines. Post a picture for students to see; then ask them to give you words that describe the picture, such as a color, an emotion, or an action word. Write their responses in a list and post it near the picture. Then ask students to write about the picture or write a story inspired by the picture. Encourage students to refer to the list of words while they write.

Marlana Howerton
Ezard Elementary
Conway, MO

I Spy a Sound!

Circle around to review beginning sounds! Seat students in a circle. In the center, place several objects representing various beginning sounds your students have learned. Start the activity by saying, "I spy something that begins with the /f/ sound." Then have a student volunteer go to the center of the circle and find the object that begins with /f/. Continue until all the objects have been identified by their beginning sounds. I spy a fish!

Michelle Brown—Gr. K
Watervliet Elementary
Watervliet, NY

I spy something that begins with /p/.

to Literacy

Vowel Song

Teach youngsters this tune with a valuable vowel lesson!

(sung to the tune of "Twinkle, Twinkle, Little Star")

Letters *A, E, I, O, U*—
These are vowels, which we all use!
Every single word we write
Needs a vowel to make it right.
Letters *A, E, I, O, U*—
These are vowels, which we all use!

Lori Magrath—Gr. K
J. T. Hood School
North Reading, MA

ABC Bottle

Help kindergartners practice letter recognition with an activity that's easy! To prepare an ABC bottle, thoroughly clean and dry a clear 20-ounce bottle. Pour in a set of small alphabet beads, such as those made for necklaces. Then fill the bottle nearly full with colored sand and use hot glue to secure the bottle cap. Make a class set of the recording sheet on page 114. Put the ABC bottle and copies of the recording sheet at your literacy center. Have a child shake and turn the bottle, find a letter, and circle that letter on a recording sheet. "Sand-sational"!

Shannon Martin—Gr. K
Children's World
Frankfort, IL

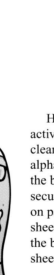

Pipe Cleaner Letters

A big bend here, a tiny twist there—now you have a letter! Have students practice letter formation with the help of some pipe cleaners. Give each child two pipe cleaners. Then call out a letter and challenge students to make that letter from their pipe cleaners. As each child finishes, she puts her letter down and gives you the thumbs-up signal to let you know her letter is complete. Check out all the creations; then start over with another letter!

Colleen Callander
Lincoln School
Brooklyn Park, MN

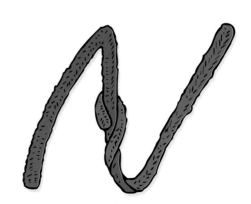

ABC Border

Want youngsters to practice ABC order? Use a length of bulletin board border! Puzzle-cut each letter length of alphabet bulletin board border. Or make your own by labeling sentence strips with the alphabet and adding a corresponding sticker or picture before cutting. Have a child correctly sequence the letters to form the alphabet. Easy!

Julia F. Simmons—Title I Reading, Aberdeen Elementary
Hampton, VA

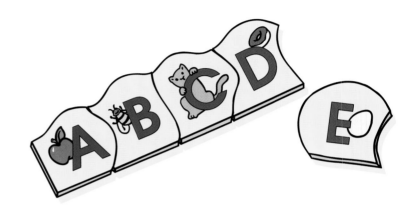

A Sticky Ending

Encourage your young writers to use punctuation in their writing by making periods special! When you do shared writing with your group, choose students to add special holiday or seasonal symbols in place of the standard periods. Have them attach heart stickers for Valentine's Day, peppermint discs for Christmas, or colored cotton balls (bunny tails) for Easter!

Katy Galewski—Gr. K
Lincoln Elementary
West Allis, WI

I Spy a Letter

This small-group game of letter location is sure to be a hit with youngsters! Have each child in the group choose a book from your reading center. Say, "I spy a(n) [letter]." Then see which child can find the letter in her book first. Vary the game by specifying capital or lowercase letters, or by asking students to locate sight words.

Danna DeMars—PreK–Gr. K
My Home 2
St. Charles, MO

to Literacy

Words of the Week

Spotlight new sight words with this fun activity! Each day, write a new word on your board, adding to the list throughout the week. Periodically during the week, blink the lights off and on. Select the first child to raise her hand and have her point to and read a word from the list. Then reward her with a small treat, such as M&M's candy or a sticker. Everyone's attention will be drawn to looking at the new words and hearing them read aloud again and again.

Millie Morris—Gr. K
Berkmar United Methodist Church
Duluth, GA

Hunting for Hearts

This colorful heart hunt is perfect for Valentine's Day—and perfect for reinforcing color words! Make a supply of colorful construction paper hearts and label each with the appropriate color word. Attach the hearts to various locations in your classroom, such as the door, the computer, the art table, or the board. Make a corresponding sheet (similar to the one shown); then duplicate it to make a class supply. Have each child hunt for the hearts and write the corresponding color word for the heart in each location. Happy hunting!

Karen Crow—Gr. K, Emerson Elementary, Lorain, OH

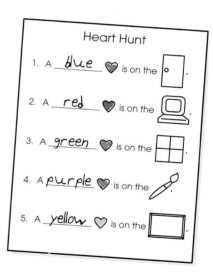

Heart Hunt

1. A _blue_ ♥ is on the [door].
2. A _red_ ♥ is on the [computer].
3. A _green_ ♥ is on the [window].
4. A _purple_ ♥ is on the [paintbrush].
5. A _yellow_ ♥ is on the [frame].

Window Cling and Words

Looking for another use for old window clings? Put them in your writing center, along with a whiteboard and dry-erase markers. Have a child choose a window cling and stick it to the board. Next, encourage him to write words that describe the picture on the decoration. Then have him read the words he's written to a friend before he erases them and removes the cling to ready the board for the next student.

Shannon Adams—Gr. K
Waxahachie Faith Family Academy
Waxahachie, TX

Journal Trade

For a twist on journal writing, have each child draw a picture on the top half of her journal page. Then have her pass her paper to a partner, who writes or dictates a story based on the illustration. Read aloud a few of the completed stories to the group and see how accurate the writer was in determining the illustrator's intent!

Christi Park
A. G. Richardson Elementary
Culpeper, VA

Author Study Booklets

Encourage reader connections to literature with these easy-to-make booklets. Choose four or more books by a particular author. Then, for each book, create a response sheet with a simple sentence for students to complete, as well as space for an illustration. If all the books have a common theme or character, such as mice, consider making shaped pages. After sharing each story, have the child write or dictate to fill in the blank and then draw a picture to accompany her response. Bind the response sheets and cover together, and include the author's name on the cover. Send the author study booklets home with students to encourage discussion about the stories with their families.

Marianne Fennelly—Gr. K
French Hill School
Yorktown Heights, NY

Coupon Matching

Take advantage of little ones' interest in various foods and snacks with this fun activity that relies on environmental print. Clip out the colored ads from newspaper coupon booklets. Cut each coupon away from its corresponding ad. Mount the ad on tagboard, leaving space for the coupon. Mount the coupon on another piece of tagboard; then attach magnetic tape to both the coupon and the empty space with the ad. Once you've prepared several sets of coupons and ads, you're ready for youngsters to read and match!

Anna Marjorie
Marrero, LA

to Literacy

A Dot? That's the Spot!

Help students understand where to begin reading with the help of some sticky dots! Place a sticky dot in front of the first word on each page of a big book. Point out that the dot shows where to begin reading the page. Also post dots at the beginning of sentences displayed in your classroom, or invite youngsters to stick or draw dots at the start of their writing. See a dot? That's the spot to start reading!

Vanessa Stultz—Transitional Gr. 1
Coolbaught Elementary Center
Tobyhanna, PA

Words and Music

Give a favorite song a literacy boost with this easy activity! Write each word of a line from a familiar song, such as "You Are My Sunshine," on a separate paper plate. Invite several children to hold the plates in front of the group and raise them in the air as each word is sung. Now music time is rhythm, rhyme, and *reading* time!

Jan Robbins
Fairview Elementary
Richmond, IN

● **Listen for directions.**

Picture Die

Help students recall details and story sequence with the help of a picture die. To make one, cover a cube-shaped box with bulletin board paper. Then draw six simple illustrations to show six different events in a story you've read aloud to your class. Tape one picture to each side of the die. Have students take turns rolling the die and telling about the story event pictured on top of the die. Or ask each child to tell what happened before or after the rolled story event.

If you're using a picture book with numbered pages, simply write page numbers on the six sides of the die. Then, when a student rolls, turn to that page in the book and have the child examine the illustration and tell about the story event.

Heidi Prouhet—Gr. K
Daniel Boone Elementary
Warrenton, MO

Lighting the Way

Early Experiences in Reading & Writing

Overhead Projector Writing

Put a twist on letter-formation practice when you have kindergartners write words and simple sentences with the help of your overhead projector! Have a child use magnetic letters (or other plastic letters) to spell a word on your projector's surface; then project the image onto your chalkboard. Have the student use chalk to trace the letters of the word onto the board. Invite her to keep going with other words or whole sentences. Write on!

DeAnna Laverick—Gr. K
Penns Manor Elementary
Clymer, PA

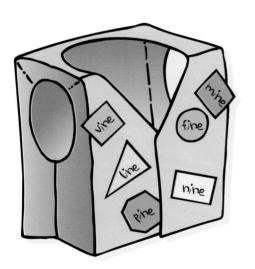

Rime Vests

Students are sure to have a "vested" interest in rime review with this idea! To prepare, cut a paper grocery bag into a vest for each child. Also cut a large number of colorful paper patches to decorate the vests during the activity. Write several word rimes on your chalkboard; then have students brainstorm words that end with those particular rimes. Give each child a large paper patch on which to write a rime; then give her a number of smaller patches and ask her to write one word from that word family on each patch. Have her glue the larger patch to the back of her vest and the smaller patches anywhere on the vest. When everyone is done and all the glue has dried, have a fashion show and invite youngsters to read the words on one another's vests.

Melissa Sherfinski—Grs. K–1
Glenn Stephens School
Madison, W

Syllable War

Build phonological awareness of syllables with this game played similarly to the traditional card game of War. In advance, prepare a stack of picture cards showing pictures of common objects that have various numbers of syllables in their names. Seat your students in a circle. Have a child draw a card and clap to determine how many syllables the word contains. Have the next child in the circle draw a card and do the same. The child whose word has more syllables gets to keep both cards and challenge the next child in the circle. If there is a tie, each child draws another picture card until one wins the cards for that round. Keep the game going until everyone has had a turn to draw a card.

Jamie Beckman
Clinton Public Schools, Clinton, CT

to Literacy

The Million-Dollar Word Club

Invite your kindergartners to report new words they hear for your Million-Dollar Word Club. When a student tells you a new word he's heard, have the class work together to determine the word's meaning through context clues or the use of a dictionary. Write the word on a sentence strip and cut out its shape. Have students clap out the number of syllables in the word and count its letters. Display the word and review it for several days; then add it to your Million-Dollar Words box. Use the collected words for a Writer's Workshop or writing practice when you have time to fill.

Karen Miller—Gr. K
Forest Avenue School
Middletown, RI

Model Sentence

Help your students improve their journal writing with a model sentence and some simple stickers. First, by hand or on a computer, write a model sentence and label important elements of a good sentence as shown. Attach a copy of the model sentence to each child's journal. Then create simple stickers with the numbers 3, 4, and 5 on them. At journal-writing time, remind students to use the model sentence to help them remember five key things about a good sentence: a capital letter at the beginning, punctuation at the end, spacing between words, writing on the line, and meaning that makes sense. When you go over the child's journal, look for those five elements. Give each child a sticker with the number of included elements circled on it. Watch your young writers improve as they strive for fives!

Pam Dunham—Gr. K
Franklin Elementary
Creston, IA

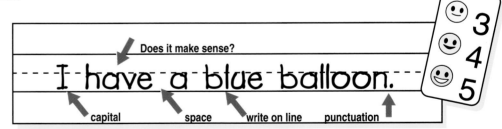

"Paws" for Sight Words

Can't bear to teach sight words the same old way? Try this twist! Cut out several bear pawprints from construction paper. Write a sight word on each one; then attach them along a path leading to your classroom door. Post at the beginning of your pawprint path the poem shown. Read the poem together whenever you and your class head toward your classroom; then have students read aloud the words on the pawprints as they step on each one. Add new words or replace old ones as the year continues.

Doreen Scheetz—Gr. K
C. A. Dwyer School, Wharton, NJ

Name _____

114

ABC Bottle

A B C D E F

G H I J K L

M N O P Q R S

T U V W X Y Z

Note to the teacher: Use with "ABC Bottle" on page 107.

OUR READERS WRITE

Our Readers Write

Superstar Welcome

Ease students' start-of-school jitters with this starry solution! Before school, send a welcome letter to each child, along with a self-adhesive star nametag labeled with the child's name, room number, and any other vital information. Wear a matching star nametag on the first day of school and decorate your classroom door with the star theme too. Although this idea is sure to make your new kindergartners feel like superstars, you could also adapt it to fit any welcome-to-school theme.

Carolyn Stein—Gr. K, Eastplain School

A Picture-Perfect Year

Create photo memories of each child's kindergarten year with this tip! Ask each child's parent to send in a disposable camera with flash at the start of the year. Throughout the year, designate one or two days per month to snap photos of children at work and play. Take photos of each child with her particular camera. Then, at the end of the year, send the cameras home so that parents can have the film developed and take a peek at what the year was like!

Cathie Rubley Hart—Gr. K, Westwood Hills Elementary, Waynesboro, VA

From Coffee to Classroom

Looking for a handy way for students to store their crayons, glue sticks, and scissors? Have parents help you save a class supply of containers from Folgers Café Latte beverage mixes. Peel off the labels; then use a permanent marker to personalize a container for each child. Have each student store her school supplies inside and then keep the container handy at her table or desk.

Brenda Saunders—Gr. K, Beale Elementary, Gallipolis Ferry, WV

Links for Lunch

Incorporate math into your daily routine with this easy idea! Make simple graph headings that show children's choices for lunch, as shown; then screw a cup hook below each one. To indicate his lunch choice, each student should attach a plastic link to the hook if he is the first child to start the graph, or add his link to the chain if the graph has already been started. Use the graph to count and compare numbers. Then add another twist by showing students how to create color patterns with the links, such as a yellow-green *AB* pattern. Watch the patterns grow more complex as the year progresses!

Cindy Stefanick—Gr. K, Roosevelt School, Worcester, MA

Colorful Kids

Review colors at the beginning of the year with a fun class book featuring your students! Divide your class into small groups; then assign each group a color. Have students wear clothing in their assigned color and gather objects of that color from home or from your classroom. Take a photo of each color group with its collected items. Once the pictures are developed, mount each one on tagboard. Label each page with the color name and then laminate the pages for durability. Bind the pages together to create a book titled "Colorful Kids."

Sue Lewis Lein—Gr. K, St. Pius X, Wauwatosa, WI

She Looks the Same!

Use a clothing clue to help your new kindergartners feel comfortable with you on the first day of school! Have someone take a photo of you wearing the same outfit you plan to wear on the first day of school. Make copies; then include a photo in each child's welcome letter, sent before school begins. Or wear your first-day-of-school outfit at Meet-Your-Teacher night before school starts. Either way, students will more readily recognize you on that important first day.

Cassie Richard—Gr. K, Kings Avenue Christian School, Brandon, FL

Christina Poulos—Gr. K, McCoy Elementary, Orlando, FL

Memory Magnet

Commemorate the first day of kindergarten by making special magnets families will use all year long! Use a Polaroid camera to take an instant photo of each child. Label the white area below the picture, as shown, to note the day; then attach a strip of magnetic tape to the back of the photo. Have each student take his magnet home to use for displaying artwork on the family fridge!

Karen Miller—Gr. K, Forest Avenue School, Middletown, RI

My first day of kindergarten
Forest Avenue School
September 2, 2003

Alphabet Guests

As you prepare to teach each letter of the alphabet, plan on inviting Alphabet Guests to visit your classroom! You might have an actor or acrobat for the letter *A,* a jogger or judge for *J,* a quarterback for *Q,* an umpire for *U,* or even a yodeler for the letter *Y!*

AnnaLisa R. Damminger—Gr. K, Mullica Hill, NJ

I am named after a poet.

Maya

Who Am I?

Encourage your students to learn one another's names and to learn more about their own names with this interactive display! To begin, send home a note with each child asking her parent to explain to her how her name was chosen. Also have each family write a clue about the origin of the child's name. Then, on a bulletin board, display a photo of each child in your class. Write each child's name clue on a sentence strip and mount it beneath the photo. Then write her name on a separate sentence strip and store the strips near the board. Talk about each child's name clue; then leave the board available so that students can match each name to the corresponding clue and photo.

adapted from an idea by Andrea Edwards—Gr. K, Hudson Elementary School, Long Beach, CA

Grand Masterpieces

Celebrate Grandparents Day with some grand artwork! Give each child an oval of white construction paper and invite her to draw a portrait of her grandparent(s). Then mount it on a larger oval of black construction paper. Attach a loop and bow of satin ribbon to serve as a decorative hanger. Then display all the finished artwork with the title "Grand Masterpieces."

Molly A. Weber—Gr. K, St. Joseph Elementary, Bellevue, IA

Kindergarten Story Quilt

Make a patchwork of pictures to tell the story of your kindergarten class! Beginning on the first day of school, periodically take photos of your students' daily routines, as well as special occasions. When you have a couple of rolls of pictures developed, arrange them on a wall or bulletin board in patchwork fashion. Both students and parents will enjoy looking over this kindergarten quilt! Every so often, take the photos down and send them home. Then make the quilt with new photos.

Jamey Gillespie—Gr. K, Aloe Elementary, Victoria, TX

Ladybug Names

Help kindergartners learn their own names and classmates' names with these lovely little ladybugs! To make one, cut a body-and-head shape from black construction paper. Then cut two wings from red construction paper. Glue a child's photo to the black body; then write his first name on one wing and his last name on the other. Attach the two wings to the body with a brad. After making a ladybug for each child, place the bugs in a bug jar (large plastic jar) at a center. Encourage a child to read the name on a ladybug and then open the wings to reveal the picture and see whether he decoded the name correctly.

Audrey McNeill, Trinity, NC

Where's the Restroom?

When families visit your classroom prior to the start of school, suggest to parents that they show their children the restroom. New students may feel more comfortable with a parent taking this role than a teacher they've just met.

Peggy Marrano—Gr. K, Boutwell School, Wilmington, MA

Picture-Perfect Puzzles

Put your classroom computer to use with this perfectly puzzling idea! Take a photo of each child in your class; then have the film developed and ask the developer to also put the pictures on a computer disk. Pull up each photo on your classroom computer, print a color copy, and cut the copy into several puzzle pieces. Store each child's photo puzzle in a labeled envelope. Invite a child to choose a puzzle; then pull up the photo on the computer screen to help her with the assembly!

Susan Schneider—Gr. K, Durham Elementary, Durham, NY

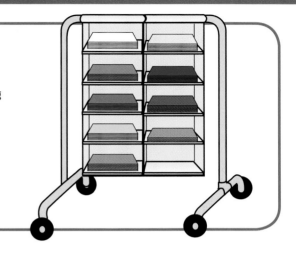

Handy Paper Holder

Keep construction paper close at hand with this storage idea! Hang two closet sweater organizers side by side on a chart stand. You'll find that half sheets of construction paper fit perfectly into each compartment. Just wheel the chart stand into your art area, and students will have easy access to a rainbow of paper colors!

Carol Chess—Gr. K, North Lauderdale Elementary, North Lauderdale, FL

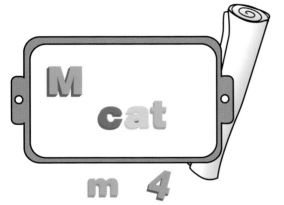

Cookie Sheet Skills

Enhance your circle time by using cookie sheets! At the start of the year, have each family send in a metal cookie sheet. Cover one side of each sheet with white Con-Tact covering. Then, each day, have students bring their cookie sheets to circle time, along with washable markers. Have students write letters, numbers, or words on their sheets as you review skills. Use a mild cleaner and a paper towel to clean the Con-Tact covering afterward. For a change of pace, try using magnetic letters and numbers on the sheets too!

Gina Barbour—Gr. K, McGee's Crossroads Elementary
Angier, NC

Teacher's Essentials

Misplaced your markers? Don't know where you stowed your stapler? Get organized with this easy tip! Purchase a spinning cake stand at your local craft store. Then use scraps of colorful tissue paper and diluted glue to cover several recycled containers, such as oatmeal canisters or instant coffee tins. Hot-glue the containers to the cake stand; then fill them with the essential items you need each day. Now they're just a spin away!

Bonnie Elizabeth Vontz—Gr. K, Cheshire Country Day School, Milldale, CT

Art Ideas on File

Don't lose track of those cute art ideas—file them away! Write up the materials and directions for an art project on a large blank index card. Then attach a miniature project sample, a photo, or a sketch to the card. Put all your art ideas in a file box and keep it handy. Later, it'll be easy to find a fresh art project.

Julie Parham, Ralph F. Wilson Elementary, Lake Charles, LA

Magic Words

Encourage good manners by taking special note of polite words. On a sheet of chart paper, write "Magic Words"; then add glitter to the letters. Keep the chart paper on display, and whenever you hear a child use polite words such as *please, thank you,* or *you're welcome,* write the words on the chart paper. Add stars next to words already on the list, and be sure to praise each child for being oh-so-polite!

Shannon Scott, Mountain Park Elementary, Stone Mountain, GA

Magic Words

Please ★★★★★
Thank you. ★★★
You're welcome. ★★
May I? ★
Bless you ★★

A Quilted Keepsake

Learn more about your little ones and at the same time create a lasting keepsake of your teaching years! Ask each student to bring in a 4" x 4" piece of cloth. (Be sure to tell parents that the cloth won't be returned.) Sew the students' squares together into a quilt; then have each child describe his square. If desired, add each child's photo or name to his square. Display the quilt in your classroom and add new squares for each new student you teach. Then just watch as your quilt and your teaching wisdom grow over the years!

Jerilynne Cook—Gr. K, La Petite Academy, Valrico, FL

Sweet Potato Frosting

Students will love making and eating this special treat made from a traditional Thanksgiving food—sweet potatoes! After preparing, use the frosting to decorate cupcakes, a cake, or cookies. Invite parents to join your class and share the treats. Before serving, have youngsters recite the poem below.

Ingredients:
2 lb. confectioners' sugar
1 c. mashed sweet potatoes
½ lb. butter
1 tsp. vanilla
¼ c. milk (if necessary)
cinnamon to taste

Directions:
1. Cream butter with one pound of sugar.
2. Add vanilla and sweet potatoes.
3. Mix in the remaining sugar and a dash of cinnamon (adding milk if needed).

Pat Davidson—Preschool and Kindergarten Special Education
Padonia International School
Cockeysville, MD

I wanted to make a special treat
For this Thanksgiving Day.
After thinking long and hard,
I chose a special way.
Not pumpkin pie or turkey or stew...
Instead I made a sweet potato treat
  for you!

Border Art

With this idea, the border surrounding your students' artwork can *also* be their artwork! Turn an old or unused border to the blank side; then invite each child to paint on a section. Laminate the dried paintings for a shiny look; then use this class-made border on a display!

Mindy Rosenthal—Junior K, Wildwood Day School, Wildwood, MO

Take Note of This Gift!

These nifty notecards make great gifts for assistants, parent volunteers, or school staff. Purchase small blank notecards; then have each child use colored pencils to draw a scene on the front of a card. On the back of each finished card, write the child's name and grade, as well as the subject of the picture. Wrap a set of notecards and envelopes together for a perfect little present!

Pam Ingram—Gr. K, Davenport A+ School, Lenoir, NC

Slip-Sliding Away?

Do your classroom tables tend to slide all over the floor? Purchase a roll of rubber matting used for lining shelves. Cut a small square of the material to put under each table leg. Now your tables will stay put!

Lynn Cutshaw—Gr. K, Westside Elementary, Clewiston, FL

Photo Cards

This holiday greeting will also be a cherished keepsake for your students! Take a class photo; then have the print made into holiday greeting cards. Send one to each kindergartner's family. What a great way to say happy holidays and help youngsters remember their kindergarten class too!

Michelle M. Betzger—Gr. K, St. Ann School, Quincy, MA

Festive Gift Bags

Here's an easy way for little hands to wrap a gift! For each student, fold over the top of a paper lunch bag; then punch two holes along the folded section. Unfold the bag and have him decorate it for the occasion with paint, crayons, markers, or other materials. Slip a gift into the bag and then refold the top. Help the child lace a piece of colorful yarn or ribbon through the holes and tie the ends into a bow. If desired, string a hole-punched gift tag onto the ribbon before tying it.

Annalisa Parent—Gr. K, Saint Mary's School, Middlebury, VT

Cocoa Cones

This gift looks like a chilly treat, but instead it provides some yummy heat! To make a cocoa cone, pour 1½ cups of hot cocoa mix into a clear, disposable pastry bag and tie off the top. Slip this bag into a second identical bag; then fill the remaining space with miniature marshmallows. Tie off the top of the outer pastry bag and attach a note with mixing directions. You'll have a parent or volunteer gift that looks like an ice-cream cone, but is perfect for warming up in cold weather!

Emily Porter—Gr. K, Garth Elementary, Georgetown, KY

Border Crowns

Store-bought birthday crowns are cute but expensive. Make your own by cutting a length of scalloped bulletin board border. Simply staple the border to fit a child's head. Border comes in lots of colors and designs, making it the crowning touch for a child's birthday or any other occasion!

Jill Berisford—Gr. K, Sherrard Elementary, Wheeling, WV

Wonderful Water Book

The snow melted.

A fresh snowfall is the starting point for this book about water. Bring in a cup of fresh snow and have youngsters observe it throughout the day, noting the changes they see. Once the snow has melted, mark the water level on the cup; then refreeze it and again have students note the changes. Let the ice melt and then watch the water evaporate over several days. All through this process, have students draw pictures and write sentences about what is happening. Put the drawings and text together in a book titled "Wonderful Water."

Joanne McCarter—Gr. K, C.F. Brown Elementary, Millis, MA

Expecting Amaryllis

Bring in an amaryllis bulb to get your students graphing, practicing calendar skills, and estimating! First, have students guess what color the blooms will be on your plant and graph their responses. Plant the bulb and then look at the information on the bulb's packaging. How long should it take until it blooms? Look at the calendar and locate the range of possible dates. Have each child guess which day the amaryllis will bloom. Then watch and wait to see whose guesses are correct!

Susan Pink—Gr. K, Children's Discovery Center, Victor, NY

Me on a CD!

Since parents love to display their children's work on the fridge, these personalized magnets make wonderful parent gifts! To make one, have a child decorate a computer CD (like the promotional ones you receive in the mail) with various colors of fabric paint. When the paint is dry, use double-sided tape to attach the child's photo to the center of the CD. Add two strips of magnetic tape to the back of the CD to complete this picture-perfect gift!

Sara Wendahl—Gr. K, St. Mary's School, Waukesha, WI

Reusable Graphing Chart

Take a bit of time to make this graphing grid, and you can use it throughout the year! Use a black permanent marker to draw grid lines on a sheet of poster board, leaving a top and left margin as shown. Then laminate the poster board. To make a hook for each square, insert one arm of a metal brad through the back side of the poster board. Tape the other arm of the brad to the back of the board. Then bend the inserted arm to form a hook. Add two more brad hooks at the top of the graph for hanging a subject strip. Make a graph marker for each child by cutting a circle (sized to fit a grid square) from construction paper. Label each circle with a child's name; then laminate the markers for durability. Use a dry-erase marker to write or draw the row headings in the left margin; then call children one by one to hang their graph markers on the grid.

Susan Bunyan—Gr. K, Linn Elementary, Dodge City, KS

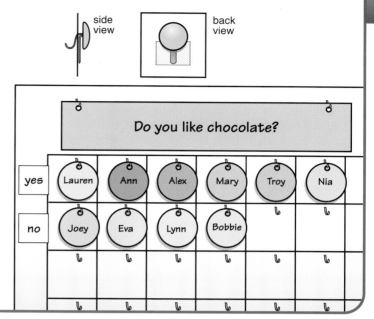

A Peppermint Present

This yummy candy makes a great holiday gift for volunteers, custodians, or office staff, and it's a good opportunity to talk about liquids and solids too! To begin, have students use wooden blocks to pound peppermint candy you've placed inside zippered plastic bags. Melt vanilla candy coating in a microwave or crock pot according to package directions. Pour the melted coating onto waxed paper, then have students sprinkle the crushed peppermint over the top. Allow the candy to cool and harden before breaking it into small pieces. Divide the pieces among plastic bags or gift bags; then have youngsters deliver the sweet treats to the recipients. Yum!

Emily Porter—Gr. K, Garth Elementary, Georgetown, KY

This Gift Measures Up

Looking for a fun and inexpensive holiday gift for your students? Purchase a tape measure for each child! Design a measuring sheet to go along with it, including instructions to measure a few common objects, such as a chair, a book, or the child's own foot. This gift encourages a little math and a whole lot of fun!

Sadie Day—Gr. K, Carbondale Attendance Center, Carbondale, KS

Table Writing

If you don't have a chalkboard in your classroom, write on the tables instead! Visit the bath and shower area of your local home improvement store. Purchase white shower wall panels, which happen to be perfect for using dry-erase markers! Ask the store to cut the panels to the dimensions of your tabletops. Then lay the panels over your tables, pass out the markers, and let the learning begin!

adapted from an idea by Lynn Porter-Whitmire—Gr. K
Eastanollee Elementary, Eastanollee, GA

Sweetheart Biscuits

Celebrate Valentine's Day with this freshly baked treat! Help each child flatten a canned refrigerated biscuit and then cut it with a heart-shaped cookie cutter. Bake the biscuits as directed. After the biscuits have cooled, instruct each child to gently pull her heart biscuit apart to make two halves. Then have her spoon a bit of strawberry jam onto one half, top it with the other half, and enjoy her snack!

Allison Pratt—Gr. K, Onalaska Kindergarten Center, Onalaska, WI

Geoboards Without the Snap

If you've had a problem with rubber bands snapping while youngsters used them on Geoboards, try this solution. Purchase some weaving loops instead (the kind used to make pot holders). They're colorful, stretchy, and safer than rubber bands.

Suzanne Clark—Gr. K, Edmunds Elementary, Burlington, VT

100 Children in Line

Mark the 100th day of school with a grand counting celebration! Have all the kindergartners assemble in your school gym or another large space. Group the children by tens; then line up the groups to see if you have 100—or more! Have students count off by ones and by tens, or even count backward and have children sit down as they're counted. Isn't 100 wonderful?

Mary-Beth Layfield—Gr. K, W. O. Parmer Elementary, Greenville, AL

Borders and Books

Here's a great way to help youngsters find and put away books on special topics you're studying. Use a length of border with a matching theme to trim the front of a shelf in your bookcase. For example, use a dinosaur-theme border to decorate a shelf; then place all your dinosaur books there during a dinosaur theme time. This will help keep these special books from getting mixed in with your regular classroom library and keep them easily accessible so everyone can check them out!

Clarese Ornstein—Gr. K, Early Education Center, Round Lake, IL

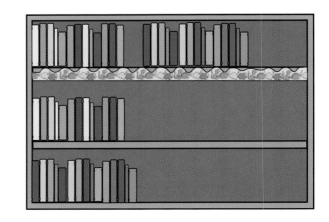

Pocket Chart Highlighters

Pocket chart highlighters sold in teacher supply stores can be expensive. As an alternative, purchase sheets of yellow or orange vellum at your local scrapbooking store. You can cut the vellum to any size to highlight letters or words.

Jennae Snow, Snow Preschool, St. George, UT

Easy-Clean Easel

Keep your painting easel looking new with this trick! Since children many times paint on the easel as well as their papers, cover the easel surface with Con-Tact covering. The covering can be wiped clean with a damp cloth.

Delores Bailey—Gr. K, Alexander Hamilton Elementary, Baltimore, MD

Tape Tip

Put a paper clip under the cut edge of a roll of clear packing tape or masking tape when you store it away. No more digging with your nails to find that invisible edge!

Kris Rogers—Gr. K, Bar-T Kindergarten Enrichment, Gaithersburg, MD

Reusable Skill Cards

If you've written on laminated flash cards or cards for games using a permanent marker, you can use this tip to reprogram them! Completely color over the writing with a dry-erase marker; then wipe the card with a dry paper towel. The old writing will disappear (a second attempt may be needed) and you can reprogram the card for a new skill.

Mary Hines—Gr. K, Trinity Lutheran School, Fort Wayne, IN

Cool Confetti

Here's a quick and easy way to obtain colorful paper sprinkles or confetti for decorating projects. Simply empty the tray on your school's binding machine—the tiny, uniform bits of paper make wonderful confetti!

Becky Gibson Watson, Camp Hill, AL

Award Labels

Take note of students' achievements or good behavior with this tip! Use your computer to type up several quick messages, such as those shown. Then print the messages out on a sheet of labels. Whenever a child deserves a bit of praise for a good day, peel off an award label and stick it to his shirt before sending him home.

Janice Moyer—Gr. K, Lester B. Pearson Public School, Waterloo, Ontario

> Ask me what a great helper I've been!

> I was a good friend today!

Reward Wristbands

Put leftover laminating film to good use with these wristbands! To make one, cut a 1½" x 8" strip of laminating film. Punch two holes (as shown) on each end. Thread a length or two of colorful yarn through the holes at one end; then fit the band to a child's wrist and tie the yarn through the remaining holes. Throughout the day (or week), give youngsters stickers as rewards for their performance or good behavior. Have them stick the stickers to their wristbands to show off to Mom and Dad when they get home!

Sister Mary Samuella, Holy Rosary School, Duluth, MN

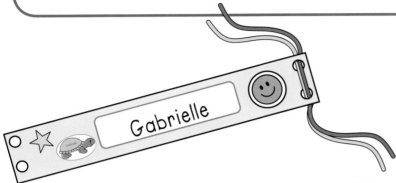

Gabrielle

Goodbye Card

Changing schools midyear can be difficult. Help your departing students remember their friends in your class with these goodbye cards. To make one, fold a large piece of bulletin board paper in half, card-style. Invite the child to choose die-cuts or stickers to decorate the front of the card. As a class, decide what the front and inside of the card should say. Then have everyone sign the inside of the card. Finally, glue a picture of the class to the back of the card and write in the year, grade, and school name below it.

Emily Flach—Gr. K, Huntington Elementary, Lincoln, NE

We'll Miss You

Magnetic Words

Make your own set of magnetic words by purchasing sheets of magnetic material, such as vent covers from your local home improvement store. Cut the material into strips; then use a permanent marker to write a series of words across the strip. Cut the words apart, and you're ready to use these "attractive" teaching tools!

Sue Lein—Gr. K, Wauwatosa, WI

Old-Fashioned Greetings

This Mother's Day card will be a big hit! Moms will love the old-timey look, and your class will love dressing up! Have each girl in your class put on an old-fashioned dress and a big flowery hat. Have her hold a big artificial flower as you take her picture with black-and-white film. Have each boy dress up in a suit coat and tie; then have him also hold the flower as you snap his photo. Develop the photos; then mount each one on a construction paper frame with the greeting shown and the child's signature.

Marla Cobb—Gr. K, Barhitte Elementary, Burton, MI

It may be old-fashioned,
But I'm here to say,
"I hope you have a very
Happy Mother's Day!"

Laura

Reading With Chopsticks

Are you always looking for fun pointers for your students to use as they read the room? Try chopsticks! They're perfect as pointers and very inexpensive. Simply glue a cap eraser on one end, and you're ready to go!

Susan Schneider—Gr. K, Durham Elementary, Durham, NY

A Magnet for Mom

Here's an attractive gift moms will love! Ask parents to help you save metal lids from cans of frozen juice. When you have a class supply, instruct each child to spread glitter glue over her lid and then place her school picture in the center. Allow the glue to dry thoroughly; then attach a strip of magnetic tape to the back. Simple and sparkling!

Janet Fraley—Gr. K, Loch Lomond Elementary, Manassas, VA

A Pot and a Poem

Plant some happy thoughts for a happy Mother's Day with this gift! Have each child use paint pens and stickers to decorate a small plastic flowerpot. Help each child add soil and plant a few flower seeds in the pot. Then attach a card with the poem shown.

Jane Tsakiris—Gr. K
Louise White School
Batavia, IL

This isn't just an empty pot.
There's something you should know.
Inside the pot there is a seed
That, just like me, will grow.

The plant that grows will someday bloom
And remind you of the seed so small.
But without your love and tender care,
The seed wouldn't grow at all.

Thanks for helping me grow!
Happy Mother's Day!

C-r-r-rack!

Here's a fun prop to help get across the idea that chicks hatch from eggs. Cut a large egg shape from poster board. Then cut out the center of the egg and tape a tissue paper circle over the opening. Use the egg and a chick puppet to dramatize the hatching process. Start with the prepared egg; then draw a black zigzag line across the egg as you describe how the chick begins to peck its way out. Then have your chick puppet break through the tissue paper and emerge!

Cindi Zsittnik, Boonsboro, MD

Water, Water, Everywhere

If you're studying Earth Day this April, teach youngsters this song about water conservation.

(sung to the tune of "Twinkle, Twinkle, Little Star")

Water, water, in the air.
Water, water, everywhere.

Water up,
Water down,
In the sky
And underground.

Do not waste it.
Keep it clean.
Water helps keep our earth green!

Peg Bruns—Gr. K
Nocatee Elementary School, Nocatee, FL

Buggy Math Mat

Spring into math practice with the help of these cute mats! To make one, cut a sheet of green felt in half; then cut a zigzag pattern along one edge to resemble grass. Sew or hot-glue the straight edge to the bottom edge of a blue felt sheet. Now you've got a grass-and-sky scene to use with plastic or craft foam bug manipulatives.

Lisa Nicklow—Gr. K, Brookwood Elementary
Houston, TX

Lovely Lattice

Add a touch of spring to a classroom display with this easy idea! Purchase a piece of white lattice at your local home improvement store. Weave artificial greenery and flowers through the lattice; then mount it on or simply lean it against a wall. Use clothespins to clip students' artwork to the lattice. Lovely!

Karen Smith—Grs. K and 1
Pine Lane Elementary Homeschool
Pace, FL

A Neat Dirt Dessert!

Here's a way to make a dirt-with-worms snack with a minimal amount of mess. Divide your class into small groups. Give each group a gallon-size zippered plastic bag with the appropriate number of chocolate sandwich cookies sealed inside. Have youngsters take turns crushing the cookies. Give the group another gallon-size bag with chocolate pudding mix and milk. Seal the bag, put a piece of tape over the opening, and then have students take turns squeezing the contents until the pudding thickens. Next, give each child a cup and spoon. Pour a bit of pudding and some crushed cookies into each child's cup; then top it off with a yummy Gummy Worm candy!

Vada Boback—Gr. K, Alliance Christian School, Morgantown, WV

Marvelous Magnets

Here's an easy and inexpensive way to make a gift parents and volunteers will treasure! Visit your local office supply store and purchase magnets intended for use with business cards. Instruct each child to create a small drawing; then cut it to business card size. Or have her draw her illustration on the back of an old business card. Peel the backing from the purchased magnet; then adhere the child's drawing. Send the magnets home to use on refrigerators for displaying notes and children's artwork.

Ellen Stubblefield—Gr. K, Bluff Park Elementary
Hoover, AL

The Wonders of Window Shades

Don't toss out those old window shades; put them to good use in your classroom! Use them as dropcloths or table coverings for messy projects, or program them for skill-building activities. Use a permanent marker to divide a shade into squares for use as a blank graph. Or make squares and then write a number and a dot set in each one. Have a child put a matching set of manipulatives in each square. Or program the shade with letters and have youngsters match small objects or pictures to the letters for beginning-sounds practice. The possibilities are endless!

Lisa Marks
Nelson County Elementary Schools
Lovingston, VA

Kindergarten Memory Bottles

Here's a special souvenir of the kindergarten year! Ask each child to bring in a clean 16-ounce plastic water bottle with the label removed and the lid on. As a group, brainstorm a list of small objects that could be put in a bottle to remind students of kindergarten. For example, a pencil or crayon might remind students that they learned to write and draw. Consider some of these items: a wood chip from your playground, a birthday candle, a reduced copy of the child's school photo, a miniature flag, and theme-related confetti from some favorite themes. Fill each child's bottle with your class's choice of items; then hot-glue the cap in place. Happy memories!

Kathy Barlow Thurman—Gr. K, Southern Elementary, Somerset, KY

Double-Duty Display

Ask your soon-to-be first graders to help you create a display that will work for both the end of this year and the beginning of next! Give each child a sun cutout. Ask her to write on it a favorite memory or favorite activity from kindergarten. At the beginning of next year, display the sun cutouts with the title "A Warm Welcome." The display will give new students and parents an idea of the fun they have to look forward to!

Anne Croxton

Bonnie McKenzie—Grs. PreK & K
Cheshire Country Day School
Cheshire, CT

Keepsake Graduation Caps

Youngsters can keep these easy-to-make craft foam caps as a reminder of their kindergarten graduation day! To make one, cut a 9" x 9" square and a 6" x 12" rectangle from a sheet of craft foam. Cut a triangle shape from each short side of the rectangle (Figure 1). Overlap the corners on each (Figure 2) short side and hot-glue them in place. Then hot-glue this fitted part of the cap diagonally across the square piece. Hot-glue a yarn tassel and a large button to the center of the top of the cap to complete it.

Kim Crane—Gr. K, Duncan Chapel Elementary
Greenville, SC

Figure 1  **Figure 2**

We saw chickens on the farm.

Annie

Here's the Scoop

Review the year with this cool display! Using the patterns on page 131, give each child an ice-cream cone and one or more scoops of ice cream. Have her write her name on the cone; then, on each scoop shape, have her write about something the class did during the year. She might recall a special event or an everyday activity. Display all the cones and scoops on a bulletin board with the title "Here's the Scoop on What We Did in Kindergarten!"

Ada Goren, Winston-Salem, NC

Thank-You Planter

Show a hardworking volunteer how much you appreciate her help with this personalized gift. Purchase an inexpensive white plastic planter at your local discount store. Use a colored Sharpie pen to label the planter with your class name and the year. Then have your students use colorful Sharpie pens to decorate the planter with their names, hearts, flowers, and butterflies. If desired, add a pretty plant and a bow before presenting the gift to your lucky volunteer!

Linda Herman—Gr. K, Knights Elementary, Plant City, FL

Mom's Address Book

Here's a handy homemade gift every mom will love! To begin, duplicate the address book page on page 132 to make 13 copies. Label the box on each of the copies with a letter of the alphabet; then copy the entire set for each child. Use your school's binding machine to bind each child's set between two half sheets of construction paper. Next, label a rectangle of white copy paper as shown and glue it onto the book's front cover. Finally, have each child decorate his mom's address book with colorful squares and gray triangles to form houses. Have him use a black marker to add windows and doors to each house. Practical and precious!

Tina Bellotti—Gr. K
George A. Jackson Elementary
Jericho, NY

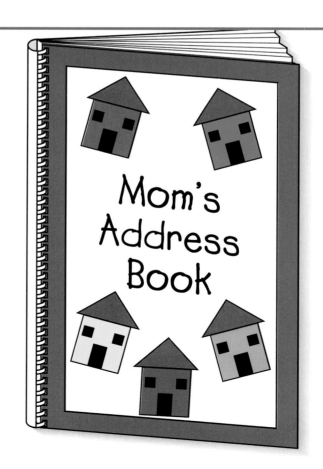

Mom's Address Book

Address Book Pages

Use with "Mom's Address Book" on page 130.

Name
Address

Phone
Email

Name
Address

Phone
Email

Name
Address

Phone
Email

Name
Address

Phone
Email

Name
Address

Phone
Email

Name
Address

Phone
Email

Name
Address

Phone
Email

Name
Address

Phone
Email

Rhythm & Rhyme Time

Rhythm & Rhyme Time

Are You Cleaning?

Make the transition from playtime to circle time with this neat little number!

(sung to the tune of "Are You Sleeping?")

Are you cleaning? Are you cleaning?
Cleanup time, cleanup time!

Pick up all the toys
Like good girls and boys!
Cleanup time, cleanup time!

Walk to the circle. Walk to the circle.
Please don't run. Please don't run!

Won't you have a seat?
Everything's so neat!
Let's begin. Let's begin!

JoAnn Lindwall
Winston Park Elementary
Coconut Creek, FL

The Bus Is Coming!

Say goodbye at the end of the day with this super school bus song!

(sung to the tune of "London Bridge")

The bus is coming—time to go,
Time to go, time to go!
The bus is coming—time to go!
Come and line up!

The bus is here; now move along,
Move along, move along!
The bus is here; now move along!
Please ride safely!

You'll soon be home all safe and sound,
Safe and sound, safe and sound!
You'll soon be home all safe and sound!
See you tomorrow!

Julie Granchell, Medina Central School
Medina, NY

It's Cool to Go to School

With the corresponding hand motions, this song is perfect to perform for moms and dads on a special school visitation day or open house night!

(sung to the tune of "A-hunting We Will Go")

I'm learning every day.
I'm learning every day.
It's oh so cool to go to school!   *Give two thumbs-up.*
I'm learning every day.

I'm learning about letters.
I'm learning about letters.
That's what I need so I can read!   *Pretend to open and*
I'm learning about letters.   *read a book.*

I'm learning about numbers.
I'm learning about numbers.
Without a doubt then I can count!   *Count on fingers.*
I'm learning about numbers.

I'm learning how to write.
I'm learning how to write.
Curves and lines suit me just fine!   *"Write" letters in air.*
I'm learning how to write.

I'm learning to make friends.
I'm learning to make friends.
I want to play with you today!   *Hug a friend.*
I'm learning to make friends.

Kathy Thurman—Gr. K
Southern Elementary
Somerset, KY

Alphabet Brew

Stir up some letter-sound practice with this Halloween chant! To prepare, place a large pot or a plastic cauldron from a party store in your circle area; then drop in a long wooden spoon. Cut a class supply of pumpkins from orange construction paper. Label each one with a different letter; then place them all facedown around the cauldron. Have one child at a time choose a pumpkin and hold it up for the group to see. Have the class chant the verse below, using the letter on the pumpkin in Line 1 and its sound in Line 3. At the end, have the child drop the pumpkin into the cauldron and give the brew a stir!

Here's [an h] to make the brew bubble.
We know its sound; we'll say it on the double.
[/h/, /h/, /h/]!
Drop it in the Alphabet Brew.
Letter sounds are magic.
Alakazam, alakazoo!

Nancy Richmond—Gr. K
New Martinsville School
New Martinsville, WV

Tree Tune

Review the parts of a fruit tree with this fun action song! Each time children sing the word *leaves,* have them wiggle their fingers. For *branches,* have them sway their arms. For *trunk,* have them touch their tummies, and for *roots,* have them touch their toes. In Line 5, have students pause after the word *blossoms* to take a big sniff and pause after the word *fruits* to take a pretend bite!

(sung to the tune of "Head and Shoulders")

Leaves, branches, trunk, and roots,
Trunk and roots.
Leaves, branches, trunk, and roots,
Trunk and roots.
Don't forget the blossoms *(sniff)* and the fruits *(bite)!*
Leaves, branches, trunk, and roots,
Trunk and roots.

Suzanne Moore
Irving, TX

Wingo

Put a turkey twist on a traditional spelling song for some fine-feathered fun! Print the letters *W, I, N, G,* and *O* on separate cards and have students hold them up. Substitute a wing flap motion as you drop each letter of Wingo's name from subsequent verses.

(sung to the tune of "Bingo")

There was a farmer who had a turkey,
And Wingo was his name-o!
W-I-N-G-O, W-I-N-G-O, W-I-N-G-O,
And Wingo was his name-o!

Karla Parker—Gr. K, Southern Elementary, Somerset, KY

135

Rhythm & Rhyme Time

Reindeer, Reindeer

Encourage your kindergartners to play the part of Rudolph as they join in this action chant. Give each child a red sticky dot to place on the tip of his nose. Ready, reindeer? It goes like this…

(chanted to the rhythm of "Teddy Bear, Teddy Bear")

Reindeer, reindeer, turn around.
Reindeer, reindeer, touch the ground.
Reindeer, reindeer, prance, prance, prance.
Reindeer, reindeer, do a little dance.
Reindeer, reindeer, line up for flight.
Reindeer, reindeer, say, "Good night!"

Karen Momrik—Gr. K
Elmira Elementary
Elmira, MI

Look and Listen

Need to get your youngsters' attention? Here's a musical method for encouraging good listening!

(sung to the tune of "If You're Happy and You Know It")

If you're listening and you know it, look at me.
If you're listening and you know it, look at me.
If you're listening and you know it,
Then your eyes will surely show it!
If you're listening and you know it, look at me.

If you're listening and you know it, fold your hands.
If you're listening and you know it, fold your hands.
If you're listening and you know it,
Then your hands will surely show it!
If you're listening and you know it, fold your hands.

Karen Mayberry—Gr. K
Northside School
Morrison, IL

What's Your Number?

Here's a tune to help youngsters review their phone numbers. Before singing, give each child a card with her phone number on it. If she can't remember her number when it's her turn to answer, she can refer to the card.

(sung to the tune of "Mary Had a Little Lamb")

Please tell us your phone number,
Phone number, phone number.
Please tell us your phone number.
[Child's name], tell us please.

adapted from a song by
Michele Tunstall—Gr. K
Cambria County Christian School
Johnstown, PA

Rhythm & Rhyme Time

Mr. Rain

When gray skies appear and raindrops fall, say this little poem with youngsters to chase the rain away!

Oh, Mr. Rain, Mr. Rain,
Mr. Dreary Rain,
Making our sky gray.
We little children,
We want to go play.
Please share the sky with Mr. Sun today.

Oh, Mr. Rain, Mr. Rain,
Mr. Dreary Rain,
Please share the sky today!

Kimberly Bush—PreK–Gr. K
Oakland Kindergarten and Pre-K Education Center
Oakland, NJ

Tell Me

Use this song to focus on the elements of a story and then encourage students to retell a story from start to finish.

(sung to the tune of "Clementine")

Can you tell me?
Can you tell me?
Can you tell me about this book?
If you tell me all about it,
I'll be sure to take a look.

Who was in it?
What was happening?
Tell me how the problem's solved.
Retell the story from start to finish.
Tell me, tell me, tell it all.

Crystal Chandler—Gr. K
Wake Forest Elementary
Wake Forest, NC

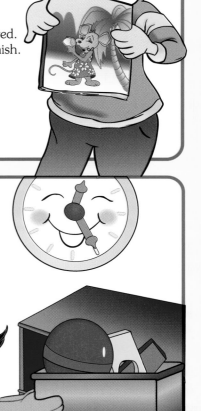

The Cleanup Song

This simple song will encourage your little ones to clean the room in a jiffy!

(sung to the tune of "Heigh-Ho")

Clean up, clean up.
It's off to clean up.
Put the toys away
For another day.
Clean up, clean up,
Clean up.

Clean up, clean up.
It's off to clean up.
We've had some fun,
But now we're done.
Clean up, clean up,
Clean up!

Lynn Hoseney—PreK–Gr. K
Pinckney Elementary
Pinckney, MI

Recycle!

Take note of Earth Day with this tune, which reminds everyone to recycle.

(sung to the tune of "Three Blind Mice")

Recycle! Recycle!
See how we save.
See how we save.
We save our paper, glass, and cans.
Everyone lend a helping hand!
We must pitch in to save our land,
So recycle!

Pauline Gould—Gr. K
Miami Gardens Elementary
Miami, FL

Come to the Circle

Help students make the transition to circle time with this lively tune!

(sung to the tune of "Take Me Out to the Ballgame")

Let's all come to the circle;
Let's all come right away!
We've got some sharing and learning to do;
There's so much fun right here waiting for you!
Oh, we've come to school for learning;
Everyone gather round!
And let's come, come, come to the circle and sit right down.

Rosalyn Harper-Jenkins—Gr. K
Marvin Elementary
St. Louis, MO

Quack! Mew! Oink!

Give pictures of the baby animals mentioned in this song to your youngsters to hold. Have each child hold up her animal as its verse is sung. And invite everyone to make the animal sounds for every verse!

(sung to the tune of "She'll Be Comin' Round the Mountain")

Oh, a baby duck's a duckling. It says, "Quack." (Quack, quack!)
Oh, a baby duck's a duckling. It says, "Quack." (Quack, quack!)
All its yellow fluffy feathers keep it warm in rainy weather.
Oh, a baby duck's a duckling. It says, "Quack." (Quack, quack!)

Oh, a baby cat's a kitten. It says, "Mew." (Mew, mew!)
Oh, a baby cat's a kitten. It says, "Mew." (Mew, mew!)
Likes to chase and scratch and purr, licks itself to clean its fur.
Oh, a baby cat's a kitten. It says, "Mew." (Mew, mew!)

Oh, a baby pig's a piglet. It says, "Oink." (Oink, oink!)
Oh, a baby pig's a piglet. It says, "Oink." (Oink, oink!)
Mud's its favorite place to play...cools it down the fastest way.
Oh, a baby pig's a piglet. It says, "Oink." (Oink, oink!)

Oh, a baby horse is a foal. It says, "Neigh." (Neigh, neigh!)
Oh, a baby horse is a foal. It says, "Neigh." (Neigh, neigh!)
Spindly legged, runs so fast, likes to eat the farmer's grass.
Oh, a baby horse is a foal. It says, "Neigh." (Neigh, neigh!)

Oh, a baby sheep's a lamb. It says, "Baa." (Baa, baa!)
Oh, a baby sheep's a lamb. It says, "Baa." (Baa, baa!)
Soft and woolly, it will stay by its mother through the day.
Oh, a baby sheep's a lamb. It says, "Baa." (Baa, baa!)

Michelle McCormick
Washington Elementary
Holdrege, NE

SIMPLE SCIENCE
FOR KINDERGARTNERS

Investigating Apples

Polish students' process skills with these "a-peel-ing" ideas. They're as easy as apple pie!

by Suzanne Moore, Irving, TX

Prior to these activities, ask each child's parents to send an apple to school.

Apple Graphing

Begin your apple study by inviting students to share their apples with the class. Have each child describe his apple, encouraging him to talk about its color, size, and shape. Next, help him weigh his apple on a balance scale. Then, on a piece of paper, have him draw his apple and the number of counters used to make the scale balance. Sort all of the apples by color and then weigh each set by placing the set in a bag and putting the bag on a bathroom scale. Write the weight of each set on an appropriately colored apple cutout. Post the cutouts and the corresponding weight records on a bulletin board to create a graph similar to the one shown. Discuss with students the results of this evaluation. Our green apples weigh more than the red ones!

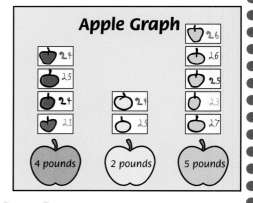

Apples—Inside and Out

Now that youngsters have collected and shared some apple data, it's time to investigate the parts of an apple. Cut an apple in half vertically. Discuss with students the stem, skin, flesh, and seeds of an apple. As you talk about each part of an apple, draw and label a diagram on your board. Then give each child a nine-inch paper plate. Help her dip one of the apple halves in red paint and then make a print on her plate. After the paint has dried, have her draw a stem and seeds on her print if they are not visible. Then, have her label the parts of an apple using your diagram as a guide. Display the prints with the title "Apples—Inside and Out."

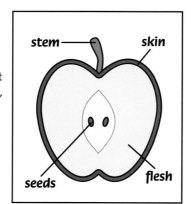

stem — skin

seeds — flesh

DID YOU KNOW?

Apples kept in a refrigerator can last up to ten times longer than those stored at room temperature.

Baked Changes

With all this talk about apples, students are bound to be hungry! Core and cut in half enough apples for each child to have one half. Give each youngster an apple half and have him place it cut side up in a personalized microwavable bowl. Instruct him to place a dot of butter in the center of the apple half and then sprinkle it with brown sugar and cinnamon. Cover each bowl with plastic wrap and microwave for three to five minutes, checking periodically.

While the baked apples are cooling, invite each child to sample a piece of raw apple and describe its crunchy texture. Then have students eat their baked apples. Did the apples' texture change? Lead students to conclude that the microwave oven's heat caused the texture to soften. Mmmm, what a yummy way to study science!

Read aloud *Apples* by Ann L. Burckhardt.

SIMPLE SCIENCE for Kindergartners

The Wonder of Webs

Capture your students' attention with these special ideas about spiderwebs.

by Suzanne Moore, Irving, TX

The World of Webs

Introduce your students to the wonder of spiderwebs by showing them photos from spider-related books and nature magazines. Then share the spiderweb facts listed below. Now that you've sparked students' interest, take them for a walk outside looking for spiderwebs—the earlier in the day, the better. Spiderwebs are very easily seen when the dew or frost is still on them. Remind students to look but not touch! Have each child record her observations by drawing the webs she sees.

- Spiders have special glands in their bodies that make silk. Each gland makes a different kind of silk thread.
- One type of silk strand is a *dragline.* The spider hangs by the dragline to drop down from high places.
- Spiderwebs can be many shapes. Some are orb-shaped, some are tangled masses, and some are funnel-shaped.

DID YOU KNOW?
Spider silk is the strongest natural fiber in the world.

Sticky Strands

All webs are made for the same purpose—to catch food. Some of the web strands are sticky, thin, and difficult for an insect to see. Its legs get stuck on the sticky strands, and it cannot escape.

How does a spider not get stuck on its own web? Try this hands-on demonstration to find out! Help each child create a loop from a six-inch length of two-inch-wide tape, rolled with the sticky side out. Have her stick one side of the loop onto a sheet of scrap paper. Explain that this loop represents the sticky threads of the spiderweb. Have each child walk her fingers across the tape. It feels sticky, doesn't it? Now have her dip her fingers into oil, such as vegetable oil or baby oil. Then instruct her to walk her oiled fingers across the tape. Now do they stick? Explain that spiders have oil on their feet, which keeps them from sticking to their own webs.

Explain to students that the strands of a web stay sticky unless the web becomes covered with dust. Finally, have each child sprinkle a bit of baby powder on her loop of tape. This web is dusty!

Funnel Fun

Different spiders spin different-shaped webs. Some spiders even spin funnel-shaped webs. Complete this project to help youngsters understand what a funnel-shaped web looks like. Begin by stretching a portion of decorative spiderweb material around a large plastic funnel. Spray it with a heavy coating of spray starch, and let the material dry overnight. The next day, carefully remove your funnel web and invite students to take an up-close look. Cool!

Read aloud *The Very Busy Spider* by Eric Carle.

It's a Cover-Up!

We've got you covered with ideas for fur, feathers, and scales.

by Suzanne Moore, Irving, TX

Prepare for this lesson by obtaining different types of animal body coverings. Museums or nature centers often have loaner samples. For example, collect or borrow rabbit fur, cowhide, alligator skin or snakeskin, feathers, and fish skin with scales. Alternately, use artificial materials (such as snakeskin fabric) that resemble the body coverings.

Body Coverings Up Close

Direct students to observe their own body coverings using magnifying lenses; encourage them to describe what they observe. Then briefly explain that their body covering is called skin, that it has different colors, and that hair may be found on most of their skin. Next, ask youngsters to think about dogs, cats, gerbils, hamsters, and rabbits. What kind of body covering do they have? Then discuss body coverings for birds and snakes. Invite small groups of students to use a hand lens to observe the different types of animal body coverings you collected or borrowed. Then discuss students' observations. (Be sure students wash their hands thoroughly after handling any animal coverings.)

DID YOU KNOW?

While mammals are warm blooded and sport hair or fur, most fish are cold blooded, have scales, and have fairly tough skin.

Furry Findings

Will animal body coverings keep an animal warm? Try this idea to find out! In advance, fill a quart-size zippered plastic bag with ice. Invite each child to touch the bag and describe how it feels—it's cold! Then cover the bag with a swatch of synthetic fur and have youngsters feel it again. Can the cold be felt through the fur? Repeat this activity using a feather pillow. Lead the group to conclude that fur and feathers help keep mammals and birds warm.

Savvy Sorting

It's what's on the outside that counts with this interactive sorting bulletin board. In advance, label a blank bulletin board "Fur," "Feathers," and "Scales."

Then have youngsters generate a list of animals of all types as you jot their suggestions on a chart. After the list has been compiled, invite each child to select an animal to illustrate. When the pictures are completed, have students categorize each illustration and mount it under the appropriate heading on the bulletin board.

Later, give youngsters some independent practice identifying animal body coverings. Give each child a 12" x 18" sheet of manila paper. Help him fold it into three equal sections; then have him label one section "Fur," another "Feathers," and the last one "Scales." Give each child a copy of page 146. Have him color and cut out the animal pictures and then glue them in the appropriate category on his folded paper.

Read aloud *Animal Skin and Scales* by David M. Schwartz

The Pump That Thumps

What's shaped like an upside-down pear, is hollow, and never rests?
Try these big-hearted activities with students to find out!

by Suzanne Moore, Irving, TX

Heart Basics

Each of your youngsters probably knows she has a heart, but does she know where it's really located and how big it is? Begin your heart study by sharing the following information: The heart is about as big as a person's fist and is located in the center of the chest, tilted slightly to the left. The heart is a pump that pushes blood through vessels throughout the body.

Next, have each child make a fist and place it in the middle of her chest. Then have her pump her fist continuously while singing the song at right. After singing, ask students whether their hands are tired from pumping. Then explain that each of their hearts beats nonstop to pump blood through their bodies all day and all night long.

(sung to the tune of "The Wheels on the Bus")

The heart in my chest goes thump, thump, thump,
Thump, thump, thump,
Thump, thump, thump.
The heart in my chest goes thump, thump, thump
Day and night.

The heart is a pump that pumps my blood,
Pumps my blood, pumps my blood.
The heart is a pump that pumps my blood
Day and night.

Exercise makes it nice and strong,
Nice and strong, nice and strong.
Exercise makes it nice and strong,
Day and night.

DID YOU KNOW?

The average heart beats over 2½ billion times in a lifetime.

The Beat Complete

What can be used to listen to a heart beat? Doctors use stethoscopes to amplify the sounds of the heart. Have youngsters create a similar effect with paper tubes. Pair students and give each twosome a toilet paper tube to share. Quiet the room. Then, in turn, instruct one youngster in each pair to listen to his partner's heartbeat. Next, have students describe the sounds they heard. Explain that the sounds are made by the opening and closing of a heart valve, and by flowing blood.

Pump It Up

After this simple demonstration, your youngsters will be eager to exercise and then check their pulses. To begin, demonstrate how to feel a pulse along the side of the neck and then have students give it a try. Next, instruct each child to put her head down on her desk and remain still for a couple of minutes. Then have her feel her pulse and note its speed. Next, have students stand up and hop 20 times. Instruct each student to check her pulse again. Then ask, "Is your heart beating faster? Why do you think it changed speed?" After students respond, explain that the speed of a beating heart changes based on the activity level of a person. Way to feel the beat!

SIMPLE SCIENCE for Kindergartners

Science "Eggs-periments"

Your little scientists will be on a roll with these egg-related experiments!

Full Circle

What keeps an egg from rolling away from its nest? Its shape! To test this, place a hard-boiled egg on a piece of bulletin board paper on the floor. Have a child use a crayon to draw a nest around the egg. Then invite another child to gently roll the egg. Youngsters will see that the shape of an egg will cause it to roll in a circle!

Peggy Campbell-Rush—Gr. K, Union Township School, Hampton, NJ

The Answer's in the Spin

How can you tell whether an egg has been boiled or not? Just give it a spin! To prepare, boil an egg and allow it to cool. Label the boiled egg and a raw egg each with a different letter. Have children gather around a table. Show them the two eggs and explain that one egg has been boiled and the other one has not. Invite each child to hold and shake the eggs and then make a guess as to which one has been cooked. Next, explain to youngsters that when you try to spin the eggs on the table, the boiled egg will spin and the raw egg will not. Spin the eggs and then crack them open to see the results.

Jan Clabuesch
Pigeon Children's Discovery Center
Pigeon, MI

Egg Parts

Youngsters learn the parts of an egg with this simple comparison activity. In advance, hard-boil several eggs. During group time, pass one egg around so students can feel the shell. Then invite students to help peel the egg. Cut the egg in half to show the egg white and yolk. Next, crack a raw egg into a clear bowl and review its parts, comparing it to the cooked egg. (Before the next step, have each child wash her hands.) Give each youngster a boiled egg half and half sheet of paper. Have her draw and label the parts of an egg and then snack on her egg example!

egg white

yolk

Katie

Randalyn Larson—Gr. K
Memorial School, Jackson, MI

SIMPLE SCIENCE for Kindergartners

Physical Changes Made Simple

To investigate the magic of physical changes your little ones won't need a special wand or a top hat—just a little powdered drink mix and water.

by Suzanne Moore, Irving, TX

Check It Out

To begin checking out physical changes, help each child in a small group scoop one-fourth teaspoon of powdered drink mix into a personalized clear plastic cup. Encourage your little ones to describe what they see, feel, and smell. Then provide each child with a hand lens and encourage him to take a closer look at the crystals. Emphasize that the powder is a solid.

Presto Change-o!

Delight youngsters with another supersimple example of physical change. Ask students what will happen if their drinks are placed in the freezer. How will the drinks change? Pop the cups into the freezer and leave overnight. (Hint: Nestle the drink cups into muffin tins for an easy no-spills trip to the freezer.)

After the drinks are frozen, give each child his cup. Have him examine its contents with a hand lens and describe how his drink looks. Explain that the liquid changed to a solid when it froze. Will the icy snack change again? After youngsters share their thoughts, set the frozen drinks aside. Presto change-o! The frozen treats will melt as they stay at room temperature, and then they'll disappear—when your students drink them!

Abracadabra

Now that your young scientists have investigated the powdered drink mix, pour one-fourth cup of water into each child's cup. Invite him to sing the following song as he stirs his water-powder mixture with a plastic spoon or coffee stirrer until the powder has dissolved into the water. Encourage students to examine their drinks with hand lenses. Ask questions such as these: Can you see any powdered drink mix? Where did it go? How do you know it's still in the water? Explain that the powdered mix only seemed to disappear when it was stirred with water. It actually dissolved. Direct each child to take a small sip of his drink. Lead students to conclude that the mix is still in the water because it has changed colors and it tastes sweet.

(sung to the tune of "Skip to My Lou")

Abracadabra. Stir, stir, stir.
Abracadabra. Stir, stir, stir.
Abracadabra. Stir, stir, stir.
Where did my powdered drink
   mix go?

Animal Cards

Use with "Savvy Sorting" on page 142.

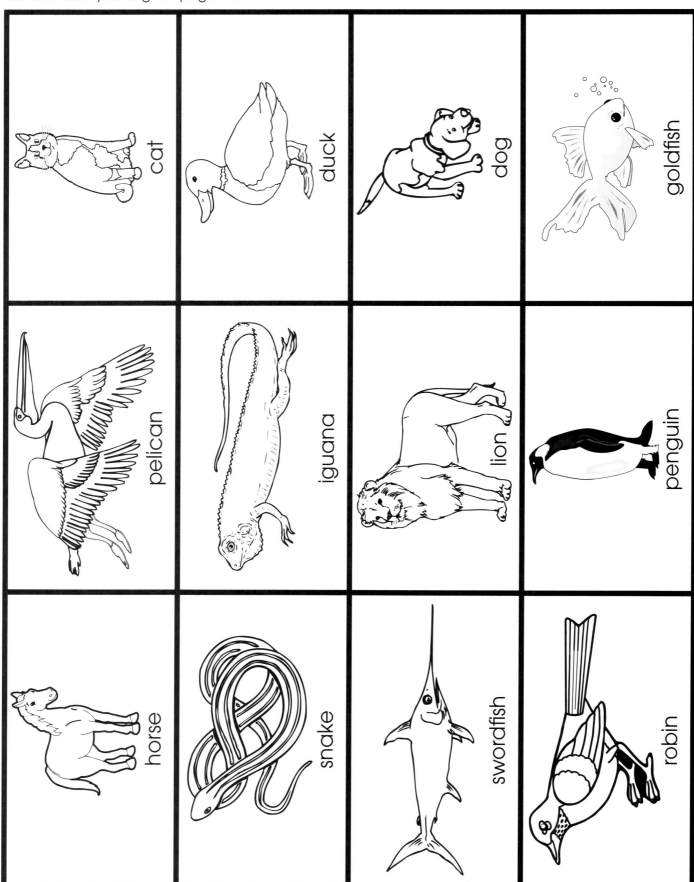

cat

duck

dog

goldfish

pelican

iguana

lion

penguin

horse

snake

swordfish

robin

BOOK FEATURES

My Crayons Talk

Written by Patricia Hubbard
Illustrated by G. Brian Karas

If crayons could talk, what would they say? Join a little girl and her crayons as they sing, yell, hoot, chirp, and laugh their way through simple rhyming text and vivid illustrations. This rollicking celebration of language is sure to make a colorful impression on anyone who has ever picked up a crayon!

Illustrating rhyming words

Time for Color Rhymes!

Have your little ones illustrate some cool color rhymes with this crafty class book! To prepare, cut a 6" x 18" white construction paper strip for each child. Then cut a supply of 6" x 18" strips from pink, red, blue, black, brown, and green construction paper. Decorate and cut each strip, as shown, to look like a crayon. Next, have each child choose a paper crayon. Then have her think of a word that rhymes with her chosen color. Give each student a strip of white construction paper and instruct her to draw the rhyming word on it. Then assist each child in writing the color name and rhyming word on the strips as shown.

Next, create a two-piece cover for the book by labeling a colored strip and a white strip as shown. Keeping the sets matched, stack the paper crayons beneath the colored strip and the illustrations beneath the white strip. Then staple both stacks to a 12" x 18" piece of white construction paper as shown. Place the book on your classroom bookshelf for students to share. It's rhyme time!

Developing fine-motor skills
Reciting a fingerplay

Five Little Crayons

Here's a creative crayon fingerplay that will challenge your little ones' fine-motor skills! To prepare, make a class supply of small construction paper triangles in yellow, blue, orange, red, and green. Tape one triangle of each color onto each child's fingers, as shown, to represent crayons. Then have the students recite the fingerplay below and act out the accompanying motions.

Five little crayons colored a scene,	*Hold hand up.*
Yellow, Blue, Orange, Red, and Green.	*Wiggle each finger.*
"Look," said Yellow, "My sun is bright!"	*Move yellow in a circle to make a sun.*
Blue said, "Great! My river's just right!"	*Wiggle blue back and forth like a river.*
Orange said, "Flowers! I'll draw a few."	*Wiggle orange.*
"Nice," said Red, "I'll add some too!"	*Wiggle red.*
"Sigh," said Green. "I'm tired of trees	*Hold up green.*
And grass and bushes and tiny leaves.	
I think I'll draw a big green cloud!	*Draw a cloud in the air with green.*
A big green cloud should be allowed!"	
The crayons all smiled and didn't think twice.	*Wiggle fingers.*
A big green cloud sounded rather nice!	*Wave hand.*

148

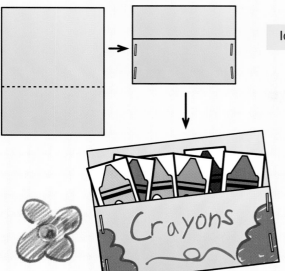

Reading a Rainbow

Your little ones will be tickled pink when they identify colors with this interactive reading activity! In advance, make a class supply of page 158. Gather a 9" x 12" sheet of yellow construction paper for each child. Fold each sheet of paper as shown; then staple the edges to create a pocket. Have each student decorate his pocket to resemble a crayon box. Next, assist students in coloring each pattern on page 158 the appropriate color. Instruct him to cut out the crayon patterns. As you read *My Crayons Talk,* have each student hold up the appropriate crayon patterns and then place them in the pocket!

A Color Chorus

Your youngsters won't be feeling blue when they sing this catchy color song! Begin by having each child gather the crayon patterns created in "Reading a Rainbow" on this page. Have each child display her crayon patterns on her workspace. Then have students sing and perform the action song below, inserting a color in Lines 1, 2, 4, and 5. Sing more verses using different colors to test youngsters' color knowledge. La-la-lovely!

(sung to the tune of "If You're Happy and You Know It")

If you see a [purple] crayon, pick it out!   *Find the crayon pattern.*
If you see a [purple] crayon, pick it out!
Stand and wiggle, give a shout!   *Stand up with the pattern; then wiggle hips and shout.*

[Purple]'s great without a doubt!   *Hold up the crayon pattern.*
If you see a [purple] crayon, pick it out!   *Sit down.*

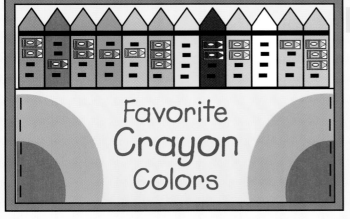

Sorting Crayon Favorites!

Get your students ready for some splendid color sorting with this interactive bulletin board! Begin by covering a bulletin board with yellow paper. Cut one 6" x 18" construction paper strip for each color represented on page 158. Then cut and decorate each strip as shown. Laminate the strips for durability and then staple each strip to the bulletin board. Staple a piece of yellow bulletin board paper over the lower half of the bulletin board to represent a crayon box. Then decorate and title the bulletin board as shown.

Next, give each child a copy of page 158. Have her select her favorite crayon color. Instruct her to color the crayon pattern and then cut it out. Laminate the patterns for durability; then place the hook side of a Velcro fastener on the back of each one. Place the loop sides of the Velcro fasteners on the crayons on the bulletin board. Put the patterns in a large resealable plastic bag. Direct children to dump out the patterns and sort them by attaching each pattern to the matching crayon on the bulletin board. Green is my favorite!

Big Fat Hen

Illustrated by Keith Baker

The vibrant illustrations and familiar text of Big Fat Hen *will have young readers clucking to read it again and again. Use this book and these activities to give your little ones something to peep about!*

ideas by Suzanne Moore, Irving, TX

Number recognition
Counting

Count Your Chickens

This egg-gathering activity will have youngsters practicing number recognition and counting. In advance, stock a sensory tub with shredded newspaper or raffia and a supply of plastic eggs with a large yellow pom-pom (chick) inside each one. (If desired, hole-punch black construction paper to make eyes, cut orange construction paper to make beaks, and glue eyes and a beak to each pom-pom.) Place a collection of small baskets near the center. Each day, post a different number at the center and invite each child to gather the specified number of eggs in a basket. After he collects the eggs, have him count the eggs and then help each chick hatch. Peep, peep!

Writing numbers
Rhyming

Thumbs Up!

Students will certainly give a big thumbs-up for this activity. Make a class set of the booklet cover on page 159. Then cut six 4" x 4½" construction paper pages for each child. Give each student a set of pages. Have her color the cover and write her name on it, below the title. Then instruct her to glue the cover to one of her booklet pages. Next, have her use yellow paint to make two thumbprints on each of the remaining booklet pages. After the paint is dry, show your group how to use a black fine-tip marker to add details to the prints, transforming them into chicks. Help each child staple the pages behind the cover. Then instruct her to write a different number in order from 1 to 10 under each chick. Next, talk about words that rhyme with *two, four, six, eight,* and *ten.* Have each youngster illustrate a rhyming word on the page opposite the appropriate numbered chick. Then help her label her drawings. Encourage each youngster to share her booklet with the class.

150

Active Antics

Your little ones will enjoy these active antics when they join you in rereading *Big Fat Hen*. Invite each child to hold up the number of fingers mentioned on each page of the book and act out the various movements listed below. Get ready, get set, get moving!

1, 2…	*Hold up fingers.*
Buckle my shoe.	*Pretend to buckle.*
3, 4…	*Hold up fingers.*
Shut the door.	*Clap hands once.*
5, 6…	*Hold up fingers.*
Pick up sticks.	*Pretend to pick up sticks from the floor.*
7, 8…	*Hold up fingers.*
Lay them straight.	*Pretend to lay sticks straight.*
9, 10…	*Hold up fingers.*
Big Fat Hen	*Flap arms like wings.*
And her friends.	*Flap arms like wings.*
1, 2, 3…	*Hold up fingers.*
4, 5, 6.	*Hold up fingers.*
All their eggs…	*Squat into a tiny ball, wrapping hands around legs.*
And all their chicks!	*Pretend to hatch, flap arms like wings, and peep.*

It's Time to Rhyme

Youngsters will slide right into matching rhyming words with a project that's just clucky! To prepare, make a class set of the project patterns on page 159. After sharing the book with your class, review the rhyming words heard in the story. Give each youngster a copy of page 159 and a nine-inch paper plate. Have him color the hen head and the egg. Then instruct him to cut out the patterns. Laminate each youngster's strips for durability and then cut them out. Have each child glue the hen head cutout to his plate and then draw the rest of her body as shown. Instruct him to glue the egg beneath the hen. Have him glue raffia around the egg to simulate a nest. Use a craft knife to cut four slits in each child's project where indicated. Then help him thread his two strips through the slits. Encourage youngsters to slide the strips up and down to match each rhyming set of pictures and numbers. It's a match!

Chicken Feed

With all this learning going on, it's certain that your little peeps will be hungry! Have each child follow these simple instructions to make his own snack of chicken feed. Instruct him to measure two tablespoons of O-shaped cereal, two tablespoons of miniature marshmallows, and one tablespoon of M&M's candies into a snack-size resealable bag. Help him seal his bag and shake it to mix the feed. Then invite him to dig in!

The Polar Express

Written and illustrated by Chris Van Allsburg

This book takes its readers on a journey to the mystical, magical North Pole, where one little boy meets Santa and receives a special gift. After reading this story, we all learn the importance of believing!

ideas by Angie Kutzer, Gr. K, Garrett Elementary School, Mebane, NC

The Train Ride
Reading comprehension, Sequencing

Work on reading comprehension and story sequence at the same time with this simple booklet. Duplicate page 160 for each child. Have her color and cut out the pages. Then encourage her to use the illustrations to sequence the story's events. Direct her to self-check by looking at the page numbers. Once the pages are in order, staple them together behind a train-shaped cover. Have the child practice reading her booklet and then send it home for her to read to her family. Choo! Choo!

The Train Ride

Name ___Kaleigh___

Ring-a-ling!
Patterning

What's better than a big silver jingle bell? Lots of jingle bells! Integrate some patterning practice by using bells to make sound patterns. Obtain three jingle bells, each a different size. Attach a pipe cleaner to each one to create a handle. Use a permanent marker to label each bell with a different letter (*A, B,* or *C*). Write several different letter patterns on separate sentence strips, such as ABAB, AABAAB, and ABCABC. Have a child choose a pattern card and ring the bells accordingly. Then have her make her own pattern and record it on an index card. Encourage her to play it for the class. Beautiful!

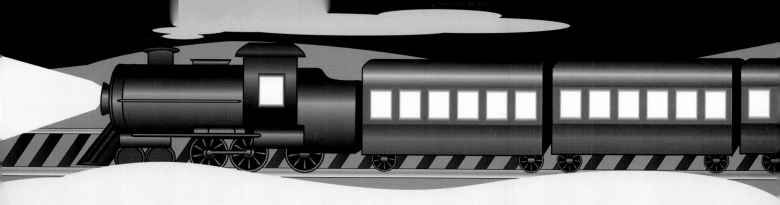

Pajama Prowess
Alphabet recognition

The children on the train have lots of fun dressed in their pajamas and nightgowns. Your students will have just as much fun matching these pajamas to practice alphabet skills. To prepare, cut simple shirt and pants shapes from wallpaper or fabric samples to make ten pairs. Use a permanent marker to label each shirt with a different uppercase letter. Then label each pair of pants with a corresponding lowercase letter. To complete the activity, a child makes pajama sets by matching the letters. To make the activity more difficult, mix the wallpaper samples when making sets. Night-night!

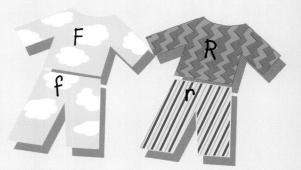

What a Sight!
Sight-word recognition

This train ride will reinforce the high-frequency words your students will encounter in the *real* world! Arrange students' chairs like train seats. Tape a different sight word to the back of each seat as shown. Obtain a wooden toy train whistle. To play, blow two short toots and have children walk around the chairs. After a brief time, blow a longer toot. At this signal, each child sits in the chair nearest to her and, in turn, reads the word on the back of her chair. Once each child reads her word, start the next round with two more short toots. Toot! Toot!

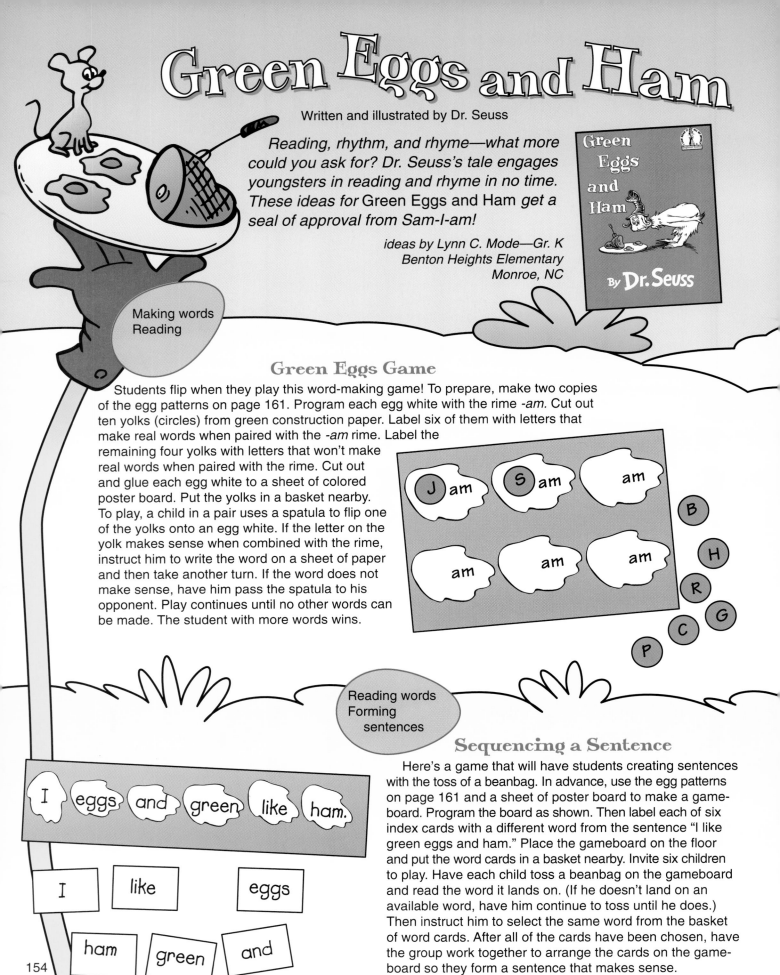

Green Eggs and Ham

Written and illustrated by Dr. Seuss

Reading, rhythm, and rhyme—what more could you ask for? Dr. Seuss's tale engages youngsters in reading and rhyme in no time. These ideas for Green Eggs and Ham *get a seal of approval from Sam-I-am!*

ideas by Lynn C. Mode—Gr. K
Benton Heights Elementary
Monroe, NC

Making words
Reading

Green Eggs Game

Students flip when they play this word-making game! To prepare, make two copies of the egg patterns on page 161. Program each egg white with the rime *-am.* Cut out ten yolks (circles) from green construction paper. Label six of them with letters that make real words when paired with the *-am* rime. Label the remaining four yolks with letters that won't make real words when paired with the rime. Cut out and glue each egg white to a sheet of colored poster board. Put the yolks in a basket nearby. To play, a child in a pair uses a spatula to flip one of the yolks onto an egg white. If the letter on the yolk makes sense when combined with the rime, instruct him to write the word on a sheet of paper and then take another turn. If the word does not make sense, have him pass the spatula to his opponent. Play continues until no other words can be made. The student with more words wins.

Reading words
Forming sentences

Sequencing a Sentence

Here's a game that will have students creating sentences with the toss of a beanbag. In advance, use the egg patterns on page 161 and a sheet of poster board to make a game-board. Program the board as shown. Then label each of six index cards with a different word from the sentence "I like green eggs and ham." Place the gameboard on the floor and put the word cards in a basket nearby. Invite six children to play. Have each child toss a beanbag on the gameboard and read the word it lands on. (If he doesn't land on an available word, have him continue to toss until he does.) Then instruct him to select the same word from the basket of word cards. After all of the cards have been chosen, have the group work together to arrange the cards on the game-board so they form a sentence that makes sense.

Green Eggs and Ham
green chickens
the green store
spray-painted green
food coloring

One day a green chicken laid
a green egg. A lade crackt
the egg and cookd it. It was
green. She put green salt on
it. Green pepper to. It tastd
good. I lik green egs.

Writing
Creating a
story

A Class Story

Did you say, "Green eggs and ham?" Is there such
a thing? Have youngsters brainstorm a list of places
green eggs and ham could come from or ways it might
be made. Record students' responses on chart paper.
Then choose one of the suggestions from the list to use
as a story starter. Encourage students to continue the
story, inviting them to help write it on the chart. After the
story is complete, read it to the class. Don't be surprised
when youngsters want to choose a new story starter
and write a different story!

Collecting data

Tasty Totals

Youngsters won't be green with envy
when they all participate in this taste test
of green foods! Provide a class supply of
samples of each of the following green
foods: lettuce, olives, kiwi, peas, and
mint chocolate chip ice cream. Give
each child a taste of each food. Have her
determine her favorite and draw a picture
of it. Then have students graph their
favorites and discuss the results. For
more graphing practice, have youngsters
also graph their least favorite green
foods.

lettuce	olives	kiwi	peas	mint chocolate chip ice cream

Waiting for Wings

Written and illustrated by Lois Ehlert

The vivid spring garden illustrations and rhyming text of Waiting for Wings will cheerfully teach little ones about the life cycle of a butterfly. Use this book and these activities to help youngsters spread their own creative wings!

ideas by Cindy Daoust

Sequencing
Retelling a story

Sequential Story

Your little butterflies will flutter around this lively sequencing activity! In advance, make a class set of the patterns on page 162. Then cut out a 1½" x 7" construction paper caterpillar for each child. After sharing the book with youngsters, review the butterfly life cycle illustrations. Give each child a caterpillar cutout and a copy of page 162. Have him color and cut out the patterns. Help him sequence the life cycle pictures and then glue them in order onto his caterpillar. Have him color his butterfly and then glue his caterpillar onto it as shown. Have pairs of students take turns using their butterflies to retell the story to each other.

Creating a life cycle model

From Egg to Butterfly

Youngsters are sure to munch their way through this tasty science activity! To prepare, gather a class supply of paper plates, a bag of pretzel twists, and a box of Corn Pops cereal. Discuss with students the butterfly life cycle as you refer to the book illustrations. Guide students to understand that a life cycle is a continuous pattern. Point out that the butterfly life cycle consists of the butterfly egg, the caterpillar, the pupa, and the adult butterfly. Give each child a paper plate, a scoop of cereal (to make the egg, caterpillar, and pupa) and a pretzel (representing the butterfly). Help her arrange and glue cereal and a pretzel onto her plate to create a butterfly life cycle model. Then have her use crayons to draw details on the plate as shown. Finally, let each youngster munch on a fresh scoop of cereal and pretzels.

Butterfly Eggs

Youngsters' rhyming skills will take flight when they help create this "egg-cellent" group game. In advance, gather a basket, a plastic egg for each pair of students, and a class set of three-inch construction paper caterpillar shapes. Give each pair of students one egg and two caterpillars. Ask each pair to think of two rhyming words and then write each word on a separate caterpillar. Check each set of rhyming words. Have each pair put one caterpillar in its egg and then place the egg and the other caterpillar in the basket.

To play the game, ask youngsters to sit in a circle and then pass the basket around for each child to remove an egg or a caterpillar. Ask one child with an egg to crack it open; then help him read the word out loud. Ask each child with a caterpillar to check his word and decide whether it rhymes. Encourage the class to help determine the correct rhyming pair. (Several children may have caterpillars with words with the same rhyme.) Repeat this process until all the rhyming pairs have been matched.

Life cycle
Parts of a butterfly

Flannelboard Flutter

Flitter and flutter to the flannelboard to teach youngsters about the butterfly life cycle. To prepare, gather four 2" pom-poms and cut the following from colored felt: four wings, six legs, one leaf, and one pupa (oval shape large enough to cover a pom-pom caterpillar). Attach the hook side of a Velcro fastener to each pom-pom, creating a butterfly egg and three body parts. Add eyes and yarn antennae to one pom-pom to make a head. Use the flannelboard pieces and the poem shown to illustrate the butterfly life cycle. Then place the flannelboard and pieces at a center and invite each child to have a turn performing the poem.

Look, look—a butterfly egg!
Crawl, crawl on caterpillar legs.
Wait, wait, little pupa.
Soon you'll be a butterfly. Super!

Place the egg on the leaf.
Use three pom-poms to make a caterpillar.
Cover the caterpillar with the pupa.
Remove the pupa; add legs and wings to
make a butterfly.

Following directions

Butterfly Garden

Watch your little artists bloom as they create this colorful flower garden that's just waiting for wings. First, make a class set of the construction paper butterfly pattern on page 162. Also gather paints, flower-shaped sponges, and construction paper. Review the beautiful illustrations in the book with youngsters. Encourage each child to use the art materials to make a flower and a leaf. Guide youngsters to use paint to create thumbprint caterpillars on their leaves, and add fingerprints to sponge-painted flowers. Then give each child a butterfly pattern and have him paint one half of it. While the paint is still wet, help him fold the butterfly in half and press down. Then lay it flat to dry. After each child cuts out his creations, arrange them on a bulletin board titled "Our Butterfly Garden."

Crayon Patterns

Use with "Reading a Rainbow," "A Color Chorus," and "Sorting Crayon Favorites!" on page 149.

purple

red

brown

green

blue

orange

yellow

black

gold

white

silver

pink

Project Patterns
Use with "It's Time to Rhyme" on page 151.

Booklet Cover
Use with "Thumbs Up!" on page 150.

My Big Fat Hen

by _____

©The Education Center, Inc.

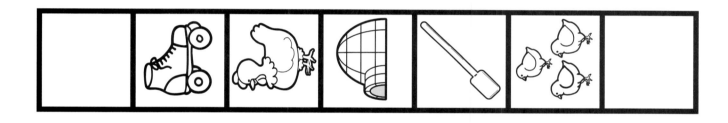

	2	4	6	8	10	

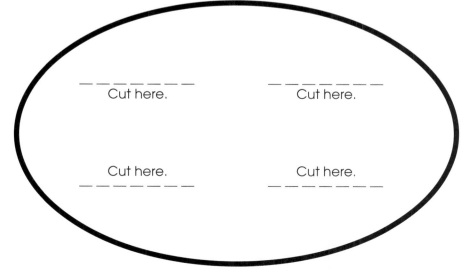

Cut here.   Cut here.

Cut here.   Cut here.

The little boy   1

The big train   2

The happy Santa   3

The shiny bell   4

The small hole   5

The best gift!   6

Egg Patterns

Use with "Green Eggs Game" and "Sequencing a Sentence" on page 154.

Life Cycle Pictures

Use with "Sequential Story" on page 156.

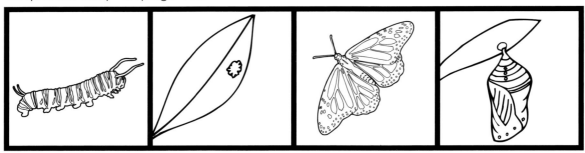

Butterfly Pattern

Use with "Sequential Story" on page 156 and "Butterfly Garden" on page 157.

LITERATURE UNITS

Back to School With BOOKS

Check out this collection of books and ideas, which will excite your students about starting school!

by Angie Kutzer, Audrey Garrett Elementary School, Mebane, NC

Wemberly Worried

Written and illustrated by Kevin Henkes

Poor Wemberly! She's a worrier. She worries about anything and everything, from shrinking in the bathtub to rusty chains on the swings. And now she has a new worry—starting school. A new friend helps to ease Wemberly's worries, and she looks forward to her next school day!

Puppet Pals

Making a craft, dramatic play

Nibblet and Petal help the girls in this story feel more at ease at school. These puppets will do the same for your students. Working with a small group, provide students with paper lunch bags, construction paper, scissors, glue, and crayons. Have each child choose to make either a cat puppet, like Nibblet, or a bunny puppet, like Petal. Then guide him in cutting paper into shapes to create his puppet, using the illustrations as a guide. Help him arrange the shapes on the bag and glue them in place. Then instruct him to use a dark crayon to draw his puppet's face.

After the puppets are complete, have youngsters use them during circle time to act out some first-day scenarios, such as introducing themselves to new friends or asking someone to share a toy.

Mousy Snacks

Fine-motor skills, making a snack

Ease your little ones' first-day worries by inviting them to make these tasty treats. Ahead of time, purchase or bake a class supply of heart-shaped sugar cookies. Then have each child turn a cookie into a mouse by frosting it with white icing and adding two chocolate chip eyes, a red gumdrop nose, and pink sugar crystal ears. Nibble, nibble, nibble!

The Night Before Kindergarten
Written by Natasha Wing • Illustrated by Julie Durrell

This analogy to 'Twas the Night Before Christmas *playfully illustrates all of the preparations being made before starting school. The kids are excited and the teacher is excited, but what about the parents? As the children get settled in the room and the fun begins, Miss Sunrise looks over to find the parents with sniffly noses and red, wet eyes. Luckily, there's a magical rug in the classroom where the parents get one final hug and are sent away with the reassurance "Don't cry, Mom and Dad; kindergarten is cool!"*

Our Night Before
Relating to literature, dictating a response

So what did your students do to prepare for kindergarten? Find out with this class book project. Discuss with students any special events that took place before starting school, such as going out to dinner, buying a special outfit, or packing a lunchbox for the first time. Have each child illustrate her activity and describe to you what she did. Write each child's dictation on her page and then bind all of the pages together. Share the book during your next circle time and store it in your book center for revisiting. Your first class book!

I went out to eat.

I went swimming.

A Cool Display
Open house display

Show parents and youngsters how cool kindergarten can be with this hallway display. Make a frozen pop and turtle pattern similar to those shown. Sketch them onto bulletin board paper. (You'll want to make several frozen pops in different colors.) During the first week of school, take photos of different activities in a kindergartner's day. Mount each photo onto a different frozen pop and then label each one. Display the turtle character and frozen treats on a wall along with the title "Kindergarten Is COOL!"

First Day Jitters

Written by Julie Danneberg • Illustrated by Judy Love

As if the first day of school isn't bad enough, Sarah Jane Hartwell is starting the first day at a new school! Her jitters make her very reluctant to get out of bed, get dressed, and head off to school. But Mr. Hartwell strongly encourages Sarah to get going. With Sarah nervously acting like any new student would, it's surprising to find out that she is actually a new teacher!

yes   no

Surprised?

Graphing, responding to literature

This clever graphing experience will show little ones which students were surprised by this story's ending. Ahead of time, prepare a T chart from poster board, as shown, and gather a class supply of colorful clothespins. After the story, ask students whether they were surprised to find out that Sarah is a teacher and not a child. Instruct each child to clip his pin to the graph to reveal his response. When the graph is complete, discuss the results. Save your T chart to use later for other graphing tasks.

Have a Great Day!

Developing character traits, making a list

Extend the story by having your youngsters generate a list of things that would make Mrs. Sarah Jane Hartwell's day a good one. Program a sheet of chart paper similar to the one shown. Then give each child an opportunity to explain a kind deed that could take place when a new teacher starts school or a substitute teacher teaches for a day. Write students' responses on the chart paper. This activity is also a good way to emphasize some of your classroom rules. It's gonna be a great day—and a great year!

First-Day Jitters
Kind Deeds

- ask to help
- give her flowers
- give her an apple
- help her with her calendar
- give her a drink
- give her a book
- be quiet
- give her lunch
- follow her directions
- give her lipstick
- say please and thank you

ABCs, 123s, and More
Books to Help Teach the Basics

From counting to the calendar, this selection of books and activities will help reinforce some basic concepts. So dive into the days of the week and leap into learning letters—all with the help of these super stories!

by Ada Goren, Winston Salem, NC

Anno's Counting Book
Written and illustrated by Mitsumasa Anno
With each turn of the page, the little village pictured in this book grows and changes—with more and more objects in each illustration. The handy tower of counting cubes in the left margin provides a clue to the sets shown on each page.

Counting
Counting With Cubes

Youngsters will naturally want to find and count the many groups on each page of this book. So gather a small group and open the book to a random page. Give each child in the group a number of counting cubes to equal the number shown on that page's tower. Then, one at a time, invite each child to cover one object set with her cubes, counting as she goes. For example, on the seven illustration, she might cover the seven cows with seven cubes. If she chooses an object set that doesn't have room to place the cubes side by side, have her build a tower atop the set.

One, two, three flowers!

Counting
Drawing
Number Pictures

Break out the cubes *and* the crayons for this artistic math activity! Give each child a tower with a random number of counting cubes, a sheet of drawing paper, and crayons. Have him count the cubes in his tower and label his paper with the corresponding number. Then have him draw sets of objects to correspond with his assigned number. For example, a child with a tower of five cubes might draw a picture with five houses, five flowers, and five clouds. Look—it's just like Anno's illustrations!

Eating the Alphabet: Fruits and Vegetables From A to Z

Written and illustrated by Lois Ehlert

A *is for* artichoke *and* Z *is for* zucchini *in this mouthwatering alphabet book! Young readers will find wonderful watercolor collages of old favorites like apples and strawberries and more unusual produce like leeks and quince.*

An Alphabet of Animals

Lois Ehlert illustrates fruits and veggies from *A* to *Z* in her beautiful book. Have your class make their own book—this time with alphabetized *animals!* Assign each youngster a letter (or two, depending on your class size). Help him think of at least one animal with a name that begins with that letter. Have him illustrate his animal on a sheet of paper labeled with his letter. Then help him write the animal's name on his paper. Bind all the pages together behind a cover with the title "Our Animal Alphabet." Keep the book in your class library for everyone to enjoy.

H h

hippo

Penny eats pizza.

Favorite Foods

Does Annie like apples or apricots best? Find out the favorite foods of your youngsters when they help you make this bulletin board display! In advance, photograph each child. Ask each child to find the page in the book that shows the first letter of her name. Have her think of a favorite fruit, vegetable, or other food not pictured in the book that begins with the same letter as her name. Provide an assortment of craft materials, such as crayons, paint, construction paper, and markers. Have each child make an artistic rendition of her chosen food. Display each child's creation next to her photograph on a bulletin board. Add a sentence strip, as shown, to each pairing. Then title the display "We Eat the Alphabet!"

The Very Hungry Caterpillar
Written and illustrated by Eric Carle
This classic tale of metamorphosis takes a caterpillar on a weeklong eating spree! Watch as the tiny caterpillar grows fatter and fatter with each passing day before cozying into his cocoon to undergo a brilliant change.

Days of the Week
Nutrition

The Very Hungry Kindergartners

The little caterpillar in Eric Carle's story seems to like fruit best, although his diet includes some typical junk food! What do your students eat each day? Find out when you ask each of them to keep a food diary for a week. Give each child a small booklet titled "The Very Hungry Kindergartner." Include seven pages behind the cover, each labeled with a different day of the week. Have each student illustrate at least one thing she eats during each day. Review the finished booklets the following week. How many students ate fruits? Vegetables? Candy? Take this opportunity to discuss healthful food choices, which are important *every* day of the week!

Days of the Week
Retelling a Story

On Monday, He Ate...

Help your little ones retell the caterpillar's story when they make a chart of his daily menu. To prepare, make a simple chart labeled with the days of the week as shown. Duplicate the chart to make a class supply. Also make a class supply of page 167. Have each child color and cut out the food patterns from page 167. Then have her glue them to her chart below the corresponding day of the week. When everyone's chart is complete, have children pair up and take turns retelling the story with the help of their charts.

How Do You Say It Today, Jesse Bear?

Written by Nancy White Carlstrom
Illustrated by Bruce Degen

Travel through the months of the year with Jesse Bear and his family. Each month's illustration contains a hidden heart or a message of love. Can your young readers find them all and discover the words that Jesse Bear says all year long?

Months of the Year
Which Month Is It?

Before reading the text for each month's illustration, have students examine the picture. Can they tell what holiday, seasonal happening, or special event is being shown? Read the text aloud; then discuss how the illustration and the event relate to that particular month on the calendar. Throughout your reading, ask students, "What do you think Jesse Bear is saying each month?" See if anyone guesses correctly before the surprise is revealed at the end of the story!

That's Halloween because they are carving a pumpkin!

In the month of *November*, and all year through...

Months of the Year
Creative Art
A "Love-ly" Card

Just like Jesse Bear, your little ones probably say, "I love you," to moms and dads all year! Help each student create a card to show his yearlong love! For each child, duplicate the card pattern on page 186. Help each child cut out his card on the bold lines and then fold it along the dotted lines. Then help him write his favorite month on the blank on the front and add his signature to the inside. Invite each child to decorate his card to reflect his favorite month, using crayon drawings or stickers, stamps, or die-cuts that you've provided. Send the finished cards home for a meaningful message moms and dads are sure to love!

Spread a Little Love With Literature

Use the following books and ideas to spread love and laughter all through your kindergarten curriculum!

by Angie Kutzer—Gr. K, Garrett Elementary School, Mebane, NC

Love Bugs

Written and illustrated by David A. Carter

Cupids, candy, flowers, love, and kisses: these traditional valentine symbols are represented here in a rather nontraditional way—with bugs! This book's creative pop-up illustrations, paired with rhyming text, add whimsy to February's favorite heartfelt holiday.

Adding

Buggy Buds

This center activity will put addition skills in full bloom! To prepare, make a supply of rosebud bugs by drawing eyes, noses, and mouths onto artificial rosebuds, as shown. Then glue on pipecleaner antennas shaped as shown. Program several plastic flowerpots, each with a different addition equation. (If desired, you may want to insert a piece of floral foam into each pot.) To complete the activity, a child reads each equation and sticks the correct number of rosebud bugs into the corresponding container. Reward efforts with a bug or flower sticker. How nice!

3 + 4 =

Following directions

Bug Bites

No need for repellent here! These bug cupcakes are a perfect follow-up to this story. To prepare, bake a batch of chocolate cupcakes. Gather the ingredients, utensils, and supplies; then guide each child to make a bug bite. Buzz! Buzz! Yummy! Yummy!

Ingredients for each snack:
chocolate cupcake
2 four-inch pieces of Twizzlers candy (antennae)
2 miniature marshmallows (antennae ends)
white frosting in a tube
2 M&M's Minis candies (eyes)
conversation heart candy (nose)
2-inch piece of red licorice lace (mouth)

Utensils and supplies:
paper plate for each child
plastic knife for each child

Directions:
1. Push a marshmallow onto one end of each antennae.
2. Push the antennae into a cupcake.
3. Use frosting to attach the eyes and nose.
4. Add a mouth.

I Love You So Much

Written by Carl Norac
Illustrated by Claude K. Dubois

Lola the hamster awakes with some special words on the tip of her tongue. She can't wait to tell them to someone! But Daddy is in a hurry, Mommy is busy, the school bus is too noisy, the teacher is preoccupied, her classmate is too annoying…it's just never quite the right time. When Lola finally shares those magical words, she gets just the right response—hugs and kisses!

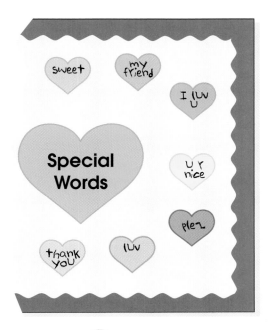

Developing vocabulary
Writing

Special Words

Warm up young minds with this brainstorming activity. To prepare, cut out a large heart from bulletin board paper and a class supply of smaller hearts from construction paper. Label the large heart "Special Words." Have students recall Lola's special words from the story. Encourage students to think of other words or phrases that are special and would make someone feel good. Give each child a construction paper heart and have her write a word or phrase on her heart. Invite each youngster to read what she has written to the class. Then display the smaller hearts around the large heart on a bulletin board for an extra special display! Encourage youngsters to use their special words often.

Following directions

The Perfect Time!

When can you share your love for others? Any time! Get students to make connections to the story's theme with this watch craft. In advance, make a tagboard copy of the watch patterns on page 187 for each child. Gather the materials listed below and then assist each student in following the directions to make a watch. Encourage youngsters to wear their watches home, tell their families about the story, and express their own magical words to a special someone. Maybe they'll get to experience the same response as Lola!

Materials for one watch:
copy of the watch patterns on page 187
brad fastener
1" x 7" red craft foam strip
self-adhesive Velcro dot
scissors
red crayon
hot glue (for teacher use)
mini hole puncher (for teacher use)
stapler (for teacher use)

Directions:
1. Color the patterns.
2. Cut out the patterns.
3. Punch holes in the watch hands where indicated.
4. Use a brad to secure the hands to the watch face.
5. Staple the watch face to the heart piece at the top.
6. Hot glue the back of the heart piece to a craft foam strip.
7. Attach a Velcro dot to opposite sides of the ends of the strip as shown.

173

Love You Forever

Written by Robert Munsch
Illustrated by Sheila McGraw

A young mother rocks her newborn son and sings a sweet chorus to express her unconditional love for him. As the boy grows, the mother continuously returns to his bedside to softly sing her love song to him. As time passes, the roles reverse. The son sings the special song to his mother and then to his own child.

Completing a caption
Reading

Sleep Tight!

In the story, the boy's bedtime routine always includes his mother's love song. Invite students to share some of the activities that occur during their bedtime routines. Give each child a copy of the booklet page on page 187. Have her illustrate and write about one thing she does before bedtime. Invite her to read her page to the class. After each child has shared, bind the pages between pillow-shaped covers cut from felt. Then place the book in your reading area for future visits. Nighty-night!

Sleep Tight!
by Mrs. Kutzer's kindergartners

Cassie 's favorite thing to do before bedtime is
(Name)
to pick a toy to sleep with .

Sequencing pictures

Growing Up

Growing up is something we all do! To prepare for this activity about growing older, cut out pictures of babies, children, teenagers, adults, and senior adults from discarded magazines. Make several different sets containing one picture from each age group and store them in a center. Revisit the illustrations in this story and point out how the boy and mother's appearances change as time goes by. Then have each student visit the center and sequence a set of pictures from youngest to oldest.

If desired, extend this activity by having each child bring in three photos of herself as a baby, a toddler, and a preschooler. Take a fourth photo of the child as a kindergartner. Have her glue her photos in order on a paper strip and then label them as shown. Mount the strips on a bulletin board titled "We're All Growing!"

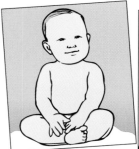

Mama, Do You Love Me?

Written by Barbara M. Joosse
Illustrated by Barbara Lavallee

A little girl finds out that her mother's love is unconditional, even when she tests the limits of her independence.

Predicting

Take a Guess

Youngsters' estimation skills strengthen when they participate in this simple activity. To prepare, gather in clear plastic bags several different collections from five to 20 items. For example, you might have one bag containing paper stars, one with a supply of gummy fish, and another with small plastic eggs. To complete the activity, simply show one bag at a time and have students predict the number of items in the bag. Then pour the contents out of the bag and have the group count as you hold up each piece. One, two, three…

Reading

I Love You Bunches!

Recognizing common words is a cinch with this fun puzzle! Make a copy of page 188 for each child. Have each youngster use the color key to color the spaces correctly to reveal a hidden picture. After coloring, instruct him to complete the sentence at the bottom of the page. Then invite each child to read his sentence to the class. Lovely!

175

Sing Me a Story!

With this particular collection of books, you can sing your song and read it too!

by Jana Sanderson, Rainbow School, Stockton, CA

I'm a Little Teapot
As told and illustrated by Iza Trapani

Whimsical illustrations and additional rhyming verses turn a favorite children's song about a teapot into a storybook of dreams.

Sharing dreams

Big Dreams

Enthusiastic shouts build for this idea centered around children's dreams. To prepare, post a large paper teacup on your board. Label the teacup "Our Dreams." Cut out a cloud of steam from white paper and attach it to the top of the cup. Invite each student to shout out his dream as you record it on the billowy cloud. You might learn that youngsters want to fly to the moon, become movie stars, build their own houses, or become the president of the United States of America. Dream big!

Fly to the moon.
Be a movie star.
Build my own house.
Be president of the USA.

Our Dreams

Steps

1.
2.
3.
4.

Following directions

Teatime

Your students will be delighted to be served tea and cookies on lace doily placemats they cut themselves. Help each student fold an 8½" x 11" sheet of paper as shown. Instruct each child to make cuts around each side of her folded paper, similar to cutting paper snowflakes. Have her unfold her paper and then use the doily to set a table for a tea party.

The Wheels on the Bus

Adapted and illustrated by Paul O. Zelinsky
Paper engineering by Rodger Smith

With bright and detailed illustrations, Paul Zelinsky creates a scene that invites readers to board the bus as it moves all over town. Turn a wheel, pull a tab, and watch the bus come alive.

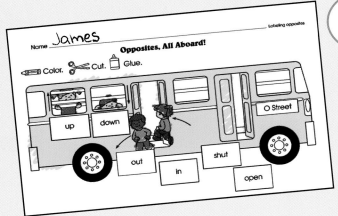

Identifying opposites

Opposites on the Bus

Youngsters get ready to practice opposites with this bus-inspired reproducible. Make a copy of page 189 for each child. Guide students to color the page and then cut out the opposite words and glue them to label the bus. Up or down—either way, this activity is lots of fun!

Patterning

People Patterning

The next stop is P Street for some patterning fun! Have children form a circle as they sing the first verse of the song from the book. Next, direct students to alternate the motions below to create patterns that go along with the verses.

up and down: The first child raises arms up, the next child holds arms down, and so on.
wipers: The first child swishes arms to the left, the next child swishes arms to the right, and so on.

The Farmer in the Dell

Illustrated by John O'Brien

To illustrate his interpretation of this childhood game, John O'Brien uses fine ink strokes to create amusing facial expressions for his characters. He clearly demonstrates the strength of teamwork when the farmer is pulled from the dell.

Using ordinal numbers

Colorful Counting

Hi-ho, the derry-o! Each child practices writing, identifying, and coloring by ordinal numbers. Make enough copies of page 190 for each child to have one copy of the characters cards. Have each student number the characters on his paper from 1 to 8. Then call out an ordinal number and a color. Instruct each child to select that color of crayon and then color the character that corresponds with the ordinal number. The activity continues until all of the characters have been colored.

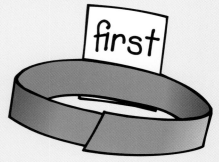

Sequencing

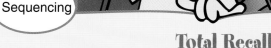

Total Recall

Nobody stands alone when children team up to recall the order in which the farm characters are introduced in the story. Photocopy one set of the characters from page 190. Color and cut out the characters; then glue each one onto an index card. Glue each card to a headband. Write ordinal number words on the back of each headband. The numbers should correspond with the order in which the characters are introduced in the story. Pass out the headbands and invite those children to the front of the class. Have the children recall the problem of the story. Ask the child with the farmer on his headband to squat down as if he were in the dell. Direct the class to recall the sequence in which the characters help pull the farmer from the dell. When they think they have the correct arrangement, ask the children to turn around one by one to see whether the ordinal numbers on the back of the headbands are in the correct sequence. If they are correct, have the group hold hands and pull the farmer up and out of the dell.

Old MacDonald Had a Farm

By Frances Cony
Paper engineering by Iain Smyth

With pop-up pages, hidden picture flaps, and moving parts, this vividly illustrated version of "Old MacDonald Had a Farm" comes alive with farmyard fun.

Old MacDonald Had...

2 pails of milk

Writing

Old "Mac-Doodle" Book

There is no telling who or what will turn up on Old MacDonald's farm when your students rewrite the story. Provide each child with a piece of paper to draw and write about something she thinks should be on Old MacDonald's farm. Invite each youngster to share her page with the class. Then bind the pages between construction paper covers. Title the book "Old MacDonald Had..." and on the final page, write "E-I-E-I-O!"

Reading
Sorting

Sorting Fun

With a black spot here and a curly tail there, here a feather, there some wool, everywhere some fun, fun! Label four berry baskets or boxes (pens) with the following animal names: "cow," "pig," "sheep," "chick." Label several sets of index cards "white wool," "pink tail," "yellow feather," and "black spot." Gather a supply of white cotton balls, yellow feathers, pink curly ribbon or pieces of twisted pink pipe cleaners, and black felt or fur spots. Combine the materials in a tub. To play this sorting game, invite students to draw a card, read the description, retrieve the item, and place it in the correct animal pen. E-I-E-I...oh, such fun!

cow

pig

sheep

chick

yellow feather

Who Took the Cookies From the Cookie Jar?

Written by Bonnie Lass and Philemon Sturgess
Illustrated by Ashley Wolff

This version of an old childhood favorite song has a Southwestern flair. Vividly illustrated desert animals question each other as to who took the cookies from the cookie jar.

Our Favorites

Chocolate Chip — Amy, Nate

M&M's Candy — Meg, Sara, Kent

Peanut Butter — Josh, Karla

Sugar — Kevin

Collecting data

Fun With Favorites

Collect some cookie data by completing this activity with students. Cut out a large cookie jar shape from bulletin board paper. Label the jar with headings of popular cookie names, such as "Chocolate Chip," "M&M's Candy," "Peanut Butter," and "Sugar." Next, cut out a supply of paper circles (cookies). Have each child write his name along the bottom of a cookie. Then instruct him to color his cookie to resemble his favorite kind. Finally, have each child glue his cookie under the name of his favorite. Count each category and compare them to determine the class favorite. To wrap up the lesson, bake a batch of cookies to match the class favorite.

Subtracting

Sweet Subtraction

This tasty activity helps your little ones practice subtraction facts. To prepare, write simple subtraction problems on index cards. Write the answer on the back of each card. Pass out a handful of minicookies or animal crackers to each student, along with one math card and a napkin. Have each child use the cookies as counters to solve her math problem and check her answer. When she is finished, invite her to switch cards with a neighbor. After the math activity is complete, invite students to snack on their cookies. Mmmmath!

$8 - 3 =$

Skip to My Lou

Adapted and illustrated by Nadine Bernard Westcott

Overwhelmed with flies in the sugar bowl, cats in the buttermilk, and a house full of farm animals, a boy gives in and joins the fun in this hilarious adaptation of the favorite folk song "Skip to My Lou." Through rhyming text, the popular playground song becomes a favorite for classroom reading.

Writing

Farmyard Funnies

Invite youngsters to draw comic strips with silly scenes similar to those in the book. Provide each child with a piece of paper and some crayons or markers. Have him think of an animal in an unusual place. Both the animal and the place should begin with the same letter, such as a bull at a ball game or a penguin at a pizza parlor. Have him draw the scene and then write to describe his picture. Next, title a bulletin board "Skip to My Lou, My Darling." Mount each comic onto a strip of bulletin board paper and post the strip above the title as shown.

Bulls at the ball game

Baboons at the ballet

Penguins at the Pizza Parlor

Flamingos at the farm

Cats in the cradle

Snakes in the swimming pool

...Skip to My Lou, My Darling

Playing a game

Skiddoo

After a reading of the book, take the farmyard fun outside to play this skipping game. Select a child to be It and stand out in the middle of the playground. Give each of the remaining children the name of an animal in the book: pig, cow, cat. It sings, "Skip to my Lou, my piggies," and all the pigs skip across the yard while he tries to catch them. If It tags someone before he skips across to safety, he can help him chase the animals during the next call. After the group has run across the yard, switch Its and play again.

181

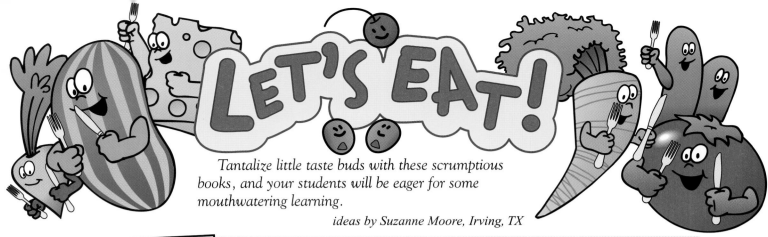

LET'S EAT!

Tantalize little taste buds with these scrumptious books, and your students will be eager for some mouthwatering learning.

ideas by Suzanne Moore, Irving, TX

Cloudy With a Chance of Meatballs
Written by Judi Barrett
Illustrated by Ron Barrett

Mashed potato snow? Mustard clouds? Jell-O gelatin sunsets? Welcome to the town of Chewandswallow, where the daily weather report is also the menu! When the weather takes a turn for the worse, the food becomes super sized. Can the people of this tiny town solve this messy problem, or will they be forced to leave?

Following directions
Reading

What's the Weather?

Students become wacky weather forecasters when they complete this fun-filled project. In advance, collect a supply of grocery store circulars. Make a copy of the weather wheel and arrow patterns on page 191 for each child. (Save the mouse puppet pattern for use with "Chomping Mouse Puppet" on page 183.) Gather a class set of brads, 9" x 12" construction paper sheets, and six-inch paper plates. Then cut a sheet of paper in fourths for each child.

Have each child cut out his weather wheel, color the icons, and then glue the wheel to his paper plate. Help him thread a brad through the center of his weather wheel and his construction paper as shown. Next, have him cut out the arrow and glue it beside the weather wheel. Then have him cut out four types of foods from a grocery store circular and glue each picture to a separate quarter piece of paper. Instruct him to write the name of the food beneath each picture. Then direct each child to stack his pages and staple them beneath the arrow as shown. Grins will shine as children turn their weather wheels and then read their mouthwatering weather forecasts!

Following directions

Tomato Tornado

The residents of Chewandswallow are horrified when a tomato tornado spins into town, but students will delight in making this version of a twister. In advance, gather a clear plastic water bottle for each child, along with liquid detergent and red food coloring. Help each child fill his bottle half full with water. Assist him in adding one drop of liquid detergent and five drops of red food coloring to the water. Screw the cap on tightly, and show him how to rotate the bottle in a circular motion to create his own tomato tornado! Lead students to discuss other types of foods red tornados could be made from.

Lunch

Written and illustrated by Denise Fleming

Sniff, sniff. A hungry little mouse smells lunch and ravenously eats its way through a bounty of colorful fruits and vegetables. Afterward, it's time for a nap—until dinner, that is!

The mouse would like macaroni and cheese.

Using descriptive language
Writing

Dinnertime

At the end of this delightful story, the little mouse takes a nap until dinnertime. Invite your crew to continue the little mouse's culinary adventures with this adorable project. First, have youngsters generate a list of foods the mouse would enjoy eating, encouraging the use of descriptive language. Then invite each child to choose a dish to illustrate. After his drawing is complete, have him make a thumbprint mouse next to his illustration, as shown, and then write a sentence about his picture. Bind the pages between construction paper covers and title the book "Dinnertime!"

Following directions
Reading sight words

Chomping Mouse Puppet

Here's a puppet project that will have your students grinning from ear to ear. In advance, make a copy of the mouse pattern on page 191 for each child. Have her color the pattern and then cut it out. Write the names of the foods in the book on individual index cards. Instruct the child to glue her pattern to a brown paper lunch sack as shown. Help her staple a six-inch length of pink yarn to her bag for a tail. Then invite your crew to don their puppets and sing the song below. Each time you sing the song, hold up a different food card for youngsters to read and then substitute the food in the last line of the song.

(sung to the tune of "The Wheels on the Bus")

The hungry little mouse goes chomp, chomp, chomp!
Chomp, chomp, chomp! Chomp, chomp, chomp!
The hungry little mouse goes chomp, chomp, chomp!
He loves [grapes]!

Growing Vegetable Soup
Written and illustrated by Lois Ehlert
The seeds, the sun, the water, the plants—the growing cycle is introduced in this vibrant book, which culminates with the best pot of soup ever.

Sequencing
Following directions

From Seeds to Soup

From seeds to soup, this book is a great resource for reinforcing sequencing skills. After reading the book, revisit the pages, emphasizing the sequence of events. Then invite each child to make her own seeds to soup book. In advance, cut paper in half so that each child will have six half sheets. Gather a supply of vegetable seeds. Make a class set of the booklet title and strips on page 192. Have each child cut out the strips. Have him glue the title and each strip to a separate piece of paper. Then guide each child to follow the directions below to decorate each page. Soup's on!

Cover: Write your name on the line. Draw and color vegetables around the title.

Page 1: Color the ground brown. Glue real vegetable seeds to the page.

Page 2: Color the ground brown. Draw water coming from a hose. Add a yellow sticky dot sun.

Page 3: Color the ground brown. Use construction paper scraps to make plants and then glue them to the page.

Page 4: Draw and color your favorite vegetables.

Page 5: Draw a large bowl. Color the interior of the bowl red. Glue bits of colorful construction paper vegetables in the soup bowl.

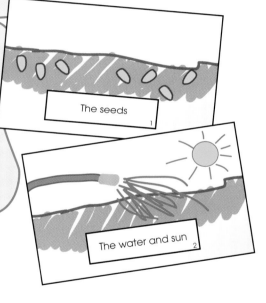

Making a list

Soup's On!

After reading this delicious book, your little soup lovers will be wishing for the real thing—so why not cook up a pot of vegetable soup in your classroom? To begin, have students brainstorm a list of vegetables needed to make vegetable soup. Make a copy of the parent letter on page 192 for each child. On each child's letter, mark the item you would like him to bring. Use the resulting collection of vegetables to stir up a batch of vegetable soup. Gather youngsters into small groups and help each child wash and prepare his contribution to the soup pot. As each youngster eats his soup, have him make a list of the vegetables in his bowl. Yummy!

Blueberries for Sal

Written and illustrated by Robert McCloskey

Join Sal and her mother on a hike to Blueberry Hill. There are lots of blueberries to pick and eat. Just ask Little Bear and his mother!

BLUEBERRIES FOR SAL
ROBERT McCLOSKEY

4

3

4 + 3 = 7

Adding
Counting

Berry Count

Sal has a good time picking and counting blueberries, and so will your little berry pickers when they play this fun addition game. Stock a center with two sets of number cards (index cards numbered from zero to five), two tin buckets (metal camp-style cups or plastic drinking glasses would work well too), and a large supply of blue beads (blueberries). To play, a student shuffles the number cards and turns them facedown. Have him draw a card from the stack, place that number of blueberries in his bucket, and write the number on a piece of paper. Instruct him to repeat this process, completing his addition sentence on his paper. Have him add the numbers together and then count the total number of berries in his bucket to check his answer. Invite him to play again. Kuplink! Kuplank! Kuplunk!

Movement
Singing a song

Picking Blueberries

Give your budding berry pickers a chance to move about and pick some pretend berries. Sing the song below and encourage each student to act it out as she sings each verse. Substitute the underlined phrases with other movements, such as *up high, down low* and *pick left, pick right*. This active idea will be a real treat—especially if you serve up a few real blueberries to taste afterward!

(sung to the tune of "Pawpaw Patch")
[Picking the blueberries], put them in the bucket.
[Picking the blueberries], put them in the bucket.
[Picking the blueberries], put them in the bucket.
Berries in the bucket make this sound: *kuplink!*

Card Pattern

Use with "A 'Love-ly' Card" on page 171.

...I say the same thing,
and that's "I love you!"

In the month of

_____,

and all year through...

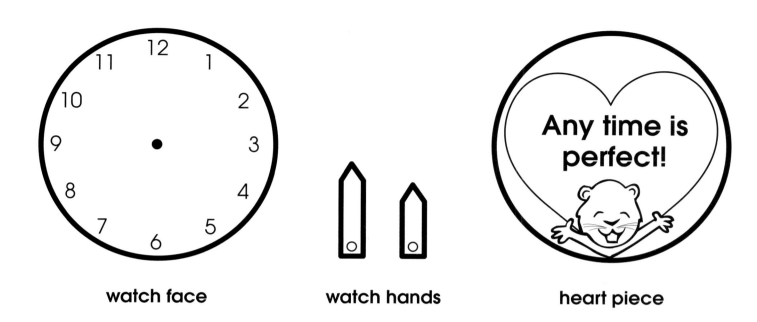

watch face   watch hands   heart piece

Any time is perfect!

Booklet Page
Use with "Sleep Tight!" on page 174.

_____'s favorite thing to do before bedtime is

(Name)

_____.

I Love You!

Read.
Color by the code.

I—gray	love—red	you—blue

Write.

I love _____ more than anything!

©The Education Center, Inc. • *THE MAILBOX®* • *Kindergarten* • Feb/Mar 2004

188 **Note to the teacher:** Use this page with "I Love You Bunches!" on page 175.

Name

Opposites, All Aboard!

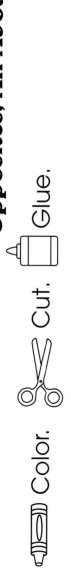 Color. Cut. Glue.

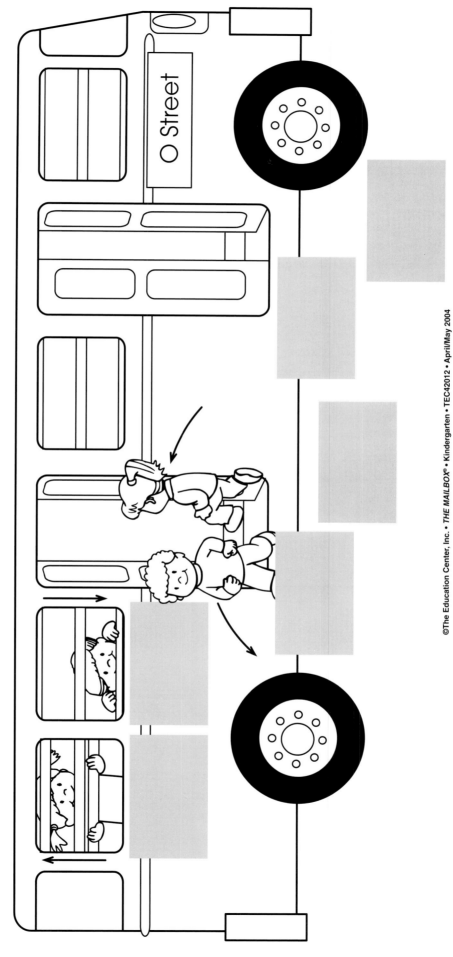

O Street

open	shut	out	in	up	down

©The Education Center, Inc. • *THE MAILBOX*® • Kindergarten • TEC42012 • April/May 2004

Note to the teacher: Use with "Opposites on the Bus" on page 177.

189

Character Cards

Use with "Colorful Counting" and "Total Recall" on page 178.

©The Education Center, Inc. • *THE MAILBOX*® • Kindergarten • TEC42012 • April/May 2004

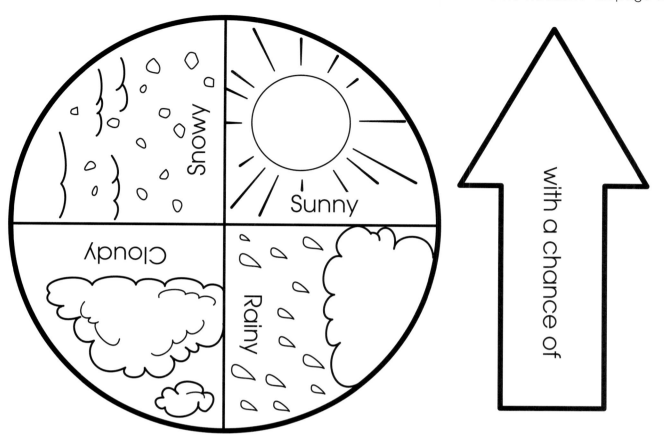

Mouse Puppet Pattern
Use with "Chomping Mouse Puppet" on page 183.

Booklet Title and Strips

Use with "From Seeds to Soup" on page 184.

From Seeds to Soup

by

©The Education Center, Inc. • *The Mailbox*® • Kindergarten • TEC42013 • June/July 2004

1 The seeds

2 The water and sun

3 The plants

4 The vegetables

5 The soup

Parent Note

Use with "Soup's On!" on page 184.

Dear Parents,

   Our class has read *Growing Vegetable Soup* by Lois Ehlert, and it's made us hungry for the real thing! Please help us make our own vegetable soup by supplying the following item(s) by

_____.

___ 1 carrot   ___ 1 can of green beans   ___ 1 green pepper

___ 1 onion   ___ 1 can of tomatoes   ___ 1 can of peas

___ 1 can of corn   ___ 1 potato   ___ 1 zucchini squash

_____

Teacher

THEMATIC UNITS AND SPECIAL FEATURES

An "A-peel-ing" Way to Start the Year

Wondering how to welcome your new kindergartners? Take your pick from these apple ideas! From nametags to notes and centers to snacks, this unit will get your classroom in apple-pie order!

by Ada Goren, Winston Salem, NC

A Wormy Welcome

Send your soon-to-be-kindergartners a note to welcome them to your class. To make one, duplicate the card cover on page 198 onto red construction paper. Next, mask the text and make another red construction paper copy. Copy the card inside on page 198 once onto white copy paper, adding your signature at the bottom. Cut out all the apple shapes; then glue the white shape to the plain red apple. Punch a hole where indicated on the card cover; then thread one-quarter of a green pipe cleaner through the hole. Tape the pipe cleaner piece in place on the back; then twist the part that shows on the front to resemble a wriggly worm. If desired, color the stem and leaf on the cover; then staple the cover to the back of the card. Tuck each card into a small kraft envelope for mailing or present the cards to your students when you make home visits.

Door Decor

There are apples aplenty on this cute door decoration, which is perfect for the beginning of the year! Begin by cutting out a bushel-basket shape from brown bulletin board paper. Mount the basket on your door along with the title shown. To make the apples, mask the text on the card cover pattern on page 198. Then duplicate the apple to make a class supply, using red, yellow, and green paper. Cut out all the apples; then label each one with a child's name. To complete the display, mount the apples as shown. Now that's the pick of the crop!

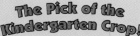

194

Apple Tree Nametags

Your new kindergartners will love wearing nametags that they help make! To prepare, duplicate the nametag pattern on page 199 to make a class supply. Cut out the nametags and personalize the top portion of each one with a child's name in bold letters. If desired, add additional programming—such as your name, a bus number, or a classroom number—on the trunk of the tree. Then invite each child to complete her nametag. Have her color the treetop green and the trunk brown. Then have her dip the eraser end of a new pencil into tempera paint and make prints over the top portion of the tree to resemble apples. Have everyone make red apples or divide the class into three groups and have one group make red, one group green, and one group yellow apples; then use the colors of the apples on their nametags to divide the students into work groups or to call them to get a snack, come to circle time, or line up.

A "Tree-mendous" Center Idea

When it's time for your little ones to pick their centers, let them pick apples too! Cut out a large apple tree from bulletin board paper and display it on a wall within students' reach, along with the title "Take Your Pick." Mount a smaller apple tree at each of your classroom centers. Then, from construction paper, die-cut a number of apples to match the maximum number of students allowed at each of your centers. Label each apple cutout with a center name; then laminate all the apples for durability. Use Velcro fasteners or Sticky-Tac adhesive to mount the apples on the large tree. When it's time for centers, have each child, in turn, pick an apple from the large tree and mount it on the corresponding smaller tree at her chosen center.

An Apple Name Game

Here's an "apple-icious" activity to help students get to know one another on the first day of school. Seat students in a circle on the floor in your group area. Show students a real apple; then ask them to brainstorm a list of foods made with apples. Next, pass the apple around the circle as you recite the chant shown. Each time you reach the end of the chant, have the child holding the apple tell the group his name and his favorite apple food. Continue passing the apple until every student has had the chance to introduce himself and tell about his favorite apple treat.

Who are you, and what do you eat?
Tell us your name and an apple treat!

195

Get-to-Know-You Graphing

Your new kindergartners will learn more about one another when you try this get-to-know-you idea that also sneaks in some math *and* an attendance display! To begin, cut an apple tree from bulletin board paper and mount it on a wall within students' reach. Add one personalized die-cut apple for each child. Next, sketch out a simple two- or three-column graph on chart paper. Each day during the first week of school, post a different apple-related graphing question (see suggestions below). When a child arrives, have her take her apple off the tree and place it on the graph in the column that represents her answer to the question. At group time, discuss the results of the graph and then extend the conversation by asking the corresponding extension question. A quick glance at the apple tree will show you if any students are absent!

- Do you like apple pie? Yes/No
  What is your favorite food?
- What is your favorite apple color? Red/Yellow/Green
  What is your favorite color?
- Have you ever bobbed for apples? Yes/No
  What is your favorite game?
- Have you ever picked an apple off a tree? Yes/No
  Tell about a favorite vacation or special place to visit.
- What is the best thing about apples? Colors/Taste/Good for You
  What is the best thing about you?

Do you like apple pie?	
Yes	No
Sam	Ari
Joe	
Keisha	

Happy Apple Smiles

Your new students will be all smiles when you invite them to make this fun snack! To prepare, cut two red apple slices per child. Have each child spread a bit of strawberry-flavored cream cheese on one side of each of her apple slices. Then have her stick a few miniature marshmallows into the cream cheese between the apple slices so that the snack resembles a smile with red lips, pink gums, and pearly white teeth!

The Apples of Your Eye

Help students—and their families—remember new classmates' names with this interactive take-home book! To begin, mask the text on the apple pattern (card cover) on page 198. Then duplicate the pattern onto red construction paper to make a class set. On each apple, mount a photo of a different child. Then glue each apple cutout to an eight-inch square of white construction paper. Attach the loop side of a small piece of a self-adhesive Velcro fastener to the leaf on each apple. Next, cut out a class supply of leaves from green construction paper. Label each one with a different child's name; then laminate all of them for durability. To the back of each leaf, attach the hook side of the Velcro fastener. Make front and back covers from nine-inch squares of tagboard. Add the title shown to the front cover. Then attach a small zippered plastic bag to the inside of the back cover. Store the cutout leaves in the bag and then bind the book together.

Have each child, in turn, take the book home for a night. Instruct her to add to each apple the leaf showing the name of the pictured child. Have her share the book, along with information she's learned about each classmate, with her family.

The Apples of Ms. Smith's Eye!

Let's Go Apple Picking!

Add a happy apple twist to your school tour by turning it into an apple-picking expedition! In advance, post a labeled die-cut apple at each location you'd like your new students to visit, such as the cafeteria, school office, music room, and science lab. Alert staff members at each room that you'll be bringing your apple pickers by to visit! Then bring out a basket and explain to your new kindergartners that you're all going to pick some apples as they get to know their new school. Take a photograph of students at each location and collect the apples in the basket as you tour the school. Later, post the apples on a bulletin board along with the photos you took. Add sentence strips with student explanations about the activities that take place in each room. What an "a-peeling" display for open house!

A Quick Note

Assure parents that their youngsters had a great first day of school by sending home these quick notes. Duplicate the first-day award on page 199 to make a class supply. Personalize and color, if desired, one award for each child and tuck the notes into bookbags before dismissal.

A Kindergarten Keepsake

Use the pattern on page 200 to make a cute kindergarten keepsake! Throughout the first week of school, snap photos of your new students at work and play. Be sure you have at least one photo featuring each child. Then duplicate page 200 onto construction paper to make a class set. Help each child glue her photo to her paper, and then help her write her name on the line. Have her color the apples. Invite her to make an apple print next to the photo by dipping half of an apple in red paint and then pressing it on her paper. When the paint is dry, send the finished projects home for families to treasure!

Card Cover

Use with "A Wormy Welcome" and "Door Decor" on page 194 and "The Apples of Your Eye" on page 196.

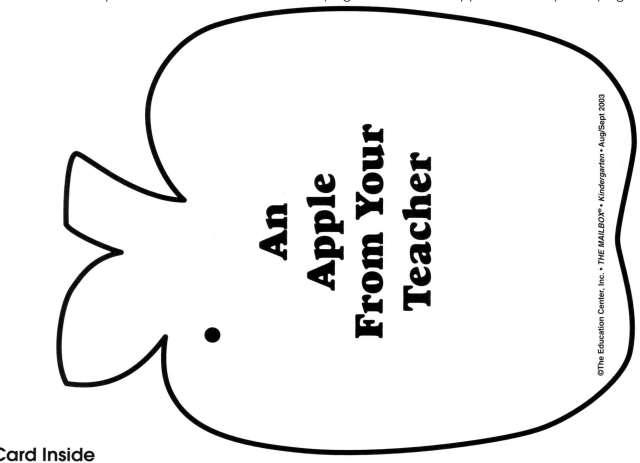

An Apple From Your Teacher

Card Inside

Use with "A Wormy Welcome" on page 194.

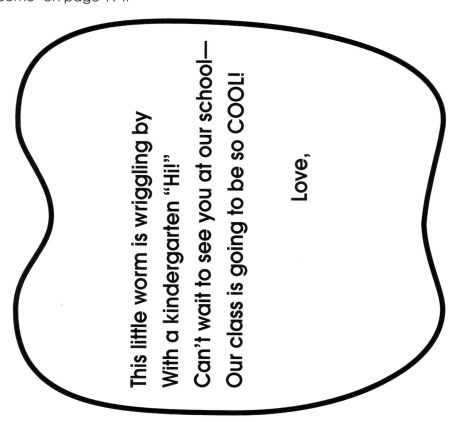

This little worm is wriggling by
With a kindergarten "Hi!"
Can't wait to see you at our school—
Our class is going to be so COOL!

Love,

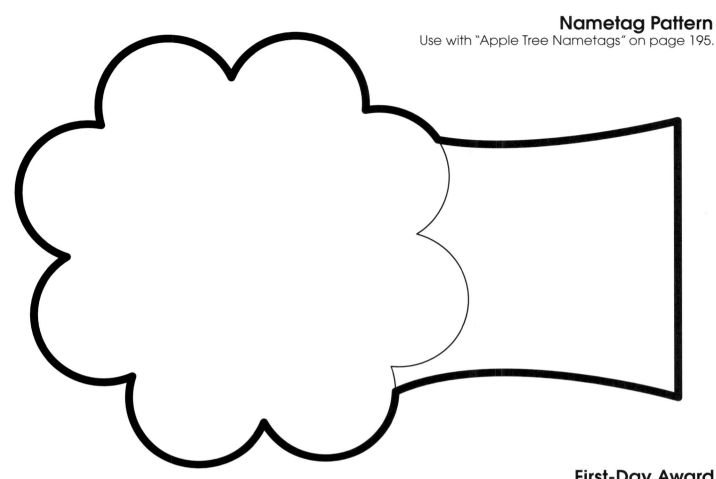

First-Day Award
Use with "A Quick Note" on page 197.

_____
child's name

had a bushel of fun
in kindergarten today!

date   teacher signature

©The Education Center, Inc. • THE MAILBOX® • Kindergarten • Aug/Sept 2003

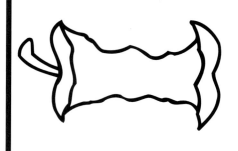

Kindergarten is good
to the core and
so is _____:

All About Me

Getting to know each of your youngsters is easy as can be with this collection of activities that will make each child say, "I'm proud to be me!"

by Lucia Kemp Henry, Fallon, NV

 Making a craft

Meet Me!

Even the shiest child will find it easy to introduce herself when the presentation is made with a stick puppet resembling herself! In advance, make a white construction paper copy of the puppet pattern on page 204 for each child. (Save the cake pattern for use with "Birthday Book" on page 202.) To begin, prompt a discussion of things that make each child unique, such as facial features, eye color, and hairstyle. Next, have each child write her name on the line and decorate a puppet pattern with crayons and collage materials to re-create herself in miniature. Have plenty of mirrors on hand so children can study their images. When she has finished, help her glue it to a large craft stick. With puppets in hand, introduce each special student to the class and have her tell one or more special things about herself. Then sing the song below. It's a pleasure to meet such unique students!

Introduction song

Glad to Meet You

Introductions will be warm and welcoming when students sing this catchy song. Repeat the song for each child, substituting his name in Lines 1 and 8.

(sung to the tune of "Bicycle Built for Two")

Hello, [child's name].
We're glad to meet you now.
You are special. You are unique, and how!
You're wonderful. Yes, it's true.
You're absolutely *you.*
We're glad to meet
A friend so neat!
Hello, [child's name]. Hello to you!

201

My Name

Since a child's name is a special part of her, she'll be thrilled to share it with classmates during this activity. To prepare, print each child's name on a sentence strip; then die-cut a set of the letters for each child's name. Put each set of letters in a small resealable plastic bag labeled with the child's name. Begin the activity by having each student, in turn, stand next to a pocket chart. Give the child her name strip and have her place it in a pocket. Then help her use the letters in her bag to spell her name. Have her display the letters in order in a pocket under her name strip. After the activity, use the strips for nametags on tables or cubbies. (Save each child's letter cutouts for "Nifty Name Banners" on this page.) This activity is n-i-c-e!

Nifty Name Banners

Make each child's name the centerpiece of this classy banner decoration. Give each child a 12" x 18" sheet of construction paper in his favorite color. Help him arrange letter cutouts for his name in the center of his paper and then glue them in place. Encourage the child to embellish his banner using crayons, stickers, craft items, and colorful construction paper shapes. Display the banners around your classroom along with one that reads "It's a Banner Day for Special Kindergartners!"

Birthday Book

Observing birthdays is a great way to celebrate the uniqueness of each youngster. Use this cooperative book to highlight each child's special day. In advance, cut a supply of six-inch paper doilies in half so that each child will have one half. Make a class set of the cake pattern on page 204. Have each child describe her favorite birthday cake. Prompt her to name the type of cake, the frosting flavor, and the decorations she likes. Write her response at the bottom of a sheet of construction paper and then write her name and birthday at the top as shown. Then give each child a copy of the cake pattern on page 204 and have her color it and cut it out. Help her glue a doily half to her programmed paper and then glue her cake to the doily as shown. Have the child glue small paper strips (candles) to the cake to indicate her age. Bind students' pages with rings. Display each birthday child's page on her big day and then allow her to take it home. Don't forget to add another candle to the cake!

Danielle
January 22

"I like strawberry cake with chocolate frosting."

Following directions
Making a booklet

My Favorite Things

What can always bring a smile to a child's face? A few of her favorite things! Help each child focus on her emerging reading skills as she makes a booklet about her favorite things. In advance, make a copy of pages 205 and 206 for each child. Guide each youngster through the directions below to complete her booklet pages. Then help her stack them in order and staple them together along the left side. Encourage each child to read her booklet to the class and then take it home to share with her family. It's sure to become a family favorite!

Directions:

Cut the pages apart on the dotted lines.

Cover: Color the words on the cover. Write your name on the line.

Page 1: Color the T-shirt your favorite color. Write the name of the color on the line.

Page 2: Draw your favorite meal on the plate. Write its name on the line.

Page 3: Draw a birthday treat on the cake stand. Write its name on the line.

Page 4: Draw something you like to see. Write its name on the line.

Page 5: Draw a picture of your face in the mirror.

Drawing
Counting

Distinctive Dwellings

Your youngsters have homes with families that are unique. Focus on family groups and basic math skills with this home-style art project. Give each child a 12" x 18" construction paper house, a 6" x 18" construction paper roof, a 4" x 9" construction paper door, and two five-inch square white paper windows. Help the child glue the roof to the house and then trim the edges to create an angled roofline. Next, have him glue the door and windows to the house as shown. Then have him draw pictures of the people he lives with on the windows. Direct the child to count the number of people that live in his home. Program each child's project with the sentence shown, making adjustments as necessary. Then invite each child to share his house with the class. Have him count aloud the number of people he lives with. Students will soon see that families can be made up of different numbers of people, which is one way each family is unique. You can count on it!

Identifying traits

Special Traits Display

Here's a handy way to help each child highlight the unique traits that make her special. First, help each child make handprints on white paper using a shade of tempera paint that matches her skin color. After the paint has dried, have her cut out her handprints and glue them to the center of a 9" x 12" piece of construction paper. Instruct her to write her name at the top of the paper. Next, encourage each child to think of a list of five or six words that describe her positive traits. Then help her type the list on a computer using a different font for each word. Print the words and have her cut them out. (For an alternative, use various colors of markers to write the words on her paper.) Next, instruct the child to glue the strips around the handprints on her paper. Display these handsome projects on a bulletin board titled "Our Special Traits." Now give your special students a hand!

Puppet Pattern
Use with "Meet Me!" on page 201.

Meet me, __!

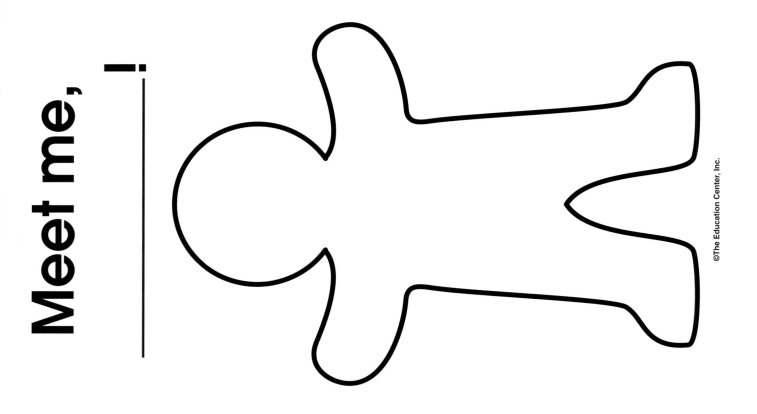

©The Education Center, Inc.

Cake Pattern
Use with "Birthday Book" on page 202.

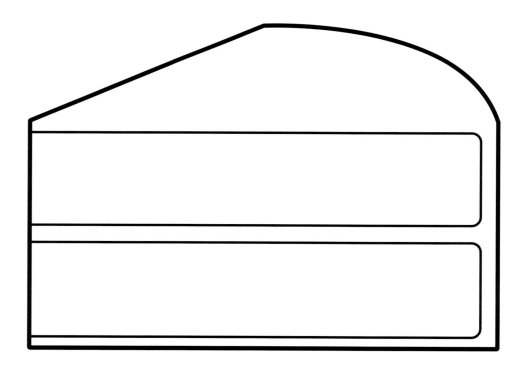

My Favorite Things

by

_____

1

I think my favorite color is cool! I like to wear

_____

clothes to school.

2

_____

is my favorite meal to eat.

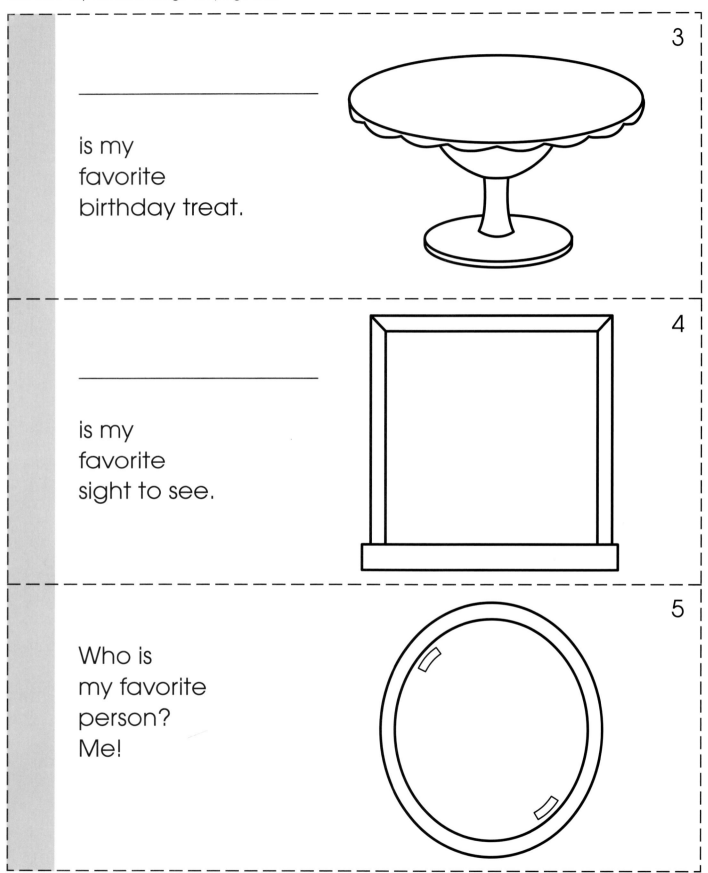

3

_____

is my
favorite
birthday treat.

4

_____

is my
favorite
sight to see.

5

Who is
my favorite
person?
Me!

Harvest Counting

Count on this crop of number sense activities to help your little ones harvest an abundance of math skills.

by Lucia Kemp Henry, Fallon, NV

Collect Your Crops

Fall is the perfect time to harvest seasonal items for a great crop of math manipulatives! Purchase or ask parents to donate ten mini pumpkins, ten short ears of dry Indian corn, ten decorative gourds, and two bags of unshelled walnuts. Then invite students to use these items in a creative cornucopia of harvest-themed math activities.

Counting to Ten

Bring in the Harvest

Start the truck; it's harvesttime! This clever truck prop and the song below will have youngsters asking for this activity over and over again. To prepare, use an opaque projector to enlarge the truck and side panel patterns on page 210 so that the truck is approximately four feet in length. Trace the patterns on pieces of bulletin board paper twice. Color and cut out the patterns and then glue them to opposite sides of a large cardboard box to make a three-dimensional truck. Cut the box as shown. Then place ten ears of Indian corn, ten gourds, ten mini pumpkins, and ten walnuts in groups on the floor to represent a farm field at harvesttime. Set out four baskets. To begin, have students imagine that they work on a farm and need to harvest vegetables and nuts to sell. Next, invite volunteers to help gather and count the pumpkins and put them in a basket as the class sings the first verse of the song. Then have students load the basket into the truck. Repeat the song, substituting the other harvest items. Now that's a successful harvest!

(sung to the tune of "Ten Little Indians")

One little, two little, three little [pumpkins].
Four little, five little, six little [pumpkins].
Seven little, eight little, nine little [pumpkins].
Ten little [pumpkins] in the truck.

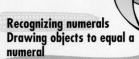

Recognizing numerals
Drawing objects to equal a numeral

Harvest Counting Booklet

Reinforce youngsters' number skills with this truck-shaped booklet loaded with harvest-themed counting! In advance, make a class set of pages 210 and 211. Cut nine 4½" x 5½" white paper booklet pages for each child. Have each child cut out his truck patterns, cover, and text strips. Instruct him to glue a different strip to each page as shown. Stack each child's pages in order behind the cover and staple them to the truck pattern where indicated. Then staple the side panel to the truck as shown. Next, have him illustrate each page to reinforce the text and then color the truck. Encourage each child to share his booklet with a classmate and then take it home to share with his family.

Writing numbers
Drawing objects to equal a numeral

Produce Posters

In the fall, produce stands display colorful signs advertising seasonal crops for sale. Invite your kindergarten counters to spruce up numeral posters with drawings of similar seasonal produce. To prepare, label ten separate cards with a numeral from 1 to 10; place the cards in a small bag. Conceal a supply of Indian corn, mini pumpkins, and gourds in a large bag. Cut one panel from the wide side of a paper grocery bag for every two students. Then have pairs of students take one number card and one harvest item from the bag. Instruct one student to use a marker to write the numeral on a corner of the pair's bag panel. Next, on white paper, have each pair draw the appropriate number of its harvest item. Instruct the pair to cut out the drawings and glue them on the panel. When the posters are completed, display them on a wall in counting order. Corn, gourds, and pumpkins make counting as easy as 1, 2, 3!

Comparing sets using more, less, and equal

Groups of Nuts

Nuts are easily gathered by little hands and fun to put in piles! Gather unshelled nuts in a bowl and use them to introduce sets and number comparison. Place two paper plates on a table along with the bowl of nuts. Working with two students, secretly instruct one child to count out a given number of nuts and put them on a plate. Have the other child do the same with a different number of nuts. Next, direct the youngsters to visually compare the nut sets and guess which set has more. Then have the students count the nuts on the plates to find out. Continue the activity with different numbers of nuts. Encourage students to compare their sets using the words *more, less,* and *equal.* What a nutty way to compare numbers!

Crop-Filled Counting Centers

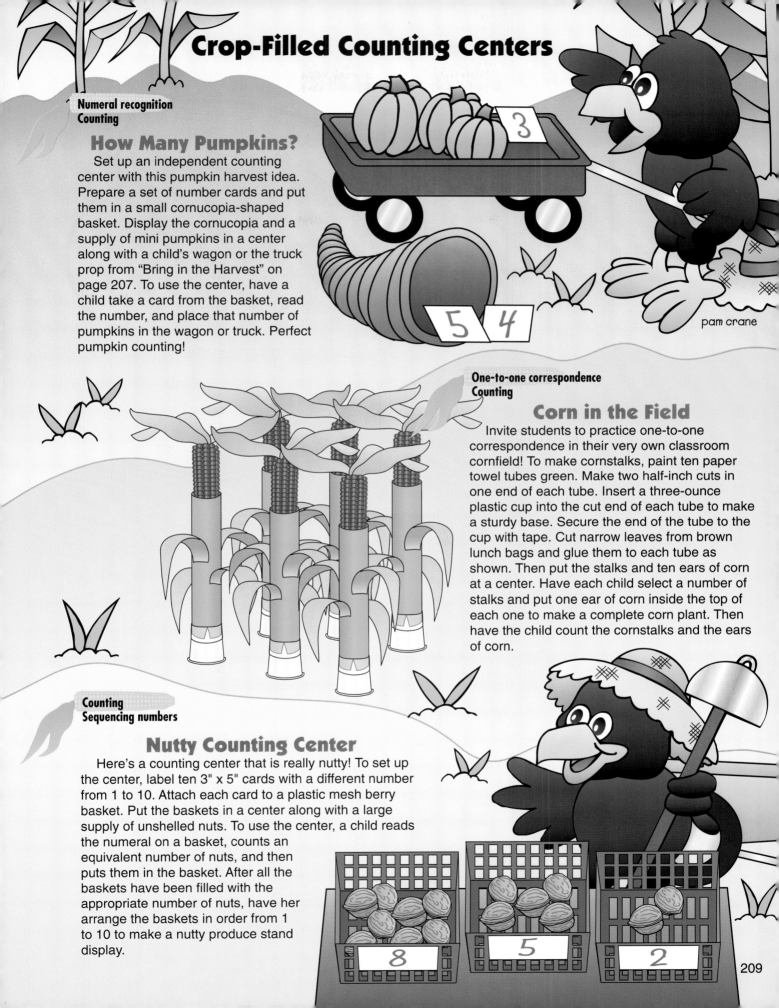

pam crane

Numeral recognition
Counting

How Many Pumpkins?

Set up an independent counting center with this pumpkin harvest idea. Prepare a set of number cards and put them in a small cornucopia-shaped basket. Display the cornucopia and a supply of mini pumpkins in a center along with a child's wagon or the truck prop from "Bring in the Harvest" on page 207. To use the center, have a child take a card from the basket, read the number, and place that number of pumpkins in the wagon or truck. Perfect pumpkin counting!

One-to-one correspondence
Counting

Corn in the Field

Invite students to practice one-to-one correspondence in their very own classroom cornfield! To make cornstalks, paint ten paper towel tubes green. Make two half-inch cuts in one end of each tube. Insert a three-ounce plastic cup into the cut end of each tube to make a sturdy base. Secure the end of the tube to the cup with tape. Cut narrow leaves from brown lunch bags and glue them to each tube as shown. Then put the stalks and ten ears of corn at a center. Have each child select a number of stalks and put one ear of corn inside the top of each one to make a complete corn plant. Then have the child count the cornstalks and the ears of corn.

Counting
Sequencing numbers

Nutty Counting Center

Here's a counting center that is really nutty! To set up the center, label ten 3" x 5" cards with a different number from 1 to 10. Attach each card to a plastic mesh berry basket. Put the baskets in a center along with a large supply of unshelled nuts. To use the center, a child reads the numeral on a basket, counts an equivalent number of nuts, and then puts them in the basket. After all the baskets have been filled with the appropriate number of nuts, have her arrange the baskets in order from 1 to 10 to make a nutty produce stand display.

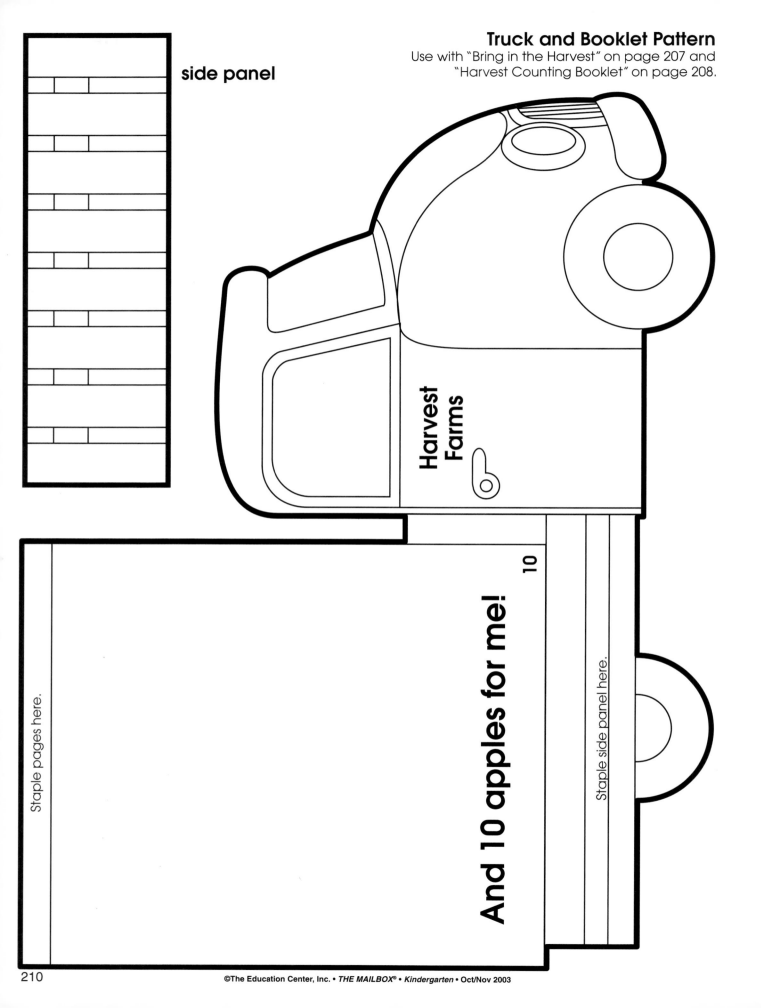

side panel

Truck and Booklet Pattern
Use with "Bring in the Harvest" on page 207 and
"Harvest Counting Booklet" on page 208.

Harvest
Farms

10

And 10 apples for me!

Staple pages here.

Staple side panel here.

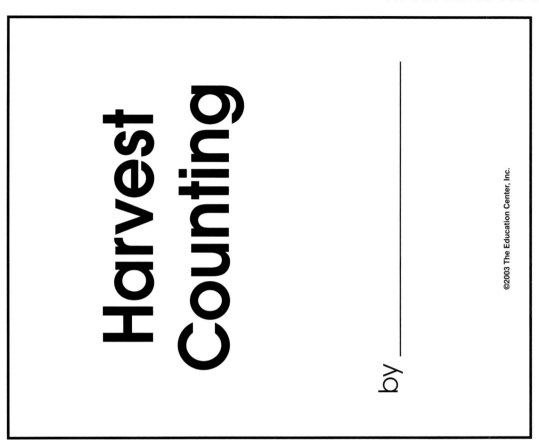

Harvest
Counting

by _____

©2003 The Education Center, Inc.

1 field 1	6 pumpkins 6
2 trucks 2	7 ears of corn 7
3 scarecrows 3	8 gourds 8
4 baskets 4	9 nuts I see 9
5 crows 5	

"Moo-ving" Toward Literacy!

Help your little ones gain important prereading skills with this collection of activities straight from the dairy library!

by Sue DeRiso, J. W. Horton Elementary School, Cranston, RI

Identifying author and illustrator
Making a craft

Occupation Exploration!

Author or illustrator? Help students discover the difference with this crafty headband! In advance, cut a 3" x 24" paper strip (headband) and a 1½" x 10" construction paper strip for each child. Staple the smaller strip to the middle of each larger strip, as shown, to create a pocket. Then gather the materials listed below. Read a book to the children, pointing out the names of the author and illustrator and identifying their contributions to the book. Then guide each child through the directions below to make his own occupation headband. After completion, have each child wear his headband showing the appropriate occupation name as he dictates or illustrates a story. When each child finishes the project, staple his headband to fit his head. No more occupation frustration!

Materials for each child:
headband
5" x 8" index card
copy of the top of page 216
crayons
scissors
glue

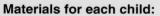

Directions:
1. Color the author and illustrator patterns. Cut out the patterns.
2. Glue the author and illustrator patterns to opposite sides of an index card.
3. Slip the index card into the pocket on the headband.

Identifying the front cover, back cover, and title page

Cover to Cover

Introduce youngsters to the parts of a book with this sticky addition to storytime! To prepare, color and cut out the book labels on page 215. Then add restickable adhesive to the back of each label. Read the poem on the front cover label. Choose a volunteer to place the label on the front cover of a book. Follow the same procedure for the title page and back cover labels. Next, read the book from cover to cover, stopping to have students follow the directions and/or answer the questions on each label. Then remove the labels and save them for use with your next storytime selection!

Recognizing appropriate book care
Singing a song

Handle With Care!

Your little ones will sing the praises of proper book handling with this catchy song!

(sung to the tune of "Twinkle, Twinkle, Little Star")

Treat a book with loving care;
It will be a gift to share.
Turn the pages carefully
And be gentle as can be.
Treat it kindly to the end;
A book will always be your friend.

Which Way?

Get students reading in the right direction with this simple activity based on a familiar nursery rhyme! In advance, program a supply of 5" x 8" index cards, each with a different child's name. Then, on individual cards, write each word in the sentence "Mary had a little lamb." Choose five volunteers and give each one an index card from the nursery rhyme sentence. Then place the students in the correct order from left to right. Read the sentence backward, pointing to each card from right to left. Discuss why the sentence doesn't make sense, leading students to conclude that words must be read from left to right. Then read the sentence correctly as the rest of the class points to each card.

Next, invite children to suggest other animals to use in the sentence. Write each suggestion on a blank index card. Make new sentences by replacing the Mary card with a programmed name card and the lamb card with a different animal card. Choose volunteers to read each new sentence from left to right. Courtney had a little cow!

Take It From the Top!

Your little ones will remember to begin reading at the top of a passage with this quick recipe reminder! To prepare, purchase milk, chocolate syrup, and a class supply of paper cups and plastic spoons. Copy the recipe at left onto chart paper; then display the chart. Explain to children that the writing on the chart is a recipe for chocolate milk. Then point to and read each word in Step 3 at the bottom of the recipe. Demonstrate this step by stirring the spoon in the empty cup. Discuss why the recipe is not working. Explain that the recipe must be read from the top to the bottom. Finally, have each child follow the directions in the correct order to make her own cup of chocolate milk. That's the tops!

Chocolate Milk

1. Pour milk into a cup.
2. Place two spoonfuls of chocolate syrup into the cup.
3. Stir until well mixed.

Picture This!

Teach youngsters the importance of matching text to illustrations with a wordless picture book! In advance, choose a wordless picture book, such as *Tuesday* by David Wiesner, and another picture book with words. Copy the first few lines of text from the storybook onto an index card. Explain to students that you have found a story to go with the wordless book. Open the wordless book and begin reading the text from the index card. Stop and discuss whether this story is a good choice for the pictures given, helping youngsters conclude that a story and its illustrations must match for a book to make sense. Next, have volunteers make up text that matches each illustration. Write the text on individual Post-it Brand notes; then place each note on the appropriate page. Read through the book using the text the children have supplied. Now that makes sense!

The cow ran to the barn.

213

First, Next, and Last

With a huff and a puff and a little bit of glue, your youngsters will practice story sequencing with this crafty pig booklet! In advance, gather the supplies listed below. Read the traditional tale *The Three Little Pigs.* Discuss the sequence of events in the story, identifying the first, next, and last house the wolf tries to blow down. Then guide each child through the directions to create a story sequence booklet. When finished, have each child take her booklet home to share with her family. They'll be blown away!

Materials for each child:
12" x 18" pink construction paper sheet accordion-folded into thirds and labeled as
　shown
8" pink construction paper circle (face)
2 pink construction paper triangles (ears)
scissors
crayons
straw
sticks
small red construction paper rectangles
glue
pink pipe cleaner half

Directions:
1. Glue the face to the front of the folded booklet. Glue on ears.
2. Cut a rectangle from the bottom of the booklet to create legs as shown.
3. Use crayons to draw a mouth, a nose, eyes, and hooves; then unfold the paper.
4. Glue straw to the section labeled "First," sticks to the section labeled "Next," and red construction paper bricks to the section labeled "Last."
5. Twist a pipe cleaner piece around a crayon. Glue one end to the back of the booklet.

Keep Them Guessing!

Stop! Think! Predict! Pleasing predictions are only a few pages away with this effortless activity. Make a copy of the bottom of page 216; then color and cut out the stop sign. Place adhesive from a restickable glue stick on the back of the sign. Then read the rhyme on the sign to the class. Next, choose a volunteer to close her eyes and stick the stop sign in the middle of the day's read-aloud book. Read through the book, stopping at the sign to choose several volunteers to predict what will happen next. Remove the stop sign to use for the next day's pleasing prediction!

"Whoo's" in the Book?

Let a wise old owl puppet help your little ones remember the characters in a book! To make an owl puppet, cut two white eyes, a yellow beak, and two brown wings from construction paper. Glue the eyes, beak, and wings to a lunch-size brown paper bag as shown. Use a black marker to make pupils and V-shaped feathers. After reading a book selection, choose a student to place the owl puppet on her hand to ask, " 'Whoo' is in the book?" Then have a volunteer name the characters in the book. Extend the activity by having the owl ask, " 'Whoo' was your favorite character? 'Whoo' had a problem in the book?" This owl is quite a character!

1. Point to the title.
2. Point to the names of the author and the illustrator.
3. Look at the picture. What do you think this book is about?

Front Cover

Let's look at a book,

A wonderful creation!

The front cover tells you

Important information.

1. Point to the title of the book.
2. Point to the name of the company that published the book.

Title Page

Did you forget the title?

Not to worry!

The title page reminds you

In a hurry.

Back Cover

This back cover

Is the end of the book.

Open it again

To take another look.

1. What was your favorite part of this book?
2. Who was your favorite character?

Occupation Patterns
Use with "Occupation Exploration!" on page 212.

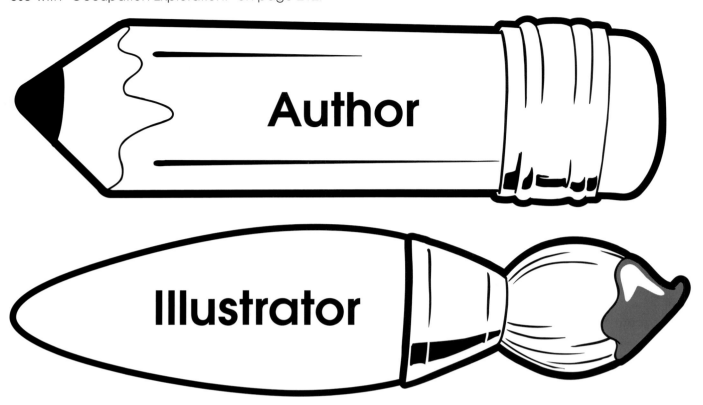

Author

Illustrator

Stop Sign Pattern
Use with "Keep Them Guessing!" on page 214.

Close your eyes;
Do not look!
Place this sign
In the middle of the book.

STOP

What do you think will
happen next?

A Spider Spectacular

Get caught in this web of clever ideas that focus on spiders!

by Jana Sanderson, Rainbow School, Stockton, CA

Writing

The Itsy-Bitsy Spider on the Move

The itsy-bitsy spider has new travel plans. Have students think of different places that the spider could climb. Then instruct each youngster to draw a picture of the spider's new destination and have him label or dictate the spider's actions. Make a yarn spider for each child by tying the end of a 12-inch length of yarn to the centers of four 6-inch lengths of yarn as shown. Hole-punch the corner of each child's paper and then tie a spider to each one. Have each child share his paper with the class, using his spider to demonstrate the action.

The itsy bitsy spider climbed up a coconut tree.

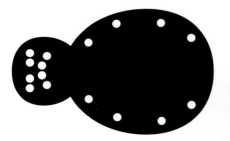

Counting to eight

Spider Spin

Here's a "gr-eight" math game for your little spider lovers! Explain to students that spiders have eight legs, and most have eight eyes. To prepare, photocopy the spinner pattern on page 220 and then laminate it for durability. Add a brad and a paper clip to the center, as shown, to complete the spinner. Make several copies of the spider body pattern, also on page 220. Cut out the patterns, glue each one to a half-sheet of paper, and then laminate them. Give each child in a small group a spider pattern and a washable marker. Have each youngster, in turn, spin the spinner and then draw the appropriate number of body parts on the spider. If a student spins more than the needed number of eyes or legs, he loses a turn. Play continues until each child has completed his spider. Everyone is a winner with this counting game!

Name Webs

Spin a web with this name-writing activity. To prepare, make a class set of the web pattern on page 221. Help each child write her name in capital letters in the center of the web so that the top and bottom of each letter touches the existing web as shown. Then, working with one child at a time, help her outline her web and name with colorful glue. Allow each web to dry. Invite each youngster to create a rubbing by placing a sheet of paper over the web and then using the side of a crayon to rub over the page. Like magic, a name web will appear!

Spin, Spider, Spin

This little ditty has youngsters pretending to be spiders catching food and spinning webs! Sing the song several times, substituting *mosquito, fly, bumblebee, ladybug, ant,* and *moth* in Lines 5 and 6. Spin, spider, spin!

(sung to the tune of "Are You Sleeping?")

Spider crawling,
Spider crawling,
Across its web,
Across its web.

Walk fingers up one arm.
Walk fingers up the other arm.

Spying a trapped [insect],
Spying a trapped [insect],
Spin, spider, spin!
Spin, spider, spin!

Make pretend binoculars.
Make pretend binoculars.
Roll arms around each other.
Roll arms around each other.

Spider Tag

This game puts a spin on an old favorite—Freeze Tag. To play the game, choose a child to be the spider; all other children will be insects. Have students fly (run) around the playground. When the spider catches an insect, the insect must stop and allow the spider to spin a web around him (turn him around one time). The trapped insect must stay in place until another insect tags him, freeing him from the web. The game continues until all insects have been caught and released from the web. When a spider gets tired, select a new one to take his place. Gotcha!

"Data" Longlegs

Display spider facts with this bulletin board idea. In advance, cut a large spider body from bulletin board paper. Make eyes by painting eight egg carton cups and then gluing them in place on the spider. Have students make eight paper chain legs from 1" x 4" construction paper strips. Attach the body and legs to a bulletin board; then add the facts shown. Discuss the spider facts with students. As youngsters learn more facts about spiders, add them to the display as well.

Spiders
most have eight eyes
eight legs
arachnid
most are hairy
eat insects
most spin webs

A Sweet Spider Treat

Spice up the end of this thematic unit with these cinnamon sugar spiders. Provide each child with a small piece of foil, 1½ refrigerated biscuits, eight pretzel sticks, eight mini chocolate chips, and access to cinnamon sugar. Have each child put his whole biscuit in the center of his foil to represent the spider's body. Instruct him to roll his biscuit half into a ball and place it on the foil next to the whole biscuit. Then have him sprinkle cinnamon sugar on the spider. Transfer the spider bodies to a baking sheet and bake according to the biscuit package directions. After baking, have him push the pretzel stick legs into the spider body and press the chocolate chip eyes into the head. Yum!

Patterns
Use with "Spider Spin" on page 217.

spinner

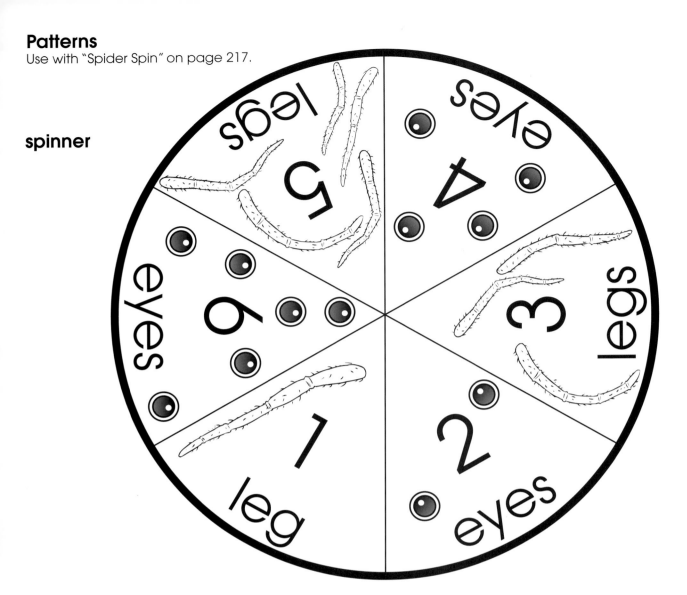

spider body

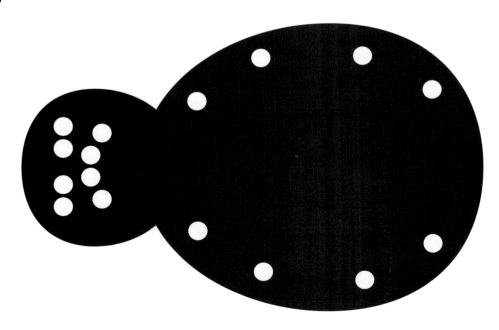

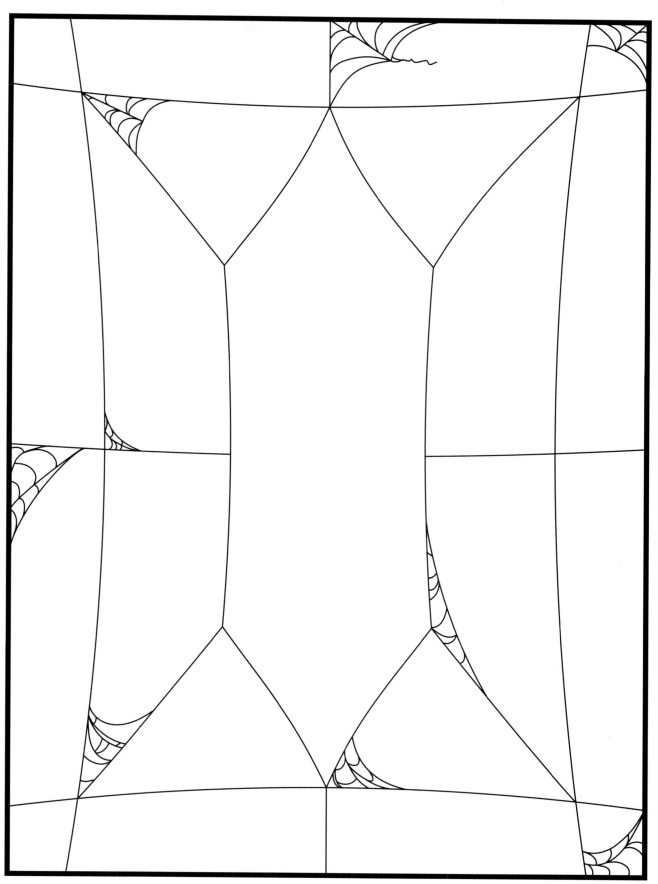

Fresh, Fun Fall!

Use the activities in this unit to enhance your study of autumn. There's something here for every area of your curriculum!

by Angie Kutzer—Gr. K, Garrett Elementary School, Mebane, NC

Fall Fun!
Emergent reading

Nothing says fall like a rowdy football game or playing in a pile of autumn leaves on a crisp, cool day! Welcome the season with this minibooklet, which is just right for reinforcing characteristics of fall and the sight words *a* and *the*. Make a copy of the booklet pages on page 225 for each child. Have him color the pictures and trace the dotted words. Next, have him cut apart the pages. Help each child arrange his pages in order. Then staple the pages together between leaf-shaped covers and add the title as shown. Read through the booklets with students, focusing on the sight words *a* and *the*. This booklet is a touchdown for literacy!

Fall Leaves

Kent

Put on a sweater. 1

my Cat

Erin

"Unbe-leaf-able"!
Creative writing

Rake up some writing skills with this autumn activity. In advance, cut out two construction paper leaf-pile shapes for each child (see illustration). Then gather a collection of colorful leaves. (You can use artificial leaves from floral arrangements, leaf cutouts from construction paper, or real leaves that your youngsters collect outdoors.)

To complete the activity, have each child glue leaves to one of her cutouts. On the other cutout, have her illustrate an animal, a person, or an object that could be hiding in the leaves. Then have her write or dictate an answer to the question "What is in the leaves?" After she adds her name, stack the leafy cutout on top of the illustration and then staple them together at the top as shown. Display the finished projects with the title "What Is in the Leaves?" on a hall bulletin board for passersby to peek under!

Falling Leaves
Music and movement, color recognition

Use this quick-and-easy tune to set youngsters in motion. To make props, cut a length of crepe paper for each child. Then glue two or three leaf cutouts along the crepe paper as shown. (To reinforce color recognition, divide your class into three groups and make sets of props in red, orange, or yellow.) Teach the song below and then give each child a prop. As you sing the song together, have each child dance with her leaves in the air and then float them gently down. When you sing each color name, instruct students holding that color to lift their leaves high one last time before making them float to the floor.

(sung to the tune of "Head, Shoulders, Knees, and Toes")

Leaves are dancing all around, all around.
Leaves are dancing all around, all around.
Red, orange, yellow
Falling to the ground.
Leaves are dancing all around, all around!

In the Fall, Fall Leaves!

High, sky, geese fly.

Bump, thump, squirrels jump.

Crunch, bunch, bears munch.

Shutter, scutter, butterflies flutter.

Skitter, Scurry...Gotta Hurry!
Rhyming, text innovation

This unique mural, modeled after Denise Fleming's *In the Tall, Tall Grass,* shows off your students' newfound knowledge about different animals' preparations for winter. To get started, share this delightful story with your students. Once youngsters catch on to the rhyming, rhythmic text, invite them to take the story a step further. Brainstorm a list of animals that are seen in the fall. Talk about how each of these animals gets ready for winter. For each animal, decide on an action word; then encourage students to come up with two words (real or nonsense) that rhyme with the action word. Incorporate each animal's name into a phrase with its three rhyming words; then help a different child write each phrase on a separate sentence strip. Divide students into small groups and instruct each group to work together using arts-and-crafts materials to create one of the animals. Display the animals with their phrases on a wall covered in large colorful leaves cut from bulletin board paper. Title your mural "In the Fall, Fall Leaves!"

What Is the Scoop?
Predicting, counting, recording

Crack into several important math and science skills with this center activity. To prepare, make a class supply of the recording sheet on page 226. Pour two bags of assorted nuts (with shells) into a plastic shoebox. Gather three different sizes of cups to use as scoops, such as a small plastic cup, a laundry detergent scoop, and a one-cup measuring cup. Place the recording sheets, nuts, scoops, and pencils at a center.

To complete the activity, have each child draw his first measuring cup in the top box. Instruct him to predict how many nuts he will scoop and then write his prediction where indicated. Next, have him scoop and count the number of nuts he actually collects in the container. Then direct him to record the number in the corresponding star. Have him repeat the process with the other two scoops. Then invite him to color his paper as he chooses. Discuss the child's results and then ready the center for the next student. Nuts to you!

223

Fall Finds
Critical thinking, sensory skills

Harvest a crop of critical-thinking skills with this mystery bag idea. In advance, gather several different pieces of fall produce (two of each kind) and a large paper grocery bag. Place one of each kind of food on a tabletop. Put the others out of sight. Cut a hole in each side of the bag as shown. Then fold down the top of the bag and staple it closed. Secretly insert a piece of produce from the out-of-sight pile in the bag through a hole. Invite a student to reach inside a hole, feel the object, and then give her classmates clues as to what kind of produce she is touching. Have students refer to the tabletop display to guess the food's identity. Now have her pull the item out and check for accuracy. Play another round with a different piece of produce and a different child. It's feeling more and more like fall!

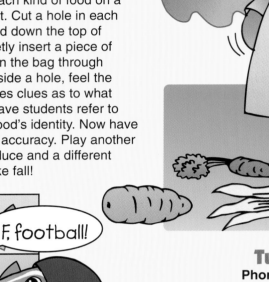

Smooth... bigger on one end than the other...

F, football!

Turn, Turn, Turn
Phonics, beginning sounds

Your little ones will leap into learning as they try to make these leaves "change" into their fall hues. To prepare, make 26 two-sided leaf cutouts. One side of each leaf should be green. The other side should be one of a variety of fall colors. Program the green side of each leaf with a different letter. Arrange the leaves in alphabetical order in a pocket chart.

To play the game, a child calls out a letter and then gives a word that begins with that letter's sound. If he is correct, turn the corresponding leaf over to reveal its fall color. Continue playing until every child has had a turn and all the leaves have been turned over. Now that's a great way to fall into phonics!

Fall Fashions
Sorting, classifying

Fall is in the air and so are cooler temperatures. Use this simple idea to have youngsters sort and classify fall clothing. In advance, gather fall clothing, such as sweaters, jackets, long-sleeved shirts, and pants. Also gather summer clothing, such as shorts, T-shirts, tank tops, and bathing suits. Place all of the clothing in a laundry basket. Discuss with students the changes in the weather from summer to fall. Then lead youngsters to talk about the differences in the types of clothing worn in each season. Next, have students sort and classify the clothing as fall clothing or summer clothing. Provide youngsters with a box so they can fold and pack away the summer clothes, and give them plastic hangers on which to hang the fall fashions.

Put on a sweater. 1

Feel the chill. 2

Grab a football. 3

Fall is a thrill! 4

©The Education Center, Inc.

Predicting, counting

What Is the Scoop?

I used	I think I will scoop	I scooped

Note to the teacher: Use with "What Is the Scoop?" on page 223.

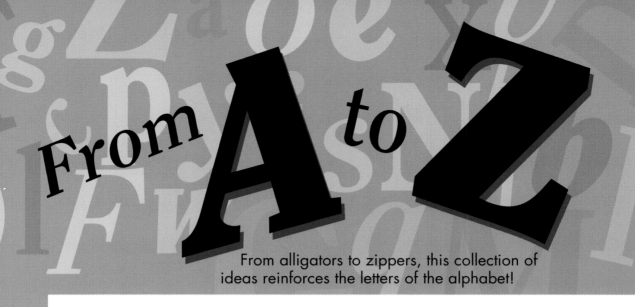

From A to Z

From alligators to zippers, this collection of ideas reinforces the letters of the alphabet!

Writing

A Is for Alligator

Youngsters will swim on over to complete this project, which focuses on writing uppercase and lowercase *a*'s. In advance, enlist the help of parents in collecting one cardboard egg carton for each child. Make a class set of the alligator patterns on page 236 on green construction paper. Have each child paint an egg carton green and then allow the paint to dry. Instruct him to cut out the alligator parts. Help him fold the pieces along the dotted lines. Have him glue the pieces to the carton, as shown, and then use a marker to write an uppercase *a* or a lowercase *a* on each egg cup. That's an awesome alligator!

Barbara Meyers
Fort Worth Country Day School
Fort Worth, TX

Identifying letter sounds
Writing

B Is for Bear

Cute bears help bind these simple *b* booklets. To prepare, make a tagboard copy of the bear pattern on page 237 for each child. Have each youngster color her bear and then cut it out. Use hot glue to attach a clothespin to the back of each child's cutout. Provide each student with several half sheets of paper and a discarded magazine. Instruct her to cut out pictures of items that begin with the /b/ sound and glue them to the booklet pages. Have her write a *b* next to each picture. Then instruct her to stack the pages and use her bear clip to secure the pages. Invite each youngster to share her booklet with the class. "Bear-y" nice!

adapted from an idea by Dawn Schollenberger—Gr. K
Mary S. Shoemaker School, Woodstown, NJ

227

Identifying letter sounds
Writing

C Is for Caterpillar

These clever caterpillars will have youngsters writing *c*'s and thinking about the /c/ sound. Give each child a sentence strip and have him write uppercase *C*s along the length of it. Then direct him to cut out small pictures of items beginning with *c* from a discarded magazine and glue them to his strip as shown. For the final touch, have him draw a face, antennae, and feet on his caterpillar. Cute!

adapted from an idea by Daphne M. Orenshein—Gr. K
Yavneh Hebrew Academy, Los Angeles, CA

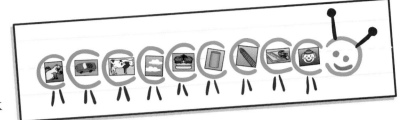

Identifying letters

D Is for Doughnut

Perfect doughnuts are boxed in this activity, which has youngsters sorting them by the letter *d*. To prepare, cut out doughnut shapes from construction paper. Label several doughnuts with uppercase and lowercase *d*'s and a few with *b*'s or *p*'s. Mark the back of each *d* doughnut with a dot for self-checking. Laminate the shapes for durability. Place the doughnuts at a center along with a pair of tongs and a clean, empty doughnut box. When forming a lowercase *d* tell students to imagine drawing a doughnut first and the stick second. Then have each child visit the center and use the tongs to place the doughnuts with *d*'s on them in the box. Follow up successful sorting with a doughnut treat!

Practicing letter sounds

E Is for Elephant

Grab your sidewalk chalk and head outside for this activity. Along a sidewalk write uppercase and lowercase *e*'s. Have youngsters pretend to be elephants and walk over the trail of *e*'s saying the /e/ sound each time they step on a letter. Repeat the walk, having students move like excited elephants, energetic elephants, and then elegant elephants. When your elephant walk is through, have your little elephants link trunks and tails (hands) and return to the classroom for a marshmallow circus peanut snack!

Jennifer Weimann—Gr. K, Dover Children's Center
Dover, NH

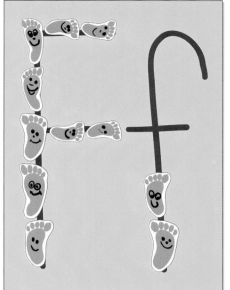

Letter formation

F Is for Funny Feet

Have youngsters kick off their shoes for this letter formation activity! To prepare, put a thin layer of paint in a shallow pan and fill a plastic tub half full with warm soapy water. On a long length of bulletin board paper, write a large uppercase *F* and a large lowercase *f.* In turn, have each child step into the paint and then make footprints on sheets of paper; for easy cleanup, have her rinse her feet with the soapy water. After the paint has dried, instruct the child to draw a face on each foot and then cut them out. Next, put the labeled bulletin board paper in the center of your group. Have each child place her funny footprints heel to toe to help form the letters. Then challenge students to form the letters without using the labeled paper. What a "feet"!

Identifying letter sounds

G Is for Garage

The parking in this garage is reserved for the letter *g!* In advance, gather a supply of small toy cars and a box. Decorate the box to look like a garage. Attach a *g* picture or sticker to all but a few cars. Put pictures with different beginning sounds on the remaining cars. For self-checking, place a sticky dot on the bottom of each car with a *g* picture on it. Have each child choose a car and decide whether the picture begins with the /g/ sound. If it does, have him drive the car into the garage. The garage is open for business. Beep, beep!

The Great Garage

Writing

H Is for Hat

Your little ones will be in style when they wear these custom-fitted hats decorated with *h*'s! To make a hat, simply place a large piece of bulletin board paper on a child's head. Push the paper down so that it forms to the shape of her head. Then wrap colorful masking tape around the crown of her head to form the top of her hat. To finish the hat, roll the edges up to make a brim. Give each child an uppercase and a lowercase *h*. Have her write the appropriate *h*'s on each cutout. Next, instruct her to glue the cutouts to her hat. Have each child wear her hat while she looks for *h* things around the room. Heart, house, and hen begin with *h!*

I Is for Insect

A swarm of cute insects is headed into your classroom in the shape of *i*'s! To prepare, use a fine-tip pen to write an uppercase and a lowercase *i* on a sheet of paper. Make a copy of the paper for each child. Give each child a copy and a bingo dauber. Have him use the dauber to make prints along the letters. When the ink is dry, instruct each youngster to add details to the prints—such as eyes, antennae, wings, and legs—to create unique insects. Then, when everyone is finished, have each student say the short /i/ sound as he touches each insect on his paper. It's an /i/, /i/ insect!

Letter and sound association

J Is for Jellyfish

These jellyfish don't sting—they reinforce the letter *j*! Gather the supplies listed below and then guide each child through the directions to make her own jellyfish. Hang the completed projects from the ceiling using fishing line.

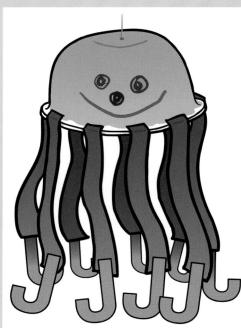

Materials for one jellyfish:
paper bowl (not foam)
access to a shallow pan containing a thin layer of blue paint
paintbrush
nine 12" lengths of crepe paper streamer
9 die-cut *j*'s
glue
markers

Directions:
1. Paint the bottom of the bowl. Allow the paint to dry.
2. Glue the streamers to the edge of the bowl. Glue one letter cutout to the other end of each streamer.
3. Use markers to draw a face on the side of the bowl.

K Is for King

Your royal subjects will be eager to complete this class book, which tells what they would do if they were kings! In advance, cut a large crown shape from bulletin board paper. Draw a duplicate crown shape on a sheet of paper and then photocopy it to make a class set. Have students generate a list of words that begin with the letter *k* and write them on the large crown cutout. Next, give each child a copy of the crown pattern. Instruct him to draw a picture of what he would do if he were king. Have each child write or dictate a sentence about his picture. Then instruct him to underline each *k* in the sentence. Have each youngster cut out the crown shape outlining his drawing. Bind the completed pages along with construction paper covers and title the book "If I Were King…"

Laurie Mills—Gr. K, Stevenson Elementary, Stevenson, AL

If I were King I would fly a Kite.

Letter and sound association
Letter formation

L Is for Letter Lasso

This simple activity will have students practicing letter formation
and searching for things that begin with the letter *l*. Cut 18-inch
lengths of rope so that each child will have one piece. Knot the ends
of each piece to prevent fraying. Gather several items that begin with
the letter *l* and a few that do not begin with *l*. Seat students on the
floor in a circle and place the items in the center. In turn, give each
child a rope and have her lasso (lay her rope in a circle) an item that
begins with the /l/ sound. Have youngsters practice the /l/ sound each
time a child encircles an item with her rope. After each child has had
a turn, collect the items and then instruct each student to use her rope
to practice forming uppercase and lowercase *l*'s on the floor.

Sherri Martin—Four-Year-Old Kindergarten, Southland Academy
Montezuma, GA

Writing

M Is for Marshmallow Moon

Craters made from marshmallows? Sure!
Your little ones will love making these moon
pictures for the letter *m*. To prepare, use a white
crayon to draw a large circle on a sheet of black
construction paper for each child. Put a thin
layer of white paint in a pan. Give each child a
programmed paper and a large marshmallow.
Have him dip one end of his marshmallow in
the paint and then make prints on his paper to
fill in the moon. If desired, outline the moon
with a bead of glitter glue. After the papers are
dry, have each child use a marker to label several prints with uppercase and lowercase *m*'s. Invite him to add foil star stickers to complete the scene.

Leanne Gibbons—Grs. K and 1, Boston Public Schools, Mattapan, MA

Identifying letters

N Is for Newspaper

Youngsters will search, search, and search some more
for the letter *n* in this activity. Give each child a sheet of
newspaper and a highlighter. Have her circle all of the *n*'s
she can find on her paper in a specified amount of time.
Then tape a sheet of newspaper to your board so that
the columns are running side to side. Demonstrate how
to write the letter *n* for students. Next, instruct students
to turn their papers sideways and to practice writing *n*'s
with a pencil or marker. Nice work on the newspaper!

adapted from an idea by Marcie Welch—Gr. K
Chireno Elementary, Chireno, TX

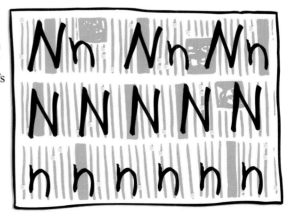

O **Is for Olives**

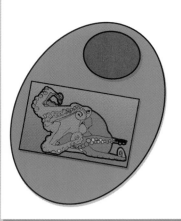

Students will like this game, which has them making olives with *o* pictures. Cut a supply of six-inch green construction paper ovals (olives) and a matching number of 1½-inch red construction paper circles (pimentos). From discarded magazines, cut out several small pictures of items that begin with *o* and a few that don't. Glue one picture to each olive. Then laminate the game pieces for durability. To play, a child says the name of the picture and determines whether it begins with *o*. If it is an *o* picture, he places a red pimento piece on the olive. Follow up the activity with an olive tasting.

P **Is for Peculiar Pizza**

These pizzas will show your youngsters' creativity. Explain to youngsters that they will be making peculiar pizzas. Provide each child with a discarded magazine, a large red construction paper circle (crust with sauce), and white shredded paper (cheese). Instruct each child to locate and cut out *p* pictures from her magazine. Then have her glue them to her crust. After her pictures are in place, instruct her to add a small amount of glue between the pictures and then sprinkle the pie with cheese. When the projects are dry, invite each child to share the pictures on her peculiar pizza with the class. Who wants a slice of pumpkin, popcorn, and parrot pizza?

Lynn C. Mode—Gr. K, Benton Heights Elementary
Monroe, NC

Q **Is for Quilt**

This group activity will have students working together to form the letter *q*. To prepare, cut fabric into three-inch squares. Give each child several squares of fabric. Have youngsters position their squares on a large piece of bulletin board paper to help form an uppercase and a lowercase *q*. Next, instruct students to glue the fabric in place on the paper. Then have each child use crayons or markers to write *q*'s all over the quilt. Display the quilt on a wall with the title "Quite a Nice Quilt."

Letter and sound association
Letter formation

R Is for Rocket

5, 4, 3, 2, 1, blast off with the letter *r!* These nifty rockets will make learning the letter *r* lots of fun! In advance, enlist the help of parents in collecting a toilet paper tube for each child. Have each student paint a tube red. After the paint is dry, have him use a marker to write *r*'s on the tube. Then have him glue a red construction paper triangle to one end of the tube and strips of red tissue paper to the opposite end of the tube to complete his rocket. Direct each youngster to hold his rocket close to the ground. Then tell students to start their rocket engines (say the /r/ sound repeatedly). Give a launch countdown and have each child lift his rocket up, making it form *r*'s in the air. That's a blast!

Letter and sound association

S Is for Submarine

When students look through the portholes in this submarine display, they'll see fish and the letter *s!* Have each child paint the backs of two paper plates yellow. Then help her cut the center out of one plate and tape a piece of blue plastic wrap over the opening as shown. Have her draw several uppercase and lowercase *s*'s on the front of the other plate. Invite her to add details to the letters to make them resemble sea creatures. Then have her glue pebbles along the bottom of her plate. Staple the plates together to form a porthole. To complete the display, cut a simple submarine shape from yellow bulletin board paper, similar to the one shown, and attach it to a wall; then add students' windows to the sea!

Roslyn Johnson—Four- to Six-Year-Old
 Kindergarten
Warrensburg Elementary School
Warrensburg, NY

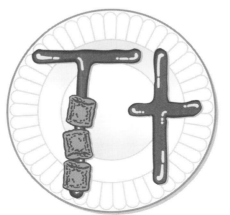

Writing
Letter and sound association

T Is for Tater Tots

This special treat will have youngsters thinking about and eating the letter *t*. Prepare a large batch of tater tots according to package directions. While the tots bake, have each child use ketchup to write an uppercase and a lowercase *t* on his plate. Then invite him to arrange tots on his *t*'s before eating them. Plan this treat for a Tuesday at 2:00!

adapted from an idea by AnnaLisa R. Damminger
Mullica Hill, NJ

233

U Is for Umbrella

Rain, rain, come today; we'll have fun in our own way! All you need for this letter identification activity is an umbrella and a large supply of paper raindrops. To prepare, cut a large supply of raindrop-shaped cutouts from blue construction paper. Label the majority of the cutouts with uppercase or lowercase *u*'s. Label a few with other letters. Have students sit in a circle. Place an open umbrella in the center of the circle with its handle pointing up. Walk around the perimeter of the circle, dropping the raindrops on students. Instruct each youngster to collect the drops that fall near him. Have him look at the drops and determine which ones have *u*'s written on them. Instruct him to put drops that have *u*'s on them in the umbrella and those that don't have *u*'s in a puddle (pile) next to the umbrella.

Varieties of Vanilla			
			Alisha
			Chandler
	Greg		Brady
	Beth	Matt	Todd
Kimi	Rachel	Katie	Chelsea
Vanilla Soda	Vanilla Wafer	Vanilla Yogurt	Vanilla Ice Cream

Phonemic awareness
Graphing

V Is for Varieties of Vanilla

This very vanilla tasting activity will reinforce the letter *v*. Provide each child with a sample of several vanilla-flavored foods, such as vanilla wafers, vanilla yogurt, vanilla soda, and vanilla ice cream. Have each youngster taste the foods and decide on her favorite. Create a graph; then have each child, in turn, come forward and vote (write her name on a self-sticking note and then place it in the appropriate column) to show her favorite. Discuss the graph with students and determine which vanilla food your students liked best!

W Is for Wagon Wheel

These wagon wheel wands will be the perfect pointers for searching for *w*'s and objects that start with the letter. In advance place uncooked wagon wheel pasta in a resealable plastic bag and add a generous amount of paint. Seal the bag and gently work the paint through the pasta. Once coated, pour the pasta in a single layer on a piece of waxed paper and allow it to dry. Give each youngster a piece of pasta and a large craft stick. Have him write his name on the stick and then glue the pasta wheel to one end. After the glue dries, have him use his wagon wheel wand to search books and the room for the letter *w* and objects or pictures of objects that begin with it.

Letter identification

X Is for X Ray

The letter *x* will be easy to spot with these X-ray glasses. To prepare, make a tagboard copy of the X-ray glasses pattern on page 237 for each child. Give each student a copy, and have her color the frames and then cut them out. Next, help each youngster cut out the lens area; then laminate the glasses. Hole-punch the frames where indicated and twist a pipe cleaner through the hole on each side. Have her put her glasses on, and then adjust the pipe cleaner arms to fit her ears. Encourage her to examine the room, looking for the letter *x*. It will certainly be easy to find while wearing these X-ray glasses!

Letter formation

Y Is for Yogurt

A few simple supplies are all you need to complete this letter formation activity. Put a large spoonful of yogurt in a resealable plastic bag for each child. Seal the bag, removing as much air as possible. Give each youngster a bag. On the chalkboard, demonstrate how to write the letter *y*. Then have each child smooth his hand over his bag to spread the yogurt into a thin layer. Invite him to practice writing the letter *y* on the bag with his finger. After several successful attempts, give him a spoon and allow him to open his bag and eat his yummy yogurt!

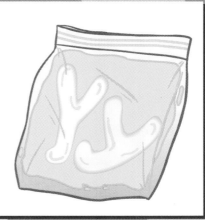

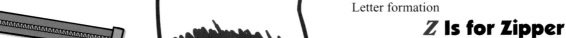

Letter formation

Z Is for Zipper

Your youngsters will be zipping right along with this *z* idea. In advance, ask parents for donations of zippers. Have students lay the zippers on the table to form the letter *z*. Encourage students to think of different ways to make *z*'s. Can a *z* be made with two unzipped zippers? After a child has placed the zippers in a *z* formation, tape them to the table. Give her a sheet of paper and have her lay it on top of the zippers. Instruct her to use the side of a crayon to make a zipper *z* rubbing. Zzzip!

Alligator Patterns

Use with "A Is for Alligator" on page 227.

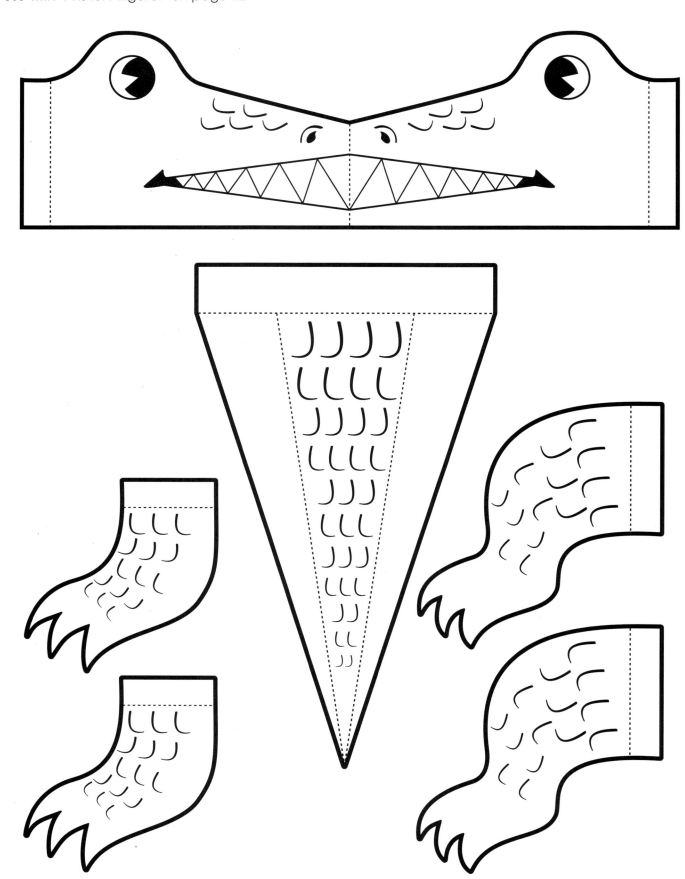

Bear Pattern
Use with "*B* Is for Bear" on page 227.

X-Ray Glasses Pattern
Use with "*X* Is for X Ray" on page 235.

Deck the Halls With Numbers!

There's a "ho-ho-whole" lot of numeral formation practice in this Christmas unit. So gather your little elves and get to work!

by Angie Kutzer—Gr. K, Garrett Elementary School, Mebane, NC

Candy Cane Puzzlers

What are red and white and loved the world over? Candy canes, of course! Use this idea to sweeten the task of forming numerals. To prepare, use a red permanent marker to draw stripes on a sheet of white craft foam. Then cut out several long sticks, short sticks, and arcs. Place a number line nearby and challenge each child to use the foam pieces to form the numerals 0 to 10. Reward his efforts with a miniature candy cane or a peppermint-scented sticker. Sweet!

A Bounty of Bows

Give the gift of numeral knowledge with this partner activity. Wrap a cookie sheet in festive holiday wrapping paper to resemble a gift. Then hot-glue a piece of magnetic tape to each of a supply of small bows of the same color. Write each number from 0 to 10 on a different index card. Instruct each child to secretly draw a card and then arrange the bows on the gift in the shape of that numeral. Have her partner name the numeral. Then have her partner draw a card and change the bows to make a different numeral. Continue in this manner for several rounds. Now that's a wrap!

Cookies for Santa

Spice up this numeral study with gingerbread! Prepare a box of gingerbread mix according to the package directions for cookies. Then give each child a piece of dough the size of a golf ball. Invite him to roll out a log shape and then form a numeral of his choice. (If the dough gets sticky, dust flour on the child's hands.) Bake the cookies and let them cool. If desired, provide white icing for decorating. Have each child show his number cookie to the class. While they probably won't make it to Santa's plate, these yummy numbers are sure to fill your little elves' tummies!

O Christmas Tree!

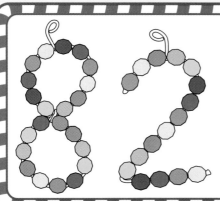

These beaded ornaments not only create beautiful decorations, but also help students work on numeral formations! Instruct each child to choose a number to create. Provide plastic beads for her to thread onto a pipe cleaner. (She may need two pipe cleaners, depending on the number she is forming.) To secure the beads, bend the ends of the pipe cleaner over the first and last beads. After the beads are threaded, help her bend and twist the pipe cleaner to form her designated number. If desired, cut a small piece of pipe cleaner and use it for hanging. Invite each child to hang her ornament on a small tree or on a bulletin board display. Beautiful!

"Lumi-numbers"

Bring the awe of Christmas lights into your study with these number luminaries. In advance, collect a small milk or juice carton for each child. Open the tops completely, rinse, and let dry. Gather the materials listed; then help each child follow the directions to make a luminary. Once the luminaries are complete, have each child bring his project to your circle area. Turn off the lights and then pass a small flashlight around, letting each child shine the light through the hole in the bottom of his luminary to light up his number. As each luminary is lit, have the group call out the number. The results of this project are bright!

Materials for one luminary:
small milk carton
dark tempera paint
paintbrush
pencil
golf tee
craft knife (for teacher use)
scissors

Directions:
1. While holding the opening flaps, paint only the sides of the carton with a dark color. (You may need to use two coats, depending on the original color of the carton.)
2. After the paint dries, lightly write a number of your choice on one side.
3. Use the golf tee to punch holes along the number.
4. Use a craft knife to cut a hole in the bottom of the carton.
5. Cut off the carton's opening flaps.

Round and Round the Reindeer

Are your kindergartners having trouble writing 5 and 2? Here's a novel way to practice! Make an overhead transparency of the reindeer on page 241. Make each child a copy of page 242. Use the text below to explain how to make each of the problem numerals as you model it with the reindeer on the overhead. Encourage each child to practice several times using the reindeer template and then write the number on his own on the back of his paper. For more fun, have student volunteers describe how to make other numbers using the reindeer. On Donner, on Blitzen!

To make a 5:
Draw a short line down through its left antler, under its eyes, and around its nose. Now draw a line from the left antler to right antler.

To make a 2:
Draw a line over its antlers, across its face, and under its nose.

Cari	③
Sam	8
Nadia	5
Ryan	③
Meg	③
Oliver	6
Rachel	③

Stocking Stuffers

Stockings are always full of surprises, and this one's no exception. Put a three-dimensional number, such as a plastic magnet, in a small stocking. During circle time, pass the stocking around and have each child feel the outside long enough to make a guess about which number is inside. Have each child write his guess on a sheet of chart paper as shown. Once all the guesses are recorded, reveal the hidden number; then have volunteers circle all of the matching numerals on the chart. Continue in this manner with other numbers.

It's Santa!

Who has a beard that's long and white? *All* of your students will with these Santa workmats. To prepare, make a copy of the Santa pattern on page 243 for each child. Then use the beard pattern on page 241 to make a beard from white felt for each child. Have students color their Santas; then laminate them. Finally, staple a beard to each Santa as shown.

To complete the activity, give each child an overhead projector marker and a wet wipe. Explain that you're going to pretend to be jolly ol' Saint Nick. Make Santa's "ho, ho, ho" sound a desired number of times. Instruct each youngster to lift Santa's beard, write the numeral for the number of times you said "ho," and replace the beard. On your signal, have youngsters lift the beards and compare numbers. With a quick wipe, they'll be ready for Round 2. Once students get the hang of it, have volunteers make the Santa sounds.

Beard Pattern
Use with "It's Santa!" on page 240.

Name

Round and Round the Reindeer

Note to the teacher: Use with "Round and Round the Reindeer" on page 240.

Celebrate Beginning Sounds

It's a party, and you and your students are invited! Use these entertaining ideas to reinforce initial sounds.

G

Identifying beginning sounds
You're Invited

Your youngsters will get these invitations ready to mail by identifying beginning sounds. In advance, label each of ten large envelopes with a different letter of your choice. Pair students and give each twosome an envelope and a large index card. Have the pair cut (from discarded magazines) pictures of things with names that begin with the letter on the envelope. Instruct students to glue the pictures to their cards. After each card has been covered with pictures, invite each pair of students to share its invitation with the class. Goat, glove, girl, and gum are on the guest list of the *G* party!

Matching beginning sounds to letters
Pop the Balloon

No real balloons are required for this activity—just chalk-drawn ones! Draw several balloons on your chalkboard. Label each one with a different letter. Gather students in your large-group area. In turn, give each child an eraser and then say a word that begins with a letter displayed on the board. Have the child think about the beginning sound and then "pop" (erase) the corresponding balloon. As the child erases, invite the remaining students to make a popping sound!

Karen Saner—Gr. K
Burns Elementary
Burns, KS

Sorting pictures by beginning sounds
HERE'S THE SCOOP

If your students love ice cream, they'll enjoy this cool game! To prepare, obtain a clean one-gallon ice-cream bucket. Glue a picture of an item beginning with a different consonant letter to the bottom of each of a supply of bowls. Then photocopy the picture cards on pages 246 and 247. Color the cards as desired, laminate them for durability, and then cut them out. Hot-glue each picture to a scoop of ice cream (foam ball) and place it in the bucket. Put the bowls, bucket, and an ice-cream scooper or two at a center. Invite each child to visit the center. Have him scoop up some ice cream, look at the picture, and then determine which bowl the scoop belongs in by matching the beginning sounds. After each child has visited the center, reward his work with a real scoop of ice cream!

Matching beginning sounds
SWITCHEROO

This simple game is sure to keep your little party guests on their toes! In advance, photocopy the picture cards on pages 246 and 247. Color the pictures, if desired, and then cut the cards apart. Have students sit in a circle, and give each child a card, making sure that there are two picture cards for each letter you are reviewing. Instruct each student to look at his card and determine the picture's beginning sound. Next, call out a word that begins like one of the pairs of pictures. The students whose pictures begin with the same sound stand up and switch seats. Periodically during play, say, "Switcheroo," and instruct all students to stand up and switch seats with someone. After students get the hang of this game, call out letters instead of words beginning with the same sound. Switcheroo!

Identifying beginning sounds
THE GOODY BAG

No party would be complete without goody bags! These bags are special because they have something in common—beginning sounds! To prepare, make 11 copies of the goody bag labels on page 248. Program each label with a different consonant letter and then color it as desired. Cut the labels apart and glue each one to a different paper lunch bag. Place the bags in your large-group area. Distribute the picture cards from "Switcheroo" (on this page) to students. Have each child sort her pictures into the bags labeled with the corresponding letters. During center time, encourage youngsters to cut pictures from discarded magazines and sort them into the goody bags too. This party was a success!

Picture Cards

Use with "Here's the Scoop," "Switcheroo," and "The Goody Bag" on page 245.

Picture Cards

Use with "Here's the Scoop," "Switcheroo," and "The Goody Bag" on page 245.

Goody Bag Labels

Use with "The Goody Bag" on page 245.

Wonderful Winter

Bundle up your youngsters; then present this collection of science-related winter ideas. Isn't winter wonderful?

by Jana Sanderson, Rainbow School, Stockton, CA

Winter Changes

Teach youngsters this song about the changes that occur during the winter season.

(sung to the tune of "Twinkle, Twinkle, Little Star")

Winter, winter, look and see
All the changes around me.
Plants are sleeping; trees are bare.
Frosty mornings, chilly air.
Winter, winter, look and see
All the changes around me.

Frigid Feelings

Here is a cool way to demonstrate the need for winter clothing firsthand. Fill a cooler with ice. Provide several articles of winter clothing, including jackets and mittens or gloves. Instruct a few children at a time to put a mitten or glove on one hand and then touch the ice with both hands. Encourage youngsters to describe their sensations. Do the gloves keep their hands warm and dry? Then instruct the children to slip on the jackets. Invite other classmates to make paper fans and wave the cool air toward the children wearing the jackets. Do the jackets block the wind? Have children discuss other types of winter clothing and why each is worn.

249

Winter Weather Watch

Show youngsters a variety of weather conditions that occur during the winter season. Gather the materials listed below and demonstrate each condition. The weather is on its way!

Weather Condition	Materials	Demonstration
wind	fan and a small flag	blow air to move flag
rain	water and paper towels	squeeze water from a wet paper towel
fog	white sheer fabric and a spray bottle filled with water	look through fabric and spray a fine mist
hail	rock salt	sprinkle salt
snow	grater and parmesan cheese	finely grate cheese

Container	Body of Water
plastic lid	puddle
segment of ice-cube tray	pond
cereal bowl	lake
large mixing bowl	ocean

An Icy Indication

Here is a slick experiment to demonstrate that depth determines the length of time necessary to freeze various bodies of water. Gather the containers listed. Then fill each one with water. Record students' predictions about which container of water will freeze first. Freeze the containers until the water in the plastic lid is frozen, approximately 30 minutes. Remove all of the containers from the freezer, observe them, and record conclusions. Talk about the containers in relation to the bodies of water they represent (see the list). Return the containers to the freezer and repeat the exercise for the ice cube tray, the cereal bowl, and the mixing bowl. Puddles freeze before ponds!

Winter Retreat

Have youngsters help you create a winter scene on a bulletin board depicting animal homes. Include a mountain with a cave, a frozen pond, a hollow log, bare trees, and holes leading to underground tunnels, all made from bulletin board paper. Read the book *Grandmother Winter* by Phyllis Root and discuss the winter animal homes from the story. Invite children to draw animals and place them in the appropriate dwellings on the board.

Brown Bear Sleeps

Brown Bear tries to explain his reasons for a seasonal slumber in this fun poem. Use this poem to reinforce bear's winter sleep. See you in the spring, Bear!

Brown Bear, Brown Bear, why do you sleep?
I sleep because there is nothing to eat.

Brown Bear, Brown Bear, you're cold as ice.
No, no, not me. With my fur I feel nice.

Brown Bear, Brown Bear, when will you wake?
Not until the snow melts, for goodness' sake!

Cool Tool

Introduce youngsters to the rise and fall of temperature on their very own thermometers. Gather a supply of tongue depressors and make a pencil mark one-third of the way up each stick. Have each child paint two sticks. He paints the large section of one stick red and the small section of the other stick red. Glue a stick to each side of a tagboard strip, making sure the red segments are facing the same direction. Have each child label the side of the strip with the short red section "cold" and label the other side "hot." Teach youngsters the song below and encourage them to hold up their thermometers as they sing about the rise and fall of temperature.

(sung to the tune of "Do You Know the Muffin Man?")

Do you know the thermometer, thermometer, thermometer?
Do you know the thermometer, which shows the temperature?

Yes, I know the thermometer, thermometer, thermometer.
Yes, I know the thermometer; it rises when it's hot.   *Stand.*

Do you know the thermometer, thermometer, thermometer?
Do you know the thermometer, which shows the temperature?

Yes, I know the thermometer, thermometer, thermometer.
Yes, I know the thermometer; it falls when it is cold.   *Sit.*

251

Itsy-Bitsy Icicle

Show children how icicles are formed with this cool demonstration! Saturate three paper towels with water and place them over a tall cup in the freezer. Check regularly and gently squeeze out more water drips from a separate wet paper towel if the icicles haven't formed or if you want to lengthen the existing ones. After your teeny-tiny icicles have formed, teach your kindergartners the cute song below.

(sung to the tune of "The Itsy-Bitsy Spider")

The itsy-bitsy icicle was formed from melted snow.
Droplets of water trickled down below.
Down went the temperature, the drips began to freeze,
And the itsy-bitsy icicle glistened in the breeze.

Melting Moments

I scream. You scream. We all scream for ice-cream sandwiches! Here is a sweet experiment to observe the varying degrees of cold. Unwrap four ice-cream sandwiches and place them on individual plates. Put one plate in the freezer, one in the refrigerator, one in a cooler cooled with ice or an ice pack, and one on a table in your classroom. Take a temperature reading from each location. Observe each ice-cream sandwich throughout the day and record the observations. Discuss the results and talk about the importance of temperature in keeping frozen food frozen. Then serve fresh ice-cream sandwiches to your young scientists.

Stash and Dash

Youngsters will go nuts over this food storage project. In advance, enlist the help of parents in collecting a class supply of paper towel tubes. Cut a hole in the side of each tube. Copy page 253 to make enough squirrel patterns for each child to have one. Staple one end of each tube closed. Have each child cut slits down the open end of her tube. Next, instruct her to bend the slits down to form branches. Have her color and cut out a squirrel pattern. Direct her to glue the pattern to her tube. Fill the trunk of each tree with a bag of nuts (cereal). Encourage youngsters to grab their trees and scurry home!

Journal Writing

Encourage writing in your kindergarten classroom with these journaling tips.

Thinking Music

Calm students and set the mood for good writing by playing soft instrumental music. Students will quickly learn that while the music is playing, it is time to think and write. What a soothing part of a writing routine!

Tammy Riche—Gr. K
Kaplan Elementary
Kaplan, LA

Writing Idea Booster

Need simple, colorful writing prompts to boost your writing time? Try decorative children's borders from wallpaper sample books. The scene choices are nearly endless, including space, animals, cartoon characters, and sports. For each child, glue a border sample to a sheet of writing paper and encourage him to write about the picture. Easy!

Debra Bousquet—Gr. K
Edward Fenn Elementary
Gorham, NH

Stick Together

To motivate writing and help manage sharing after journal-writing time, try placing a sticker on the next clean page in two students' journals each day. Each morning, youngsters will rush to discover who has the stickers. The lucky students get to share their entries for the day with the class. Every once in a while, add a thrill by placing stickers in four journals. This idea helps students look forward to journal time and encourages them to share their ideas. Sounds like a winner!

Kim A. Minafo
Cary, NC

Look Again!

These bookmarks are just the thing to keep your little ones focused on proper writing. To begin, teach students to start sentences with capital letters, to include spaces between words, and to end sentences with punctuation marks. Then make a class set of the bookmarks on this page. Give one to each child to remind him of these important points without having to say a word. Have each child refer to the icons on the bookmark after each writing experience to reinforce each step. After he's checked his writing, have him mark his place in his journal for the next day. What a great writing reminder!

Anna Marie Conaway—Gr. K
Davis Elementary
Malone, NY

Bookmarks
Use with "Look Again!" on this page.

Look Again

C Did you start with a capital letter?

____ * ____ * ____

* Did you leave spaces between words?

. ? ! Did you end with a punctuation mark?

©The Education Center, Inc. • *THE MAILBOX® • Kindergarten* • Feb/Mar 2004

Look Again

C Did you start with a capital letter?

____ * ____ * ____

* Did you leave spaces between words?

. ? ! Did you end with a punctuation mark?

©The Education Center, Inc. • *THE MAILBOX® • Kindergarten* • Feb/Mar 2004

Graphs Galore!

Make math a hands-on process for youngsters with this group of attention-getting graphing ideas that can be used over and over.

by Lucia Kemp Henry, Fallon, NV

Concrete Graph

A supersize graphing mat makes it easy for youngsters to create great concrete graphs. Use colored duct tape to divide a solid-colored rectangular vinyl tablecloth into columns and rows to make a large, reusable graphing mat. Have students classify and organize real objects (shoes, building blocks, silk flowers, etc.) on the graph. Then simply fold it and store it until your next graphing experience.

Yes-or-No Chart

Need a simple and effective way to display data? Make this reusable chart to display student answers to yes-or-no questions. Use double-sided tape to attach a wide ribbon down the middle of a pocket chart, dividing it into two columns. Label one column "yes" and the other one "no." Have each child place her name card on one side or the other to indicate her response to yes-or-no questions.

Choice-of-the-Day Graph

Invite youngsters to exhibit their opinions about classroom activities with this simple graphing idea. To make a graphing mat, glue part of a sentence strip to one edge of a 9" x 12" sheet of construction paper and then laminate it. Place two mats on a table along with a class supply of plastic milk jug lids. Add a strip with the title shown to the display. If youngsters are to choose a book for storytime, place a different book on each mat. Invite each child to place a plastic lid on one of the sentence strips to indicate her choice for storytime. Have two volunteers count the lids to determine which title is the day's winner. Use the graphing mats over and over to make choices for snacks, music selections, and art projects. Majority rules!

Choice of the Day

Three Little Pigs

Good Night, Little Bear

A Slice of the Pie

There's no baking required for this pie! Teach students about reading data on a pie graph with this easy idea. To prepare, cut a large red circle and a large yellow circle of the same size from poster board. Cut each circle into same-size wedges that equal the number of students in your class. Then pose a question to students, such as "Do you like pepperoni or cheese pizza?" Instruct each child to choose a wedge to represent her choice (red for pepperoni and yellow for cheese). Then have youngsters place their wedges on the floor in a pie shape, keeping the red ones side by side and the yellow ones side by side. Explain to youngsters that the part of the pie with the most wedges of the same color indicates the majority's favorite. Now that's a perfect pie!

Favorite Things Picture Graph

Youngsters love to graph when the data displayed focuses on student favorites. Use colorful corrugated border strips to divide a bulletin board into a horizontal headline space and four columns. Divide the columns into rows by drawing lines. Use the headline space to display a question, such as "What is your favorite pet?" Display a word card at the top of each column as shown. Ask each child to draw and color a picture to represent her favorite; then have her cut out the picture and attach it to a column on the board. The board can be used again and again to graph favorite foods, colors, or hobbies.

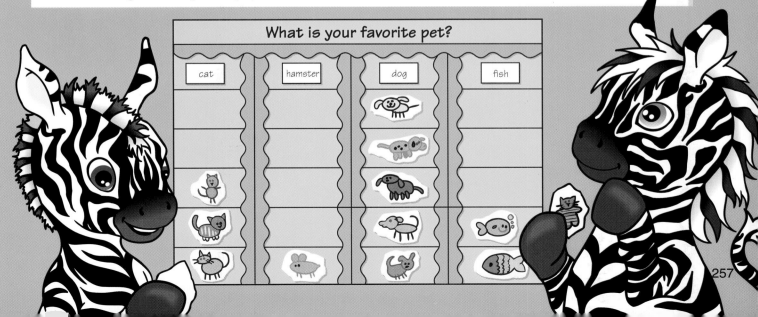

What is your favorite pet?

| cat | hamster | dog | fish |

257

Name _____

A Great Graph

Sort.
Graph.
Count.

Note to the teacher: Program the graph as desired for student use.

Graph and Count

Sort.
Graph.

10						
9						
8						
7						
6						
5						
4						
3						
2						
1						

Note to the teacher: Program the graph as desired for student use.

Valentine Rimes

These ideas will help Cupid do his job when it comes to developing a love for learning to read. A kindergartner and literacy skills? What a perfect match!

by Angie Kutzer—Gr. K, Garrett Elementary School, Mebane, NC

Identifying rimes

Kindergarten Cupids!

If your youngsters aren't familiar with who Cupid is, give them a brief explanation about this mythological character. Then use his tactics to pair students up with rime endings. Purchase a toy bow and arrow set that has suction cups on the ends of the arrows. Draw several large hearts on your whiteboard. Program each heart with a different rime ending. To play, a child shoots an arrow at one of the hearts. He says a word that has the same ending as the one on the heart. Continue until each child has had a turn. On another day, use different rimes and play the game again. That's right on target!

R. Saunders

Will You Be Mine?

Making words · Reading

Let your students play matchmaker with this word-making game. In advance, cut out seven large hearts from red craft foam. Then cut the hearts in half. Program each of the right halves with a different rime and each of the left halves with a different consonant. (See the list below.) Give each member of a small group one of the left halves. Randomly pick a right half to hold. If a child can make a word with his half and your half, he gets a point. Continue for several rounds and then tally up to see who's a really fine valentine. Reward all efforts with valentine stickers!

-an
-at
-ot
-ip
-ap
-ug
-it

Match Me

Matching rimes

Make these easy matching puzzles to keep up with the current character favorites of students. Ahead of time, ask parents to send in any of their child's leftover valentines or buy an extra box in advance. Copy and cut out the rime pictures on page 263. Glue a pair of matching rime pictures on the back of a valentine and then cut the card in half. Mix up the cards and store them in a heart-shaped box. Have each child pair the pictures with matching rimes and then self-check by turning the pieces over to view the preprinted image on the valentine.

Reading

Loving Literacy

Give students an opportunity to show off their reading skills with this clever valentine. Copy the heart pattern on page 264 onto red construction paper for each child. Next, from white or pink construction paper, cut a supply of small 1" x 2" cards (several for each child) and larger 2" x 2" cards (one for each child). Give each student a copy of the heart pattern and the cards. Have her choose a rime, write it on her large card, and glue it where indicated on her heart. Then instruct her to write on each of her small cards a different letter that creates a word when combined with her chosen rime. Next, instruct her to cut out her heart. Then help her stack the cards and staple them to her heart where indicated to complete her project. Encourage each child to read her words to the class. Cat, mat, pat—I can read!

I love to read!
Yes, it's true.
Let me read
These words for you!

c -at

Big, pig. They rhyme!

| got | man | hat | pig | not | cat |
| can | big | pan | lot | fat | dig |

Reading
Identifying matching rimes

Shake, Shake, Shake

This fun game will help reinforce rimes for your students. To prepare, gather a sanitized foam egg carton and two heart-shaped beads. Use a permanent marker to label the eggcups with words from three or more different rimes, similar to the carton shown. Add two beads and close the carton. To play, one child shakes the carton and then opens it. She reads the words under the beads. If the two words have the same rime, she takes another turn. If the words do not end with the same rime, play continues with the next student. Ready, set, shake, and read!

car	jar	five	hive
can	fan	map	cap
pen	hen	sheep	jeep
box	fox	pot	dot
jam	ham	sled	bed
sink	wink	tire	fire

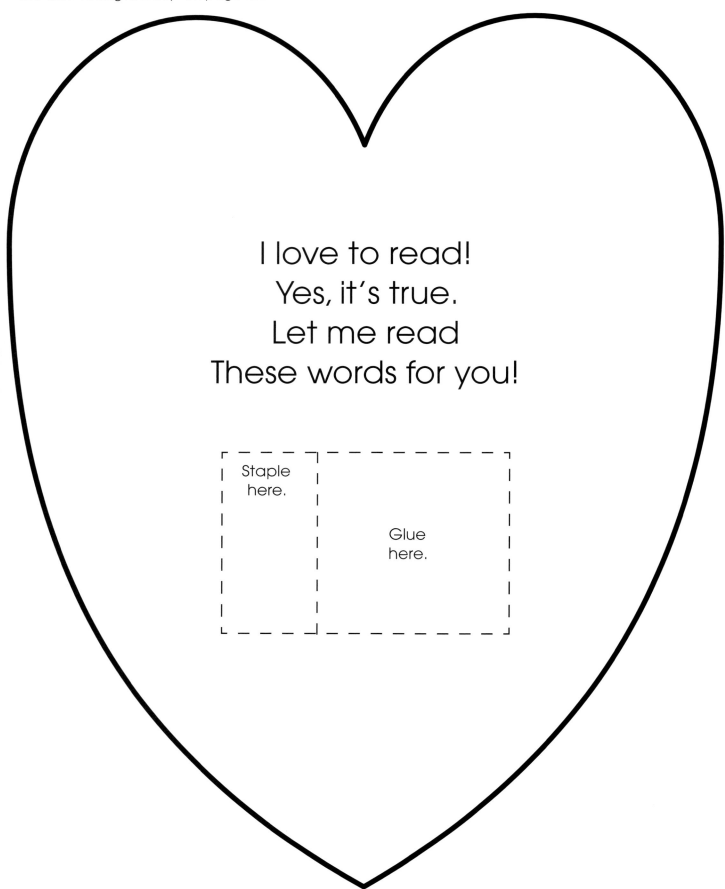

I love to read!
Yes, it's true.
Let me read
These words for you!

Staple
here.

Glue
here.

Special Delivery

This post office unit is positively the best for cross-curricular fun and learning!

by Jana Sanderson, Rainbow School, Stockton, CA

Signed, Sealed, and Delivered

Start your post office unit with this little ditty. Then get ready to sort all kinds of mail!

(sung to the tune of "Three Blind Mice")

Mail, mail, mail.
Mail, mail, mail.
All kinds of mail.
All kinds of mail.
Cards, bills, letters, and coupons to share.
Boxes and magazines handled with care.
Mail is delivered by foot, truck, and air.
Mail, mail, mail.

Mail Call!

Here is a first-class activity for sorting fun. Cut several large manila envelopes into house shapes, leaving the opening of the pocket at the top as shown. Draw windows and doors and label each house with a house number. Staple the houses to the bottom of a bulletin board titled "Mail Call!" Gather a supply of mail (newspapers, magazines, letters, postcards, etc.) and attach a mailing label to each piece, addressing it to one of the houses. Invite students to sort the mail and then deliver it by inserting each piece into the pocket of the correct house.

265

You've Got Mail

Got mail? Sure thing! And here's an idea for a faux leather bag to carry it in. Gather a class supply of large brown grocery bags. Trim each bag into a 13" x 28" piece as shown. Have each child crumple his paper to give it a leather look. Then instruct each child to paint his paper with blue watercolor paint. Hang each paper to dry. When the paint is dry, help each child fold his paper to form a bag with a flap. Then use a hole puncher to make a row of holes along each side of his bag. For each side, help him tie a length of yarn through the bottom set of holes. Then have him sew each side of his bag and tie it closed. To create a strap, help the child tie on an additional length of yarn to the top holes on each side of his bag. Add a Velcro fastener to close the flap if desired.

13"

28"

Postal Hats

These hats are the crowning feature for your little letter carriers. Create a hat pattern similar to the one shown. Have each child trace the pattern on blue construction paper and then cut it out. Help each child fold her hat to make a brim. Instruct her to write "U.S. MAIL" on the hat above the brim. Staple each child's hat to a blue construction strip and then size the strip to fit her head. With a mail bag on her shoulder (see "You've Got Mail" on this page) and a hat on her head, it's mail-collecting time!

U.S. MAIL

U.S. MAIL

Lick-'N'-Stick Stamps

Your students will get to experience a favorite pastime as they make, trade, and collect stamps. Give each child a sheet of paper. Have each youngster draw several different stamp designs on his paper. Then instruct him to turn his paper over and paint a coat of sticker solution (see recipe below) over the entire sheet. When the solution is dry, have students use decorative scissors to cut their stamps apart and then trade with their classmates. Provide each child with a waxed paper envelope or stamp-collecting booklet to preserve his new collection. To use a stamp, he simply licks the back and positions it on an envelope.

John

Tina

Sticker Solution

1 tsp. unflavored gelatin
1–2 tsp. cold tap water
½ c. boiling water

Stir the gelatin and cold water together until the gelatin dissolves. Then stir in the boiling water. Cool the solution, allowing it to thicken before painting.

Stamp of Approval

Young postal workers will enjoy stamping the postmark on envelopes to prepare them for delivery. Gather a supply of clean milk jug lids and hot-glue a cork to the top of each one to make circle stamps. Stock your dramatic-play area with the stamps, black ink pads, mail, and pencils. Hang a calendar in the area. Encourage youngsters to postmark letters as they use the post office center each day. Instruct them to stamp the circle on the envelope, write the date inside it, and then draw wavy lines over the stamp to cancel it. At the end of each day, cross out the date on the calendar and circle the next number to use as a reference the following day.

Postal Peekaboo

Kindergartners will love delivering and collecting mail with these classroom mailboxes. Enlist the help of parents in collecting a 7½" x 10½" empty cereal box for each child. Cut off the flaps from the open end of each box. Then cut around the bottom of each box, leaving one small side intact to make a door. Tape the boxes together to form mail slots. Cover the sides of the group of slots with white bulletin board paper. Lay the group of slots on its side so that the doors hang down. Write each child's name on a different door and at the back of the same slot as shown. Hole-punch the bottom of each door flap and loop a piece of yarn or pipe cleaner through the hole to make a handle. Encourage youngsters to make cards and write letters to deliver to their classmates. (Occasionally write a note to each child to ensure that everyone gets mail.) Have a child place the mail in the correct slots at the back of the postal center. At the end of the day, have each child check her mailbox. Peekaboo—there's mail for you!

267

Delivery!

It's delivery time! This game has youngsters counting and delivering packages. In advance, make four copies of page 270. Color, laminate, and cut out the game strips and mail trucks. Tape each truck to the side of a berry basket. Fill each truck with six cubes, representing packages. To play the game, have each of four children, in turn, roll a die, removing a package from his truck and delivering it to the matching house on his game strip. If a number is rolled twice, the player loses his turn to deliver a package. The game continues until a child has successfully delivered a package to each house in his neighborhood.

U.S. Mail

Mail Magic

Abracadabra! Every child in the class will receive a letter in the mail with this idea. Begin by using a marker to divide a sheet of paper into different puzzle shapes. Then photocopy the page for each child. Write each child's name on a slip of paper. Have each student draw a name and write or dictate a letter to that child on the back of the puzzle page. Instruct each child to cut her letter into puzzle pieces and place the pieces in an envelope. Then have one or two of your little letter carriers deliver the envelopes to the appropriate children. After the envelopes have been delivered, invite each youngster to open her mail, put her puzzle together, and then read her message.

Kate,
You ar a good frend. I lik you.
Matt

268

Delivery Directions

Learning cardinal directions is fun with this activity! Address several envelopes with pretend names and addresses but with real states. (The return address on each envelope should be from a different state.) During group time, hang a large map of the United States on your board. Write "North," "South," "East," and "West" around the map on the board. Find the state where the envelope was sent from; then find the state where the envelope was sent. Use chalk to lightly trace the path in which the letter traveled. Next, draw an arrow on the board in the same direction. Have students determine which direction the letter traveled. It traveled east!

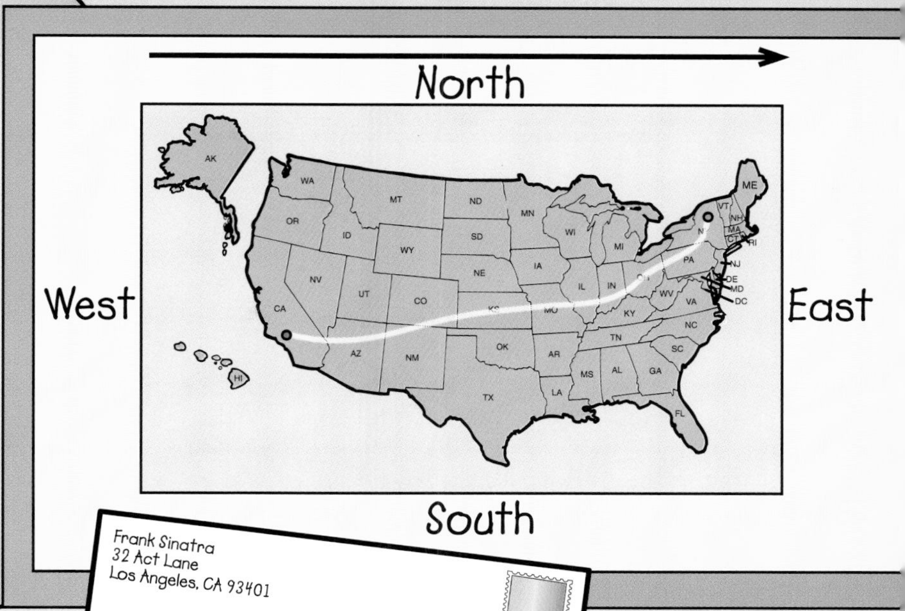

North

West

East

South

Frank Sinatra
32 Act Lane
Los Angeles, CA 93401

Tom Jones
63 Sing Way
New York City, NY 32169

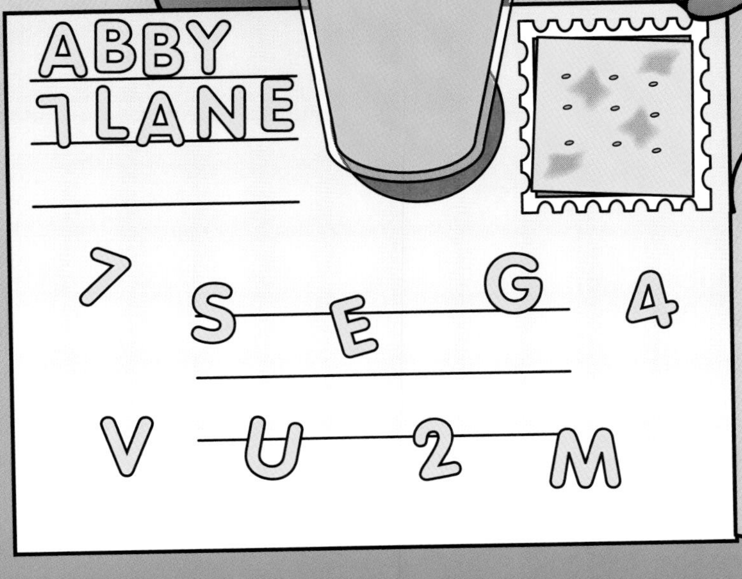

ABBY
1 LANE

7 S E G 4

V U 2 M

Edible Addresses

Who knew addresses could be so tasty! In advance, make a class set of the placemat on page 271. Give each child a small square cracker to serve as a stamp on her placemat. Have her place a small cup of juice over the postmark circle. Give each child a scoop of Alpha-Bits cereal to address the envelope with invented spelling, creating pretend names and addresses on the lines. After the envelope is complete, invite each youngster to have a snack. What a delicious delivery!

Truck Pattern and Game Strip
Use with "Delivery!" on page 268.

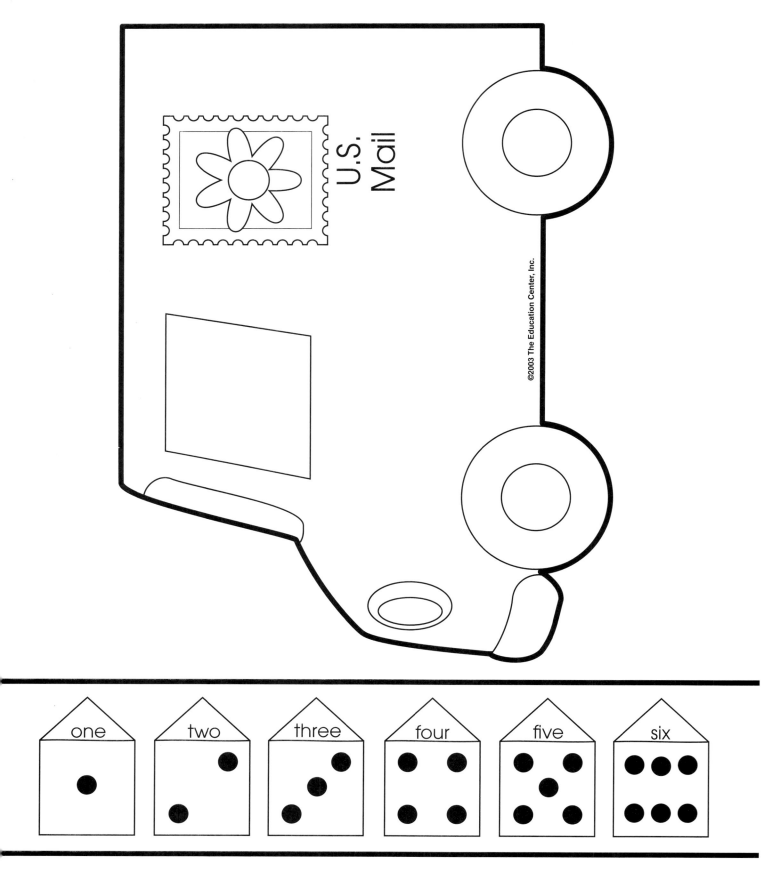

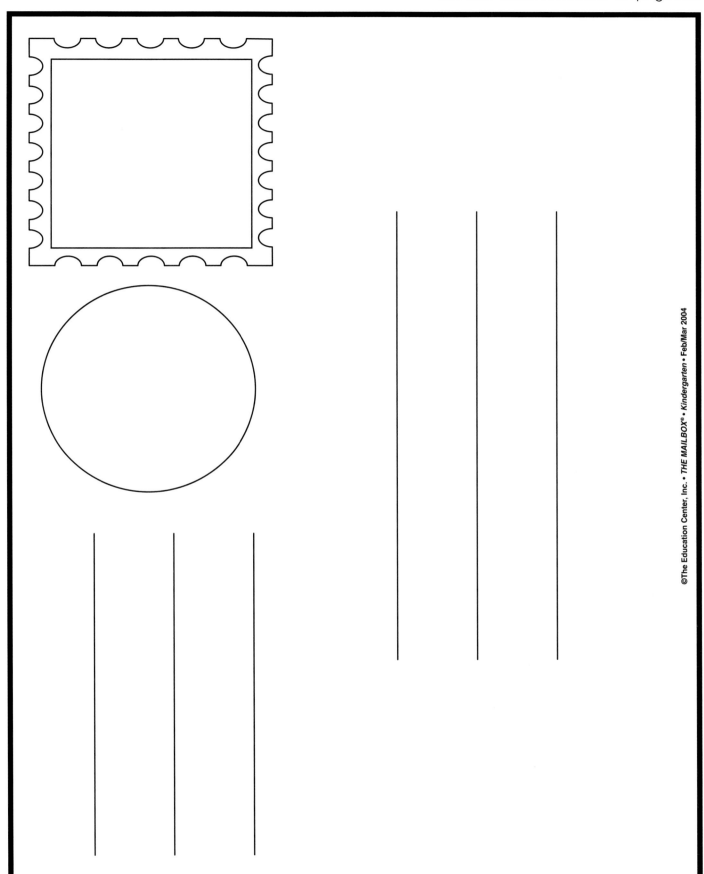

Name _____

Air Mail

Color.

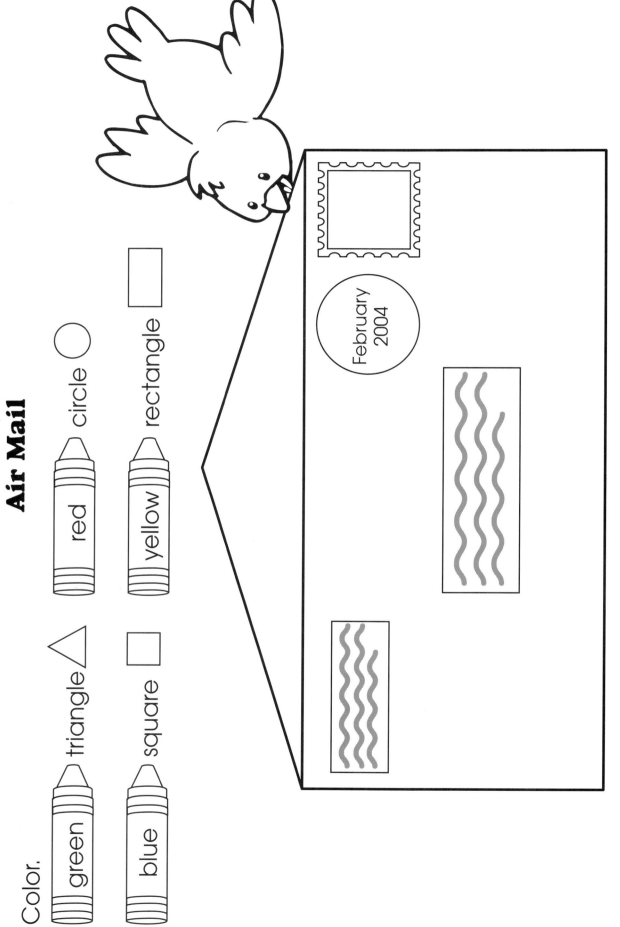

green △ triangle   red ○ circle

blue ☐ square   yellow ☐ rectangle

February 2004

Note to the teacher: Use with the activities on pages 265–269.

Springtime Science

Invite your little sprouts to celebrate the season with this set of springtime explorations. Your youngsters' science skills will blossom as they investigate rain, plants, trees, and wind.

by Lucia Kemp Henry, Fallon, NV

Charting Changes

Curious students are natural scientists thanks to their excellent observation skills. Introduce a scientific investigation of spring by sharing *When Spring Comes* by Robert Maass with your little ones. As you read, ask students to observe and discuss the springtime scenes described in the book. Then encourage your youngsters to share their ideas about how they know that spring has sprung! Jot students' responses on a large tulip shape cut from bulletin board paper. Finally, invite students to sing the suggested verses of the song; then add their charted ideas to the lyrics.

(sung to the tune of "Go in and out the Window")

How do we know it's springtime? How do we know it's springtime?
How do we know it's springtime? How do we know it's springtime?
We know that it is springtime, we know that it is springtime
When we see [raindrops fall], when we see [small seeds sprout].

Sing two more verses of the song using the following phrases: *cold snow melt, new leaves grow, flowers bloom,* and *baby birds hatch.*

a breeze blowing
green leaves and grass
melting snow
flowers blooming
baby animals being born
rain
birds building nests

Spring Scenes Display

Invite students to use this bulletin board idea to classify seasonal weather, flowers, and baby animals that are common in spring. In advance, use a die-cutter to make a supply of cloud, duck, and tulip shapes. Place the shapes inside a large plastic flowerpot. Write "Weather," "Baby Animals," and "Flowers" on separate sentence strips. Display each strip on a different section of a large bulletin board titled "Spring Sights." To begin, read the text on the bulletin board to students. Help them review the chart from "Charting Changes" on page 273 to find ideas to match each category on the board. Next, give each child a 9" x 12" sheet of white construction paper. Have her use crayons to illustrate an idea from the chart or one of her own that fits one of the categories. When all the pictures have been completed, lay them out on the floor or on a large table in front of the bulletin board. In turn, ask each child to draw a spring shape from the flowerpot. Have the child find a picture to match the theme of her shape (weather, animal, or flower). Then help the child attach the picture to the board below the matching sentence strip. What a fun way to spring into science classification skills!

The Soil in Spring

Mild spring temperatures and rainy days change the cold, dry ground into a warm, damp place where seeds can sprout. To demonstrate how spring weather changes soil, place a big bowl of potting mix in the freezer overnight. Set the chilled bowl of soil on a table. Have each child in a small group use her hands to explore the soil as the group discusses how it feels. Next, use a spray bottle to add rain to the soil a little at a time as students mix it with their hands. Have students discuss how the soil changes as they mix it.

When the soil is damp but not soggy, cover the bowl with plastic wrap and place it in the sun. After several hours, uncover the bowl and invite youngsters to investigate and discuss the soil once more. Write student descriptions of the warmed-up soil on the chart; then use the findings to discuss how soil changes in the spring.

Spring Thaw

When the rainy, warm days of spring arrive, snow begins to melt. Help youngsters investigate this seasonal thaw with a comparison activity. In advance, gather several empty salt shakers and two large, shallow plastic containers. Fill the shakers with water and set them aside. To begin, pour two cups of finely crushed ice in each plastic container to represent mounds of snow. Set one container on a table, set the other one inside your water table, and invite each child to describe the contents. Next, explain that students will use the shakers to sprinkle rain on the snow in the water table. Ask your group to decide which will melt faster—the snow sprinkled with rain or the snow left alone; write predictions on chart paper. Then have each child take a turn shaking raindrops on the snow in the water table. Encourage each child to describe what happens! Finally, write students' findings on a chart as youngsters compare the two snow mounds and discuss their discoveries about how raindrops help make snow melt in the spring.

Windsock Project

Spring weather changes are often ushered in with brisk breezes. It's windsock season! To make a sturdy windsock, give each child a 10" x 18" piece of bulletin board paper. Invite the child to decorate her windsock with sponge-printed flower designs. While the paint dries, have the child cut streamers from plastic grocery bags. Help her glue the streamers along one long edge of the paper. Reinforce both long edges of the paper with wide masking tape. Roll the paper and tape the ends together to create a cylinder-shaped windsock. Next, punch four holes along the edge opposite the streamers. Complete the windsock by threading yarn through the holes to create a hanger as shown. Then invite each child to use her windsock in the simple wind measurement activity in "Measuring the Wind" on page 276.

Spring Sprouts

Now that your little ones have explored the warmed-up soil with "The Soil in Spring" activity on page 274, it's time for spring planting! Have each child put ¼ cup of the potting soil inside a zippered plastic bag. Give him a lima bean that has been soaked in water overnight. Help him plant the seed so that it is sandwiched between the soil and the side of the bag. Use a permanent marker to write the child's name on his bag. Then use masking tape to secure the bag to a warm, sunny window inside the classroom. Plant a seed in an additional bag of soil, seal it, and place it in the freezer. Once students' seeds are growing roots, bring the frozen seed out for students to compare; then return it to the freezer. When the beans have sprouted, have youngsters compare them to the frozen sample again. Wrap up the activity by having each child draw a picture of his sprouted seed. Then have him write a description of the changes that have taken place in his springtime experiment!

Dandelion Discovery

You know when dandelions reappear that spring is here! Since these common plants are thought of as weeds, digging them up for a study of plant parts won't be a problem! In advance, scout around your schoolyard for dandelion plants. Then take students outside on a dandelion hunt. Encourage students to look for dandelion plants with buds, with flowers, and without flowers. Dig up several large flowering dandelion plants for further classroom study. (Alternately, bring in plants from home.) Lay the plants on a large table for student observation. Ask students to find and discuss the root, leaves, stem, and flower as you name them; write the vocabulary on sentence strips. Then have each child draw, color, and label a large picture of a dandelion to illustrate the four important parts of the plant. Display the completed diagrams on a bulletin board along with the vocabulary words. Spring is in flower!

Measuring the Wind

Now it's time for students to test their windsocks! Ask a volunteer to hold his windsock in front of a 3-speed fan. Turn the fan on low to simulate a light wind; prompt students to discuss the movement of the windsock. Next, turn the fan on medium and have your youngsters discuss changes in the windsock's position. Then turn the fan on high to simulate a brisk breeze. Use what students have discovered in your demonstration to talk about wind speed and the effects of wind. Discuss how we can observe wind moving things such as leaves, flags, and kites. To extend the activity, invite your little weather watchers to take their windsocks outside on a breezy day for a session of wind measurement! Direct each child to grasp the strings of his windsock with one hand. Ask him to stretch his hand and arm out at shoulder height. Next, have him move around until the wind catches the windsock. Then have your little weather watchers observe the windsocks' movement. This activity is a breeze!

Spring Tree Model

Spring means that the leaves on trees begin to grow. Blossoms begin to bud and cover the trees with color. Take your budding scientists for a walk around the school or a nearby park to take a peek at the trees! Encourage students to look for trees in different stages of spring growth; trees with leaves, trees with blossoms, and trees that are bare. Help youngsters identify the trunk, leaves, and blossoms of different trees. Then invite each child to use her observations to make a 3-D model of a tree. Each child will need a 9" x 12" sheet of brown construction paper, a 6" x 9" piece of white paper, a 6" x 9" piece of green construction paper, and a 4" x 4" piece of cardboard. Help each child roll her brown paper into a tube and secure it with tape to create a tree trunk. Have her cut one-inch slashes in one end of the tube and fold them out to make roots as shown. Assist the child in cutting four *V* shapes in the other end of the tube to make branches. Help each child staple the roots to her piece of cardboard. Next, have each child cut a treetop shape from the green paper. Have her use a small leaf-shaped sponge and green paint to print leaves on the treetop. Then give the child a cotton swab and pink paint to decorate the treetop with dot-shaped blossoms. Help each child use a stapler to attach the treetop to the branches. To complete her project, have each child make a simple key to identify the trunk, leaves, and blossoms as shown.

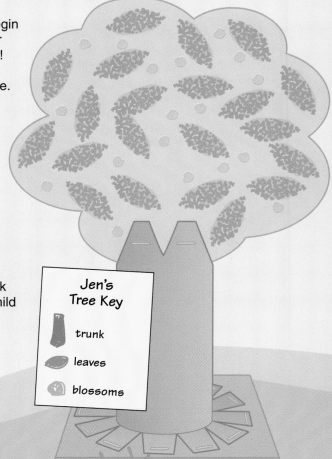

Jen's Tree Key

trunk

leaves

blossoms

A Sight Words Spectacular

Your young readers will get some great practice reading sight words with the clever ideas in this unit. So grab your sight word list and get started!

Scrolling Sight Words

This idea takes very little preparation but will greatly benefit youngsters learning to read sight words. Simply type the sight words you want your students to practice in a large font on your computer. Then set the text on a scrolling marquee or slide show application. During center time, start the scrolling list and just watch. Youngsters will flock to the computer to read the next word on the screen. Periodically add to your scrolling list to build more sight word mastery!

Rachel Chavez—Gr. K
Dalton Early Childhood, Uvalde, TX

Word Walk

You'll need some music for this activity, which has students moving, grooving, and reading! To prepare, make several copies of the feet patterns on page 280. Program each pattern with a different sight word you want your students to practice. Laminate the patterns for durability and then cut them out. Place the patterns on the floor in a circle. As music plays, have students walk around the circle. When the music stops, instruct each child to stop on a foot pattern. Have each student read the word on her pattern. Continue play until students have read most of the words.

Maureen Behrs—Grs. K–1
Linkhorne Elementary School
Lynchburg, VA

Sharon Leavins—Gr. K ESL
Heritage Elementary
Houston, TX

Sight Word Dice Are Nice

Students read and reproduce words with this activity. To create a word die, label a cube-shaped box with different sight words you want your students to practice. Place the die and a supply of letter tiles in the center of each small group of students. In turn, have each child roll the die and read the word on top. Instruct her to use the tiles to re-create the word and then read it again before passing the die on to the next person.

Katie Zuehlke—Gr. K, Bendix Elementary, Annandale, MN

COMING SOON

COMING SOON

Thumbs-Up for Sight Words

This clever idea will keep youngsters on their toes and listening for a specific sight word. Use a washable marker to write a sight word on the thumb of each student. Instruct each child to give a thumbs-up whenever she hears her word spoken throughout the day by anyone at school. Students love it and so do their thumbs-up recipients!

Mark Giufre—Gr. K

Squirting Words

This is one sight word activity your students will ask for again and again! In advance, collect several squirt bottles with adjustable nozzles that spray in a stream. On a warm, sunny day head outside with youngsters to a long sidewalk. Give each pair a squirt bottle. In turn, have one child use the bottle to squirt a word on the sidewalk. His partner reads the word and then the partners switch roles and repeat the activity. As a variation during winter, fill the bottles with tinted water and have youngsters squirt letters and words into fresh snow. Squirt, squirt, read! Squirt, squirt, read!

Mark Giufre—Gr. K,
Perkins Elementary School, Newark, NY

Famous Words

Everyone is a winner with this reading game! Copy the gameboard on page 282, color it, and then laminate it for durability. Gather two game pieces and a die. Program a set of index cards with different sight words. Place the gameboard, game pieces, word cards, and the die at a center. Invite a pair of students to play the game. In turn, have each child choose a word card and then roll the die. Have him read the card. If he reads the word correctly, he gets to move ahead the same number of spaces he rolled. If he doesn't read the word correctly, his turn ends. Continue play until both students have crossed the finish line.

Jill Jaronik—Gr. K, St. Philip Neri, Indianapolis, IN

up →	down		yes →	black
run	it		can	me
off	stop		and	see

Stop.

Stuck on Signs

This activity helps youngsters cling to reading words—really! In advance, purchase a suction cup ball from a local discount store. Make two copies of page 281. In each grid space, write a sight word you want students to practice. Tape the pages together to make a larger gameboard as shown. Laminate it for durability. Post the gameboard on a wall at students' eye level. Dampen the ball; then have each child, in turn, toss the ball at the gameboard. Instruct her to read the word in the space in which the ball stuck. If the ball lands on a line, the child reads each word whose space touches that line. Sounds like a hit to me!

Sharon Leavins—Gr. K ESL
Heritage Elementary, Houston, TX

Literacy Lineup

Add a little reading to lining up with an idea that has youngsters matching words. Tape the footprints from "Word Walk" on page 277 to the floor where you typically have students line up. Label a supply of index cards with the same words as those on the floor. When it's time to line up, have each child choose a card, read the word on it, find the matching word on the floor, and then take that place in line. Who knew that literacy could be practiced so easily while lining up!

Marietta Canalizo—Gr. K, Pines Elementary School, Plymouth, NC

am   see   blue

I   the   run

Feet Patterns

Use with "Word Walk" on page 277 and "Literacy Lineup" on page 279.

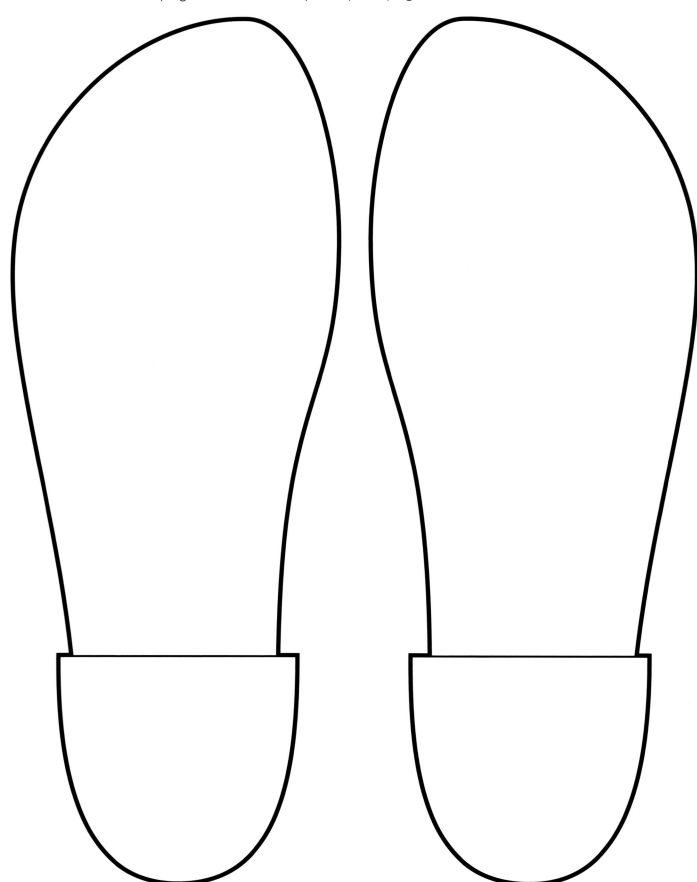

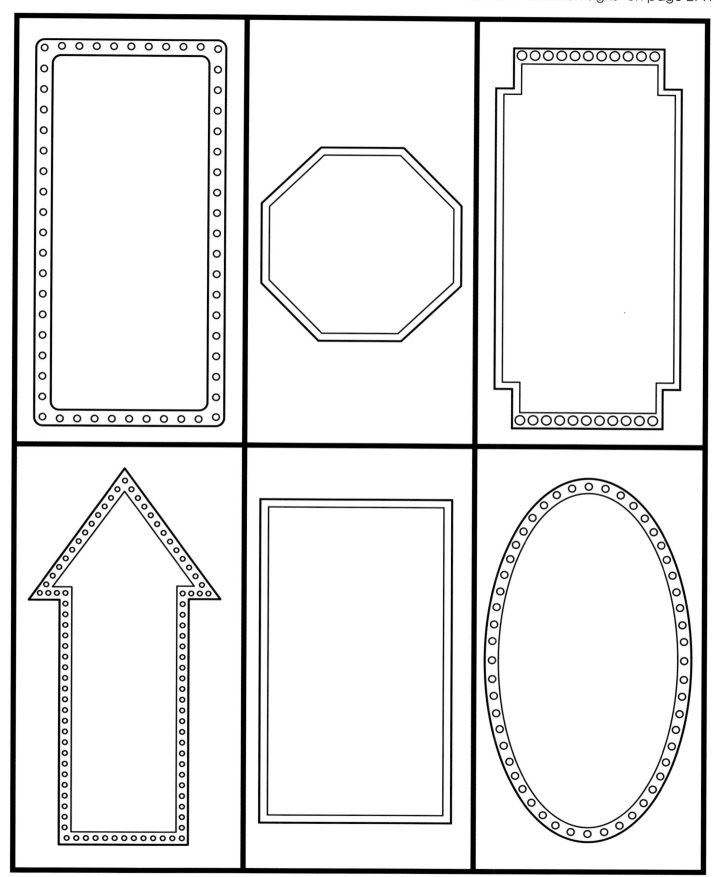

Famous Words

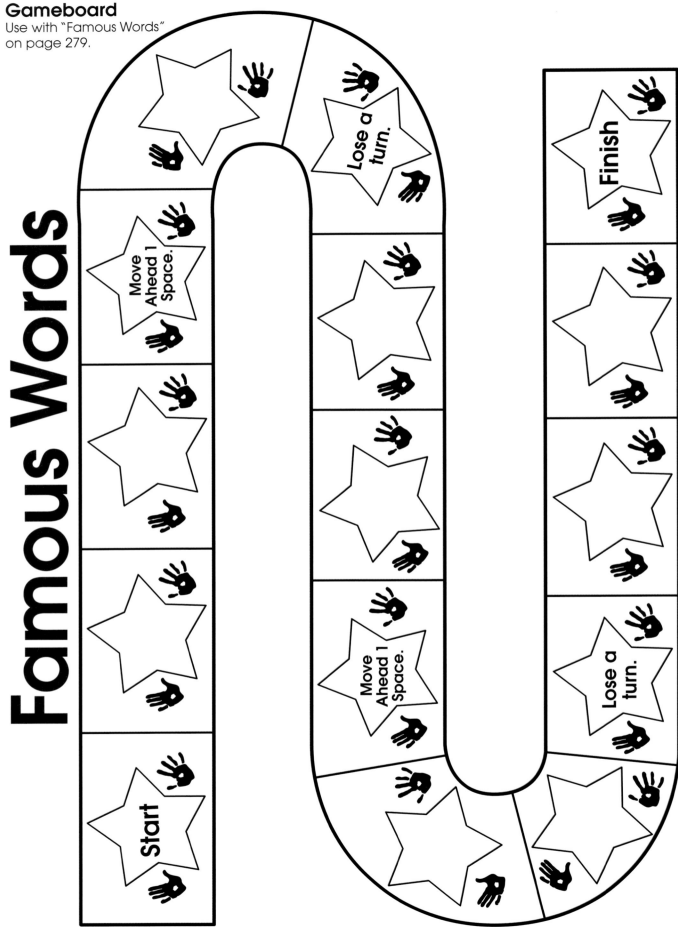

©The Education Center, Inc. • *THE MAILBOX*® • Kindergarten • TEC42012 • April/May 2004

Bunnies Sum It Up

Have your little ones give these "egg-cellent" addition activities a try. They'll be "hoppy" to practice addition with these festive ideas!

by Suzanne Moore, Irving, TX

> Two hops and three hops equals five hops in all.

Bunny Trail Hop

Here's a fun addition activity that even Peter Cottontail would love. In advance, cut 11 large egg shapes from colorful bulletin board paper. Number each egg cutout with a different numeral from 0 to 12. Decorate the eggs if desired and then laminate them for durability. Next, create a number line with the eggs by taping them to the floor. Make several sets of the card patterns on page 286. Color and cut out each card; then glue it to tagboard. Laminate the cards if desired. Now your little ones are ready to hop, hop, hop down the bunny trail! Invite a volunteer bunny to stand on the egg labeled "0." Have another youngster select one of the cards and then direct the bunny to hop along the number line the same number of times as indicated on the card. Have the child repeat by drawing a second card and then instructing his bunny friend to hop some more. Have youngsters count to discover how many hippity-hops the bunny makes down the bunny trail. Repeat the activity until each child has had a chance to be the bunny. Hop to it!

0 1 2 3 4 5 6 7 8 9 10 11 12

Cottontail Totals

Totaling up cottontails during center time will add up to be a basketful of fun for your little bunnies. In advance, pile 20 cottontails (large white or pink cotton balls) into a large basket. Invite each student to grab a handful of cottontails in each hand. Have him count each handful of cottontails separately. Then direct each youngster to combine his cottontails and count the total. Last, instruct students to return the cottontails to the basket and start again!

Egg Roll

Here's an independent activity that will make your little ones cheep with excitement. Begin by converting an empty tissue box into a large die. Make a copy of page 286; color and cut out each card. Wrap the tissue box with adhesive-backed paper and then glue or tape one card to each side of the cube. Stock a center with the die, three baskets lined with Easter grass, and a clean foam egg carton containing 12 plastic eggs. To use the center, the child rolls the die and places the appropriate number of eggs in the first basket; he rolls again and places that number of eggs in the second basket. Then encourage him to make up an oral story problem, such as "The Easter bunny left three eggs in the first basket and two in the second basket. How many eggs are there in all?" As the child counts the eggs to determine the answer, he moves them to the third basket.

The Easter Bunny left three eggs in the first basket and two in the second basket. How many eggs are there in all?

3 + 6 = 9

Spilling the Beans

Here's a sweet addition activity that uses a traditional Easter favorite—jelly beans! In advance, duplicate the jelly bean patterns on page 287 for each student. Have each child color all of her beans one color of her choice. Next, direct her to cut out her jelly beans, flip them over, and color the other side of each bean a second color. Have each child place the completed jelly beans in a paper lunch bag. Now it's time for your students to spill their beans and do some addition! Invite your crew to pour their jelly beans from their bags. Then have each child count the number of each bean color. Demonstrate how to create an oral addition problem by counting the beans, such as "I have three pink jelly beans and six green ones. How many do I have in all? Nine!" Have students return the beans to their bags and spill them again to create new addition sentences.

After completing this activity orally, encourage each student to record her findings (drawing the correct number of jelly beans of each color to represent her number sentence) the next time she spills her beans. Sweet!

A Family Affair

Youngsters will have an "eggs-tra" good time discovering the related number families for the numbers 5 to 10. In advance, gather six plastic Easter eggs. Using a permanent marker, number each egg with a different numeral from 5 to 10. Inside each egg, place the appropriate number of chicks (yellow pom-poms). Stock a center with an Easter basket filled with the eggs; place paper and pencils nearby. Encourage each child to select an egg, pop it open, and arrange the chicks in as many ways as possible to show all the addition facts for the number on the egg. For example, if a student were to select 9, she would form number partners 8 + 1, 7 + 2 , 6 + 3, etc. Encourage students to write the number sentences they create. Good addition skills are hatching!

Magi

8 + 1 = 9
7 + 2 = 9
6 + 3 = 9
5 + 4 = 9

$$3 + 5 = 8$$

Hide-and-Seek

How many colored eggs will be hidden in the grass? It's up to each of your little ones. Stock a center with a supply of 3" x 9" lengths of green construction paper, markers, scissors, the die used in "Egg Roll" on page 284, and a colorful stamp pad. Invite each child to fringe-cut one long side of the green paper to represent grass. Have him roll the die twice and make a set of the appropriate number of fingerprints on his paper for each roll. Instruct him to write the appropriate number sentence on his paper as shown. Have him total the number of eggs hidden in the grass and complete the number sentence. Use the projects as a grassy border for a seasonal bulletin board.

Beautiful Baskets

Here's the perfect project to capture the creative interests of your lively students while they practice addition skills. Stock a center with a class supply of the basket pattern on page 287, a large supply of small die-cut ovals (eggs), crayons, glue, and Easter grass. Place the large die used in "Egg Roll" on page 284 at the center. Invite each child to color a basket pattern and then glue a few strands of Easter grass atop the basket. Next, have her roll the die. The number on top of the die indicates how many Easter eggs she will glue in her basket.

After all of your youngsters have had an opportunity to create their baskets, pair students and have them count the number of eggs in each basket and then add them together. What's the total? Have the pair switch papers and add the eggs in the baskets once again. Is the total the same? Explain that no matter which basket of eggs comes first, the answer is always the same. Save these projects to create "Bunny's Big Addition Book" on this page.

Hey! Three plus six and six plus three both equal nine!

Five plus four equals nine.

Bunny's Big Addition Book

Use the projects completed in "Beautiful Baskets" on this page to make this nifty addition book. Begin by dividing the basket pages in half. Stack each set atop a 9" x 12" sheet of tagboard; top each stack with a title page as shown. Next, staple the stack on the right along its right margin; staple the left stack along the left margin. Demonstrate how to flip the pages on the left and right to create a bounty of baskets and eggs to count and then add.

Bunny's Big Addition Book

Egg Cards

Use with "Bunny Trail Hop" on page 283, "Egg Roll" on page 284, and "Hide-and-Seek" and "Beautiful Baskets" on page 285.

Jelly Bean Patterns
Use with "Spilling the Beans" on page 284.

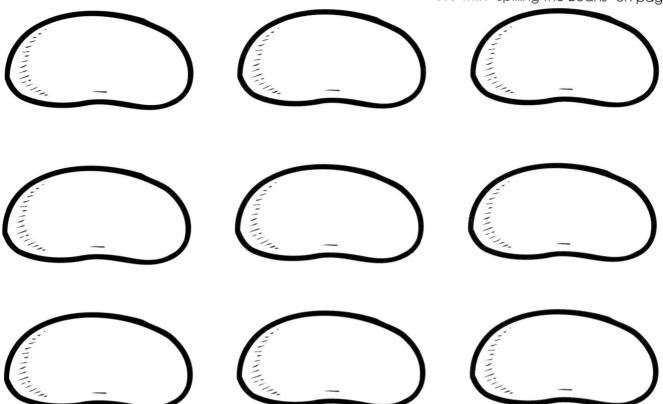

Basket Pattern
Use with "Beautiful Baskets" on page 285.

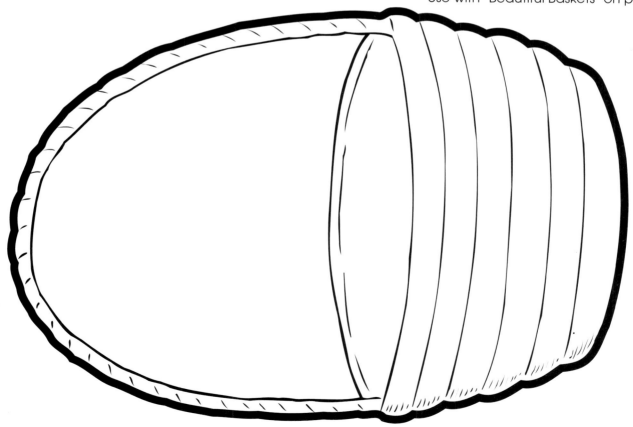

Fun on the Farm

Youngsters will be ready to head on down to the barn for these cross-curricular farm-related ideas. Don your overalls and best straw hat, and let's get going!

by Angie Kutzer—Gr. K, Garrett Elementary School, Mebane, NC

Reading
Labeling a scene

Reading Round the Barnyard

Take advantage of a busy barnyard scene to practice high-frequency words with this labeling activity. Use a decorative farm bulletin board set to create a barnyard scene on a magnetic board. Program cards with descriptive words or picture names and then attach a strip of magnetic tape to the back of each one. Store these cards in a tin pail near the scene. To use the center, a child reads each word and then attaches it to a corresponding location on the board. After using all of the labels, have him read the words and then remove the labels to ready the board for the next student.

Phonics

A Phonetic Farm

Create some barnyard banter with this letter and sound adaptation of the traditional song "Down on Grandpa's Farm." Grab a set of alphabet cards and make sure that the uppercase and lowercase letters are shuffled together. Hold up one letter card and then sing the verse below to the familiar tune, inserting your name and the designated letter's name and sound where indicated. Continue in this manner for several rounds, allowing students to take turns showing letters and singing the verse with their names. What fun!

We're on our way; we're on our way, on our way to [Kutzer's] farm.
We're on our way; we're on our way, on our way to [Kutzer's] farm.
Down on [Kutzer's] farm there is a(n) [uppercase T].
Down on [Kutzer's] farm there is a(n) [uppercase T].
The [T], it makes a sound like this: [/t/, /t/].
The [T], it makes a sound like this: [/t/, /t/].

In the Mooood for Math?

Practicing addition facts to ten is "udderly" cool with this idea. In advance, save ten emptied and cleaned half-pint milk cartons from the cafeteria. Make a copy of the reproducible on page 291 for each child. Put the cartons, the copies of page 291, and crayons in the math center. Have each child who visits the center use the cartons as manipulatives to solve each problem on the sheet. Then instruct her to color the spaces according to the code.

Here, Piggy, Piggy!

Challenge your students with the question "How heavy are piglets?" Then give youngsters the opportunity to explore the answer with this activity. To prepare, pour sand or rocks into a lidded container to equal about three pounds. Then tape a picture of a pig to the container. Bring in a bathroom scale (digital is ideal) on the day of the activity. To begin, have students guess the weight of a newborn piglet; then inform them that farm pigs weigh approximately three pounds at birth. Pass the weighted container around the group so that students can get a feel for what three pounds is. Then invite each child to find an object that he thinks is equal to the piglet's weight, such as a stack of books, a collection of blocks, or a tape player. Weigh each set of objects on the scale. Have the child determine whether it is more, less, or equal to the pig's weight; then list the object on a chart similar to one of those shown. When a three-pound object is found, be ready for squeals of delight!

A piglet weighs more than...

– a pencil
(Jake)
– a marker
(Dani)
– my glue
(Isabel)

A piglet weighs about the same as...

– my boots
(Cesar)
– 3 books
(Aaron)
– the tape player
(Kathy)

A piglet weighs less than...

– the easel
(Cathy)
– the trash can
(Casey)

Horsin' Around With Sight Words

It's sight word feeding time for your little workhorses! Make a class supply of construction paper hay bales from the patterns on page 292. Program each bale with a sight word that your students need to know. (Make a duplicate set of word cards for calling cards.) Arrange students in a circle. Choose one student to be the horse, and have her stand in the middle of the circle. Next, give each child a programmed hay bale. Then show the group a card from your pile. Have them recite the chant shown, inserting the designated word where indicated. Direct the horse to find the child holding the chosen word and switch places with him. Then repeat the game with the new horse.

A hungry little horse
Is looking for some hay.
Find some with the word [big].
Neigh, neigh, neigh!

big

Compound Words: Words to Crow About!

This flock of compound words is about to land in your sensory table! To prepare, write several different compound words on separate yellow sentence strips. Cut the words apart and mix them up. Fill your sensory tub with raffia and hide the word cards in it. For added effect, mount a scarecrow near the materials. Reproduce page 293 for each child. Review compound words with your youngsters and then instruct a small group to visit the center. Encourage each child to find word cards to make four compound words. Have him write the words on his recording sheet. Finally, compare lists to see how many different words were made. Outstanding!

Barn Basics

With this activity, students practice writing as you review the basic concept of inside and outside. In advance, glue a large barn cutout, similar to the one shown, on a sheet of bulletin board paper. Instruct each child to think of one thing that might be inside the barn and one thing that might be outside. Encourage her to illustrate each choice and write a sentence for each picture. Have her cut around her pictures and sentences. Then have the child glue her illustrations to the appropriate places on or around the barn. Display the finished mural for all to admire. Wow, your students really know the ins and outs of writing and directionality!

The hay is inside.
The sun is outside.
The tractor is outside.
The cow is inside.
The duck is outside.
The horse is inside.
The pig is outside.
The puddle is outside.
The pond is outside.

Farm "Fun-due"

Finish up your farm study with this fun graphing opportunity. Ahead of time, arrange for a parent volunteer to make chocolate fondue and cheese fondue. Have other parent volunteers send in bite-size portions of foods that come from a farm, such as apples, strawberries, carrots, cauliflower, and broccoli. Provide wooden skewers for children to use to taste each fondue. Prepare a two-column chart and then have youngsters vote for their favorite fondue. Or, for a higher-level math activity, work together with youngsters to figure out how many combinations could be made with the different foods and fondues. Then have them choose their favorite combination. Any way you dip it, farm food is fantastic!

Our Favorite Fondue

Chocolate   Cheese

Name _____

Let's "Cow-culate"!

Color Code

7 = yellow   8 = green   9 = blue   10 = brown

Add.
Color by the code.

5 + 4 =

3 + 5 =

5 + 5 =

4 + 6 =

5 + 2 =

1 + 8 =

6 + 4 =

4 + 4 =

4 + 4 =

7 + 1 =

1 + 7 =

291

Note to the teacher: Use with "In the Mooood for Math?" on page 289.

Hay Bale Patterns
Use with "Horsin' Around With Sight Words" on page 289.

Scarecrow Surprise

Note to the teacher: Use with "Compound Words: Words to Crow About!" on page 290.

The Season of Summer

While the sun is blazing, ignite your students' understanding of summer with these sizzling science activities.

ideas by Lynn C. Mode

Generating a list
Following directions

Warming Up to Summer

A little sunshine inspires youngsters to think about characteristics of summer and things they might see in summer. To prepare, make a copy of page 296 for each child. On a sunny day, take students outside and bring along a sun-shaped chart. Have youngsters make a list of summer words or phrases, and record their responses on the chart. Then discuss why or how each response relates to summer. After returning to the classroom, give each child a copy of page 296. Use this fun summer sorting sheet as a follow-up and a review of the brainstorming session.

Name _____
Summer Sorting
Sorting summer items
🖍 Color.
✂ Cut.
🧴 Glue summer things.

sun   swimming
hot   picnics
beach
shadows
camping
sunbathing

Making predictions
Observing

A Melting Moment

On a sunny day, try this predicting and melting exploration with students. In advance, gather six things that will melt, such as a crayon, chocolate chips, an ice cube, a birthday candle, a piece of freezer pop, and a scoop of ice cream. List each item on a chart and then place each one in a different cup of a muffin tin. Give each child a strip of paper and have him predict the order in which the things will melt by drawing them on his strip. Venture outside with the tin and have youngsters observe the effects of the warm sun on the items. Every few minutes have students check their predictions with the actual results. It's melting!

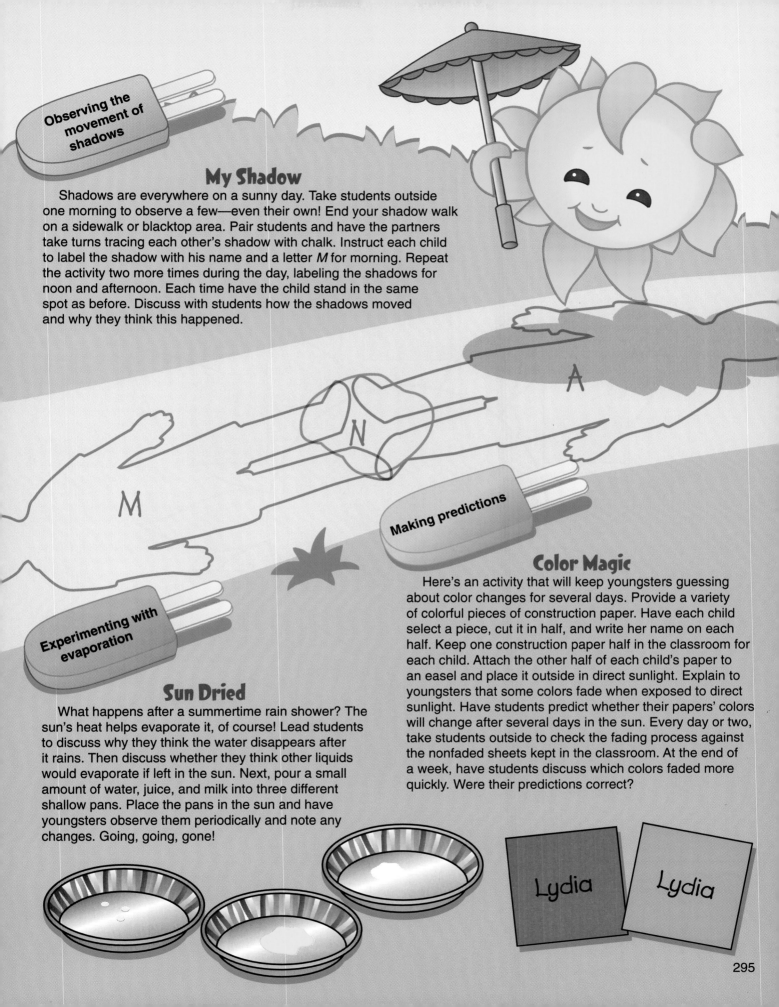

My Shadow

Shadows are everywhere on a sunny day. Take students outside one morning to observe a few—even their own! End your shadow walk on a sidewalk or blacktop area. Pair students and have the partners take turns tracing each other's shadow with chalk. Instruct each child to label the shadow with his name and a letter *M* for morning. Repeat the activity two more times during the day, labeling the shadows for noon and afternoon. Each time have the child stand in the same spot as before. Discuss with students how the shadows moved and why they think this happened.

Color Magic

Here's an activity that will keep youngsters guessing about color changes for several days. Provide a variety of colorful pieces of construction paper. Have each child select a piece, cut it in half, and write her name on each half. Keep one construction paper half in the classroom for each child. Attach the other half of each child's paper to an easel and place it outside in direct sunlight. Explain to youngsters that some colors fade when exposed to direct sunlight. Have students predict whether their papers' colors will change after several days in the sun. Every day or two, take students outside to check the fading process against the nonfaded sheets kept in the classroom. At the end of a week, have students discuss which colors faded more quickly. Were their predictions correct?

Sun Dried

What happens after a summertime rain shower? The sun's heat helps evaporate it, of course! Lead students to discuss why they think the water disappears after it rains. Then discuss whether they think other liquids would evaporate if left in the sun. Next, pour a small amount of water, juice, and milk into three different shallow pans. Place the pans in the sun and have youngsters observe them periodically and note any changes. Going, going, gone!

Summer Sorting

 Color.

✂ Cut.

🖊 Glue summer things.

©The Education Center, Inc. • *The Mailbox®* • Kindergarten • TEC42013 • June/July 2004

Note to the teacher: Use with "Warming Up to Summer" on page 294.

Clever Assessment

These simple assessment ideas will help you gather valuable information on the progress your students are making.

Brain Checkups

Have student progress information readily available for parent conferences, intervention meetings, report cards, and memory books by giving your students monthly brain checkups! Around the first of each month, give each child a sheet of paper with a seasonal border and have him complete several tasks, such as writing his first and last name, writing numerals (as high as desired), drawing shapes, writing sight words, or writing a sentence. These simple monthly assessments can be adapted to record a multitude of skills. It's thrilling to see the growth these brain checkups capture!

Bobbie Redd-Hallman
Don Stowell School
Merced, CA

Charlie Smith
1 2 3 4 5 6
7 8 9 10 11 12
13 14 15 16 17
18 19 20

Anytime Assessments

Capturing student progress is easy with this daily assessment method. Program a sheet of large mailing labels with students' names. Then place the sheet of labels on a clipboard. As you monitor students, keep the clipboard handy to record student behaviors, work pace, participation, choices, and skill mastery. Mark each label with the date and attach it inside the appropriate student's folder. The labels can be used for quick references for scoring report cards, making notes for parent conferences, and assessing students' needs. This assessment technique becomes an ongoing process that enables you to better meet the needs of all of your students.

Jennifer Skrivanek—Gr. K
Bowen Elementary
Bryan, TX

6/1/04
Joletta
• good behavior in music
• counted to 20
• wrote a sentence

The Everything Notebook

Putting in a little time up front on this notebook makes things go smoothly when you are ready to assess your students. Make a test or list a task for all the skills you will need to assess throughout the year. Put each sheet in a page protector and place each one in a notebook. When you are ready to assess a student, simply turn to the appropriate page and let her show you just how smart she is!

Tracey Bomar—Gr. K
Cottage Grove School
Cottage Grove, TN

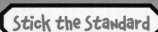

Sight Words
at
the
and
on
this

Mark

State Goal 3: Write to communicate for a variety of purposes

My Birtday
I had a parte for my birtday. I got a biK. We ate cake. It was choclat. I liK choclat caK.

Stick the Standard

These stickers make assessing students' work quick and easy! Prepare a class set of mailing labels with the standard you want to assess, such as "State Goal 3: Write to communicate for a variety of purposes." After a child writes a brief story, attach the sticker to his work. Later, the work sample is ready for conferences, student evaluation, or district assessment. Easy!

Peggy Wieck—PreK
Litchfield Prekindergarten
Litchfield, IL

Who Wants to Earn a Treat?

A Gummy Bears treat surely motivates youngsters to share all that they know about various skills! Mark a sheet with several skills you want to assess. In turn, have students answer questions relating to the skills. For each correct answer, reward the child with a bear treat and then mark her name under the skill she has mastered. Sweet!

Michelle Bowman—PreK
Noah's Ark
Lima, OH

Writer's Award

Presented to

_____

for excellent writing!

_____
(date)

_____
(teacher)

Writer's Award

Presented to

_____

for excellent writing!

_____
(date)

_____
(teacher)

Wee Ones Write

Make writing exciting by presenting these ideas to your little writers!

Thematic Word Charts

These useful charts with helpful picture clues will encourage youngsters to write about a particular topic. When working on a thematic unit, create a chart with related words as a reference. Beside each word on the chart, attach or draw a picture that depicts the word. Post the chart in your writing center and watch students' stories appear on paper!

Beach
- shell
- sand
- wave
- beachball
- chair

Tangible Story Characters

Give students story characters that they can hold in their hands—plastic animals! Distribute a piece of story paper and a plastic animal to each child. Have her write a story about the animal and then draw a scene from the story at the top of her paper. Laminate the stories for durability. Hole-punch the corner of each child's paper. Help her tie one end of a length of yarn to her animal and the other end to the hole in her paper. Invite each child to manipulate her animal as she reads her story.

Anna

My Horse
My horse lives on a farm. He liks to run around the tree. He sleeps in the brn. His name is Spike.

A Window to Writing

Students bring the outdoors in with this writing idea. Cut a square frame from bulletin board paper and tape it to a window. During the day, invite each child to look through the frame and write a story about what he sees outside. At the end of the week, have students share their stories. Youngsters will be amazed at how different their stories are even though they were looking out the same window!

Listening for Stories

Recordings of various sounds inspire youngsters to write! Tape-record sounds such as a train passing by, falling rain, or ocean waves. Have students close their eyes and listen as you play one of the recordings. Encourage them to use the sounds they hear to think of a story and then incorporate the sounds into their writing. The sounds of falling rain just might take a child's imagination to the rain forest!

Magic Pencils, Pens, and Markers

Make writing time fun by providing students with special pencils and other writing instruments to complete their stories. Place colorful pencils, markers, and metalic pens in a treasure chest (colorful box). Explain to youngsters that these writing utensils are magical and will help them write wonderful stories. After each child has completed a story, have her use a metallic pen to sign her name on her work before sharing the story with the class.

Travelin' Time!

Summer is the time when little tykes and their families make vacation travel plans. Plan your own travel-themed itinerary with activities to gear your youngsters up for travelin' time!

ideas by Lucia Kemp Henry, Fallon, NV

Problem solving

Travel Guessing Game

Embark on your classroom travel plans with this vacation-themed guessing game. Display two small suitcases and a backpack, each with different-themed contents for a trip to the beach, a theme park, or a campground. Challenge students to guess the travel destinations according to the contents of each bag. Write "beach," "theme park," and "campground" on a chart; then invite students to suggest more vacation destinations. Have each child secretly think of his favorite vacation destination. Then wrap up the activity by reciting the chant below once for each child in your class. Each time, select a child to sit in a chair in front of the group. At the end of the chant, invite students to guess his favorite vacation spot!

Vacation Destinations

beach
theme park
campground
grandma's
mountains
cruise
spa

Vacation, vacation. Guess my destination!
I could camp, go to the beach, or visit many theme parks.
Vacation, vacation. Guess my destination!
My bags are packed, I'm in the car, and I'm ready to travel.

The Places We'll Go

When it comes around to vacation time, how do your youngsters get to their destinations? Find out by inviting students to think about how their families get to favorite vacation spots. To prepare, die-cut a class set of car, plane, boat, and train shapes from construction paper. Place the die-cuts in a small suitcase. Discuss the different forms of transportation families might use to travel to places nearby and far away. Then instruct each child to select a die-cut from the suitcase. Instruct him to draw his face on his transportation shape. Next, give him a 9" x 12" sheet of construction paper and have him glue his shape in the center. Have him name a vacation place he could visit using that form of transportation. Program each child's paper as shown and then have him complete the sentence by filling in the blank. Attach the pictures to a bulletin board and title the display "The Places We'll Go!"

Michael can travel in an ✈ to Disney World.

Pack Up!

Packing for a vacation is almost as important as planning where to go! Set up a suitcase-packing center so that your little travel-lovers can polish their reading and packing skills. Place a large basket of accessories such as shorts, T-shirts, button-up summer shirts, flip-flops, a towel, and a deflated beach ball at a center along with a small suitcase. Also include several items that wouldn't be taken on a beach trip. Then make a list of the items to be packed for a beach trip. Photocopy the list to make a class set. Have each child read each item on the list and then carefully fold each item and check it off on the list before packing it in the suitcase. You'll be pleased with the expert readers and packers this center produces!

✓ T-shirt
shorts
flip-flops
shirt
✓ towel
ball

Suitcase Stories

Since your well-seasoned travelers now know their way around a suitcase, they'll love making this 3-D mini rolling bag booklet. To make a booklet, give each child an 8¾" x 5¾" clean foam tray, two brads, a ¾" x 5" construction paper strip (handle), crayons, pencil, glue, and white construction paper copies of pages 305, 306, and 307.

Have each child cut out the cover, booklet pages, and wheel patterns. Help him stack the cover and pages in order. Then instruct him to write his name on the luggage tag on the cover. Have him color the cover and wheel patterns. Next, have each child draw a picture to illustrate the text on pages 1, 2, and 3. Then, on page 4, instruct him to illustrate a special item he would like to pack and write its name on the line. Help each child glue his cover and booklet pages together where indicated. Then accordion-fold the pages so the cover faces up. Assist the child in gluing the back of page 4 to the bottom of his foam tray. Have him glue the wheels to the bottom of the tray as shown. Help each student attach a handle with his brads as shown. Invite each youngster to read his booklet to the class. Have bag, will travel!

This bag belongs to
Andy

A Suitcase Story

Hometown Vacation

No time for long-distance travel? Encourage students to view their community as a tourist would and take a vacation in their own hometown! In advance, gather postcards for each special destination in your area, including beaches, parks, lakes, campgrounds, historic buildings, museums, theme parks, and zoos. Begin by sharing the postcards with youngsters. Discuss each place and the special things visitors see there. Next, place several postcards in the bottom row of a pocket chart to set up a graph. Give each child a die-cut car shape labeled with her name. In turn, have each student place her cutout in the pocket chart to indicate her favorite local vacation place or a place she would like to visit. Use the graph data to compare the attractions and determine the class favorite. If possible, arrange a field trip to the attraction or invite a representative from it to speak to your students. Your little ones will be ready to explore their community!

Following directions
Matching sight words

Travel Snacks

Top off your vacation unit with an easy-to-make snack that really travels well! Place shelled, roasted sunflower seeds; chocolate chips; and chopped dried fruit or raisins in separate bowls. Put a tablespoon in each bowl. Give each child a treat bag. Have him scoop a spoonful of each ingredient into his bag. Seal each bag and place it on a serving tray. Line up your classroom chairs in rows with a center aisle as on an airplane. Label each chair with a different sight word. Make a matching set of word cards (tickets). Give each child a ticket and instruct him to find his seat on the plane by matching the word on his card with the word on his seat. After all students are seated, offer each child a juice box and a bag of snack mix. Invite each child to enjoy his mini feast as he listens to you read a favorite travel tale!

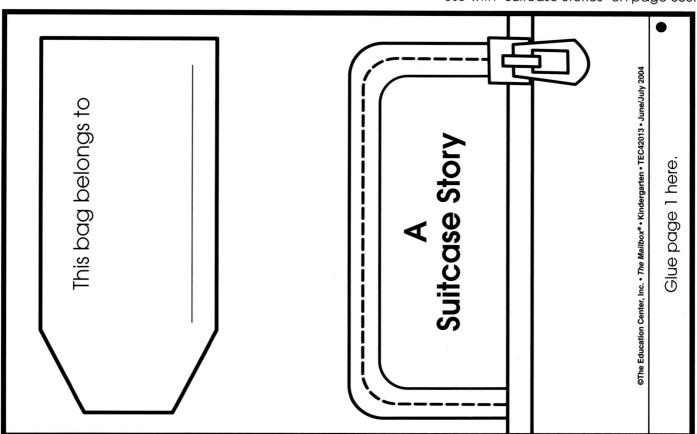

This bag belongs to

A
Suitcase Story

Glue page 1 here.

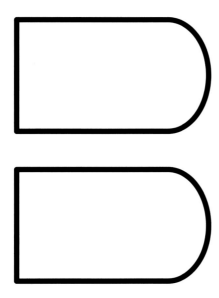

Booklet Pages

Use with "Suitcase Stories" on page 303.

my shorts,

2 ■

Glue page 3 here.

●

I pack my shoes,

1 ◀

Glue page 2 here.

Then I pack my _____ and I'm ready to go!

4

and my shirts just so.

3

Glue page 4 here.

Plant the Measurement Seed

Plant the seed, measure the growth, and harvest the knowledge your youngsters gain for nonstandard measurement with the ideas in this clever unit!

ideas by Jana Sanderson, Rainbow School, Stockton, CA

Singing a song

As Cool As a Cucumber

Math is *cool* when you trade in your rulers for seeds, vegetables, or worms! It's even cooler when you get to sing about it! Kick off your measuring unit by singing the song below. Repeat the song, using the words *vegetables* and *worms* in the third line.

(sung to the tune of "Pop! Goes the Weasel")

Let's all do some measuring now.
We don't need a ruler.
We lay [seeds] end to end.
Garden measuring is cooler.

Using nonstandard measurement
Ordering lengths

Tubular Tubers

This measuring activity is totally tubular! In advance, enlist the help of parents in collecting a large supply of toilet paper tubes. In a center, tie four different, long lengths of thick yarn to a table leg (plant stem) to represent plant roots. Working in pairs, invite students to thread cardboard tubes onto the lengths of yarn and hold the last tubes in place with clothespins. Instruct students to count the number of tubes on each root and then sequence the roots from shortest to longest. After completing the activity, have students remove the tubes and mix up the yarn pieces to ready the center for another group.

Diggin' the Distance

Your kindergartners will dig this measuring activity! Trace a shovel on one long edge of a piece of bulletin board paper. Provide access to various colors of paint in shallow pans and halved vegetables, such as a carrot, a squash, a radish, and a mushroom. In turn, have each child use a vegetable to make prints along the length of the shovel outline until there is a row for each vegetable (as shown). When dry, have the children count each row of vegetables and make comparisons as they sing the song below.

(sung to the tune of "Where Is Thumbkin?")

How long's the shovel?
How long's the shovel?
It's [21] [mushrooms] long.
It's [21] [mushrooms] long.
That's more than the [squash].
That's more than the [squash].
But less than the [radish].
But less than the [radish].

Making comparisons
Ordering by length

Garden Vegetable Medley

Youngsters measure and sequence the length of vegetables with this idea. To prepare, gather the paint pans and cut vegetables from "Diggin' the Distance" on this page. Have each child make a vegetable print on paper. When the paint is dry, have him use Unifix cubes to measure the height of his print. As a group, have students count each stack of cubes and order the prints by height from shortest to longest.

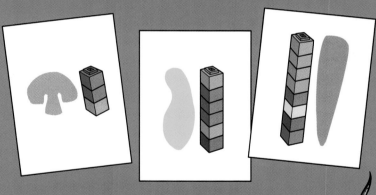

Counting
Using nonstandard measurement

Rainbow Garden

These colorful flower stems are fun to measure—and munch! To prepare, glue a craft foam flower or a paper flower to one end of a long wooden skewer (pointed ends cut off). Give each child a flower and have him thread Froot Loops cereal onto the stem. Instruct him to place a mini marshmallow at the end of his skewer to hold the cereal in place. Have him count the cereal pieces to determine the length of his edible flower stem. Hey, this stem is 35 cereal pieces long!

Using nonstandard measurement

Measuring Garden Rows

Turn your classroom into a greenhouse and watch the measuring fun grow, grow, grow! In advance, enlist the help of parents in gathering a supply of toilet paper tubes, paper towel tubes, and wrapping paper tubes. Cut each tube in half lengthwise. Attach vegetable stickers, as shown, to each tube half. Purchase a supply of rubber fishing worms. Have each child position the tube halves in rows on the floor to represent garden rows. Have her use the worms laid end to end to measure the lengths of her rows. Encourage youngsters to repeat the activity, making more rows and measuring again!

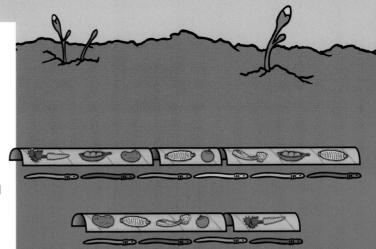

Following directions
Labeling length

Lengthy Literature

Cultivate an understanding of measurement with this child-made book. To prepare, cut out a class set of 2" x 10" construction paper strips (booklet covers). Then give each child a copy of page 312 and have him cut the pages apart along the dashed cut lines. Instruct him to complete the drawing on each page. Next, stack each child's booklet pages and accordion-fold them along the gray fold lines. Separate the pages (keeping them folded); then staple them in a folded booklet cover. Direct each child to title and personalize the booklet cover as shown. Then have him complete his booklet by writing *short* and *long* on the lines of each page to describe the picture when the pages are folded and unfolded.

Using nonstandard measurement
Sorting

Flower Garden Fun

Your youngsters will become experts at measuring and sorting flowers from the garden. To prepare, gather a supply of long-stemmed silk flowers, six 2½-inch plastic flower pots, and five 16-ounce plastic water bottles. To make five vases, remove the labels from the water bottles and number each one 2, 3, 4, 5, or 6. Next, cut each flower to a different length: five inches, 7½ inches, ten inches, 12½ inches, or 15 inches. At the center, instruct each child to choose a flower, lay it on the table, and then measure its length using the small pots as shown. Have him count the pots and then place the flower in the vase labeled with the corresponding number. Encourage youngsters to continue measuring flowers and filling the vases. Beautiful!

Happy Trails

These edible snails create trails that are deliciously measurable! In advance, purchase a class supply of Little Debbie Pecan Spinwheels sweet rolls (snails). Pour maple syrup in a bowl. Give each child a sweet roll, a white paper placemat, and a small handful of raisins. Instruct her to dip her snail in syrup and then drag it across her placemat to make a snail trail. Then have her measure her trail with raisins! Lead students to discuss the lengths of their snail trails and then invite them to snack on their snails!

Measuring Length With Leaves

Enthusiasm for measurement grows as your kindergartners help measure Jack's beanstalk. In advance, spray-paint a supply of dried lima beans green to represent leaves. Next, draw a simple castle in a cloud shape on tagboard. Color and cut out the pattern and then laminate it for durability. Hole-punch the top and bottom of the pattern; then thread a piece of thick green yarn through the holes to represent the beanstalk. Use tape to secure the ends of the yarn around a piece of heavy cardboard. Read or tell the story of *Jack and the Beanstalk.* Invite each youngster to move the castle up or down the yarn and then lay leaves along the length of the stalk leading up to the castle. Have her count the leaves. Instruct her to remove the leaves, reposition the castle, and remeasure the length of the beanstalk. Fee! Fie! Foe! Fun!

Edible Earthworms

Your little ones take a bite out of a lengthy lesson when they measure these edible worms. Give each child a refrigerated biscuit on a piece of waxed paper. Have each child roll his biscuit into the shape of a worm and then sprinkle it with pink sugar crystals. Bake the worms according to the package's directions. When the worms are done, invite each kindergartner to measure his worm by counting how many bites it takes to eat it. Mmm, tasty measuring!

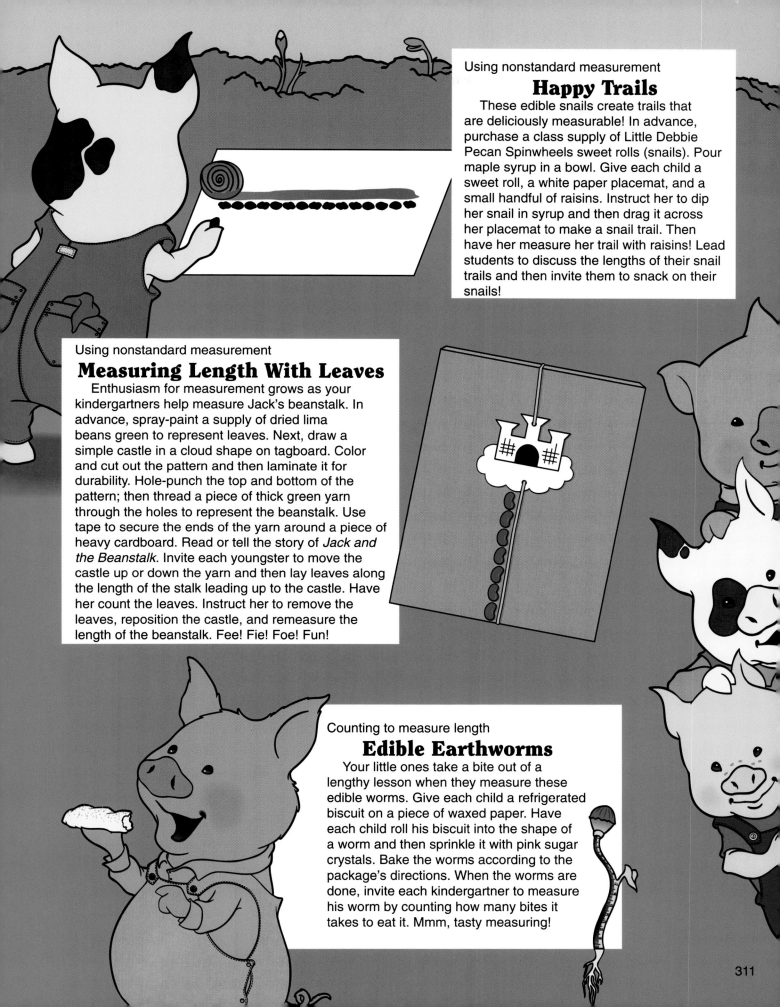

Booklet Pages

Use with "Lengthy Literature" on page 310.

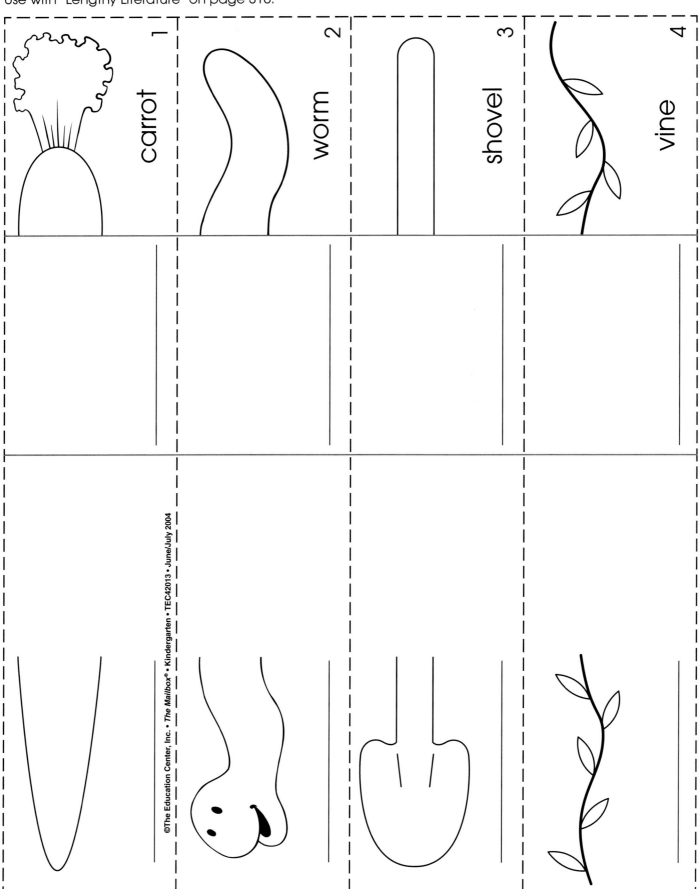

carrot 1

worm 2

shovel 3

vine 4

©The Education Center, Inc. • *The Mailbox®* • Kindergarten • TEC42013 • June/July 2004

Index